FOR ANYONE WHO WALKS THE
WOODS AND FIELDS AND WANTS TO
LEARN ABOUT LIVING THINGS HE HAS
OFTEN LOOKED AT BUT NEVER SEEN

"Hal Borland,
Sunday nature columnist of the New York *Times*
and author of 15 books,
lives on a Connecticut farm by the Housatonic
where woodlands, meadows, a bog and the river
itself are his for the exploring.
He and his wife watch deer feeding at dawn,
otters and foxes at play on a sleepy afternoon
and May flies dancing by the million
on a moonlight night.

"They know where and when to look for the
first anemones and the first returning redwings
and where—though this they tell nobody—
flowering arbutus may still be found.
And still, year by year, they go on making
new discoveries.

"With a refreshing absence
of the dogmatism and coyness
that so often mar books in the first person,
the author shares his discoveries,
old and new."
..*AUDUBON MAGAZINE*

# BEYOND YOUR DOORSTEP

*A Handbook to the Country*

## Hal Borland

AN AUDUBON/BALLANTINE BOOK
An Intext Publisher
NEW YORK

THE NATIONAL AUDUBON SOCIETY
1130 Fifth Avenue, New York, N. Y. 10028

BALLANTINE BOOKS, INC.
101 Fifth Avenue, New York, N. Y. 10003

FOR
*Barbara*
*for whom I pick the first violet*

# Contents

1. The Country House      1
2. The Rural Roadside      17
3. Pastures and Meadows      33
4. The Woodlands      49
5. The Bog and the Swamp      69
6. Flowing Waters      83
7. The Miniature World      103
8. An Assemblage of Animals      119
9. A Badeling of Birds      135
10. Sun, Moon, Stars, and Weather      153
11. Biotopes and the Lay of the Land      171
12. No Need To Go Hungry      187
13. Out of This Nettle, Danger      201
14. Month by Month: What To Look for and When      215
15. The Names and the Naming      239
     An Armful of Books      269

# Foreword

*This is a book* about the outdoors, the natural world where plants grow, birds sing, insects buzz, fish swim, and animals live out their lives with little help and only moderate interference from man. It is primarily about the countryside, not the wilderness; countrysides are common and within the reach of almost everyone, but wildernesses have become rare and usually are remote.

I wrote this book for two broad groups of readers, appreciators and participators. Those I think of as appreciators do most of their outdoor exploring vicariously, sometimes by choice more often because of circumstance. For them, I hope to serve as eyes and ears that will enrich their understanding or refresh their memories. Those I think of as participators have the inner urge and can create the opportunities to go and see and do for themselves. For them, I hope this book will be an informal guide and companion.

Most beginners and newcomers to the outdoors say: "But there is so much to see! Where do I begin?" I have tried to answer that question by suggesting areas and indicating starting places. No one can comprehend a dooryard, a meadow, and a woodland in one excursion or even one

Summer vacation. Even after years of life in the country, I find it best to investigate one natural area at a time and to look for birds or insects or wildflowers on separate occasions, not all at once. This book is organized with such a program in mind. It starts with a country house and its dooryard, then explores the roadside, the meadow, the woodland, the bog, and other areas, one at a time. It takes up birds, animals, edible and poisonous plants, and other aspects of the outdoors in turn.

I have not attempted to write a field guide. Instead, I have tried to indicate what to look for and where and when. For identifying detail, the differences between a bay-breasted warbler, say, and a chestnut-sided warbler, or between sweet goldenrod and swamp goldenrod, the reader should turn to the guidebooks to birds and wildflowers. Their function is identification. This book's function is recognition of the natural world and its broader outlines and relationships. If it lures the participating reader to the guidebooks in a search for more knowledge of the world around him and his place in it, my purpose will have been fulfilled.

To a large degree, these chapters are about the countryside where I live. But my own area is typical to the extent that it consists of meadowland, woods, bogland, ponds, and riverbanks that can be approximated elsewhere. Readers almost anywhere in the eastern half of the United States can duplicate most of my observations. The seasons vary from place to place, but where I mention specific times, those times can be converted for other areas by using a simple formula explained in Chapter 14.

Since I am writing primarily for the layman rather than the specialist, I have used the common names for plants, birds, and animals throughout the text of this book. In Chapter 15, however, is a list of those common names with the accepted scientific names for those who wish to make absolute identification.

Obviously, a book of this length is less than encyclopedic in scope. Aside from the limitations of space, there are two primary reasons. First, my knowledge is by no means boundless. Second, my purpose is to rouse and share interest in the subject and suggest its scope rather than to exhaust it. At least half the satisfaction of acquaintance with the natural world comes from discovery.

At the end of this volume, under the title: "An Armful of Books," I have listed some of the available field guides and other books I have found especially interesting or useful.

I believe that one of man's deepest needs is to feel at home in this world where he lives and that the only securities are those achieved when man has reached a degree of understanding of life and time and is at peace with his environment. Since man will always be a minority member of the living community on this earth, he would be wise to know something about his co-inhabitants here. Despite the insistent spread of urbanization, even the most obstinate apartment-hermit cannot completely isolate himself from nature. The cities have their birds, their insects, their skulking animal life, their insistent weeds and wild plants, as well as wind and weather, sky, sunset, and stars. And just beyond every city lies the countryside, if not a refuge at least a reminder of man's minority status, the rootbed of life itself.

I wish I could thank all those, both professionals and amateurs, who over the years have helped to broaden my knowledge of the outdoors. But that would call for a roll of the friends and acquaintances of a lifetime. I must disclaim for all of them, however, any responsibility for the opinions or dogmatic statements in this book. Those are my own.

Finally, I must quote a few lines from Linnaeus:

"If you have remarked errors in me, your superior wisdom must pardon them. Who errs not in perambulating the realm of nature? Who can observe everything with accuracy? Correct me as a friend, and I as a friend will requite with kindness."

H. B.

*Weatogue*
*Salisbury, Connecticut, 1961*

# Chapter 1

# The Country House

THE NEWCOMER to the country will find the first signs of "wild life" in his own house. Even before he explores the dooryard he can sharpen his eyes indoors. He may be surprised at the outsiders who want to share that house with him.

*There was a time* when "nature" meant every living thing on earth, the earth itself, the air, the water, the weather, even the stars and planets. In that unsophisticated age, the "naturalist" was a man interested in all such natural phenomena. But times change, and as man urbanized his life he came to think of nature as alien if not, indeed, hostile. And the naturalist became the person who specialized in some aspect of that strange, alien nature.

But nature has its own insistence. The urban tides ebbed as well as flowed, and many returned to a natural environment. With characteristic human zeal to understand the new, the strange, the alien, some of them were fascinated by the natural world around them. And even some of those who persisted or were trapped in the urban environment looked about them with new interest in such things as birds, insects, plants, and animals. A whole new legion of naturalists, in the old sense, appeared. Since the old term had lost its essential meaning, we couldn't call them naturalists, so we granted some of them the name "bird watcher." "Animal watcher" and "plant watcher" still are strange to the tongue, logical though they are, but "nature watcher" suggests itself for all of them.

In that sense, there now are millions of nature watchers. They live everywhere, in cities, suburbs, small towns, and country. Some of them are specialists to a degree, but most of them are interested in the broad picture of nature and the interrelationships of life. Some of them study birds and insects on a penthouse terrace in the heart of the city. Some

2

of them study wild life in a city park. Some explore botany and entomology in a suburban backyard. And many of them take every chance they find to go down a highway, leave the highway for a side road, quit the road for a country lane, and finally come to a place where wild plants far outnumber tame ones and human beings are vastly in the minority in the community of living creatures. Some, who are either dedicated or specially fortunate, go to the country to live.

I am one of the fortunate ones. I live on a hundred-acre farm with a riverfront, an area of fields and pastureland, a relatively wild mountainside of brush and timber. We came here to live in part because I have been a nature watcher all my life and in part because as a writer I have a degree of leeway in my choice of residence. Underlying these reasons is the belief that close acquaintance with nature is essential to a balanced and reasonable philosophy of life, and such a philosophy seems important to me.

The ideal time to go to the country, to live or to visit and explore, is March. March marks the beginning of the natural year. Spring peepers peep, the earliest wildflowers bloom, trees prepare to open bud, migrant birds return, and the first of the insect hordes are hatching. From that beginning one can follow the season into Summer with its growing leaves, burgeoning fields, nesting birds, and birthing animals. As Summer passes one can see how nature matures, with reddening berries, young birds in flight, insects swarming, flowers turning to seed heads, nuts ripening. One can watch and wonder through golden September and into the magnificence of October, know the falling leaves, the honking geese, the silken flight of milkweed floss and thistledown. One can know the new horizons of bare-branched Indian Summer, settle into Winter's hush, live with snow and ice, and prepare to watch Spring again.

March, I say, is the ideal month. But it isn't always practical. March usually is muddy if not icy underfoot and wet and cold overhead. March has uncomfortable and inconvenient aspects, even for the resident countryman and especially for the newcomer. So the sensible advice is to go to the country in your own comfort and convenience and eventually come to know March, with its whims of weather and its rewards of new beginnings.

We came to this farm not in March but in late July. We moved here from another country place, and the timing was dictated by details of living and legal necessities of sale and purchase. You buy a place when you find it for sale, and you move in when you get possession. In any case, we didn't come here merely to watch one Spring arrive. We came here to live and to work, and I expected to see quite a number of Springs mature into Summer, Summers ripen into Fall, Falls fade into Winter. I could be patient. If there is any outstanding lesson to be learned in the country it is that patience is a virtue. Nature seldom hurries.

I shall be writing in some detail about this farm and the nearby hills and valleys, not because I live here but because one aspect or another of this small area is broadly typical of much of the American countryside north of the Carolinas and east of the Mississippi. Even the house and dooryard have their typical aspects.

The day we came to take possession, while we awaited the arrival of the furniture van, we went through the house from cellar to attic. I had made an inspection of the house as a structure before we bought it, and I had not been unaware of its few non-human inhabitants. But I had taken no census, so to speak. Now there was time to make a casual survey of those with whom we would have to share this house. Every house has its own population, especially country houses, and the people who live there are fortunate if that population is, as the ecologists say, in balance, a balance favorable to human habitation.

In the cellar I saw a mouse scurry. I had only a quick look, but I saw that it had big, rounded ears, a rather blunt nose, and whitish feet and belly. It was a white-foot mouse that had come in from the fields, quite different from the European house mouse that infests so many houses. The white-foot is essentially a clean creature and a friendly neighbor, but the house mouse is a dirty nuisance. I found no signs of house mice.

In the kitchen we found no cockroaches, centipedes, millipedes, or water bugs. An old ant trap in one of the kitchen closets proved that this house, like every country house I ever knew, had its ant invasions now and then. But there were no ants in sight. In the bathroom there were no silver fish and again no water bugs. In one corner of the ceiling there was a small spider web with two dead flies trapped in it. And in the living room were two more such webs, both small, both relatively new. Spiders are everywhere, but we seemed not to be overrun by them. Not downstairs at least.

The bedroom closets smelled of moth balls. I looked for cocoons, found none, nor did I find any clothes moths. I decided the moth balls had been prevention rather than cure, and thanked our predecessors.

Finally we went to the attic. There I was aware of a faintly sweet odor and looked for bat droppings. I found a few, dark brown granules something like coarse coffee grounds. There were no obvious openings through which big bats could get in, so ours probably were the little brown bats that live unsuspected in houses almost everywhere in the United States. These little bats are the size of small mice and can creep through incredibly small crevices. I once found one that had squirmed between the sashes of a half-open storm window, a crack so small I couldn't force a lead pencil into it. The few droppings indicated that we had a pair or two in our attic.

Then I saw a mud-dauber wasp nest on one of the open rafters. There were half a dozen such nests, but I was sure we had only a minor wasp population. Bats tend to rid a place of wasps. Looking for more wasp nests, I saw spider webs here and there among the rafters. Were we overrun by spiders in the attic? No. Wasps kill spiders, paralyze them with their sting, and stuff them into their nests to feed the young wasps when they hatch.

So, within half an hour, I knew that the wild population in our house was quite well in balance. Which spoke well for those who lived here before we came. There were no signs of invading birds or squirrels or chipmunks. If we were lucky, and if we worked at it, we probably could maintain that balance, though we would always remain in the minority, surrounded by insistent nature.

Since then we have had a few invasions, but none crucial. Two or three times the house mice have appeared, probably from the big barn where they thrive on waste grain and litter. I got rid of them with traps. From time to time ants have got into the kitchen, usually in late Spring, and they had to be discouraged with poison in covered traps—I refuse to use open poison, even for ants. Almost every year a few mud-daubers seem to think the open front porch is an ideal place for their nests, and every year a few paper-maker wasps build a few open-celled nests there. I have to take steps, since I regard the porch as ours and we don't like wasp stings. And each September a few black crickets get indoors, hide under the bookcases, and stridulate well into Winter.

Before hard frost came, that first Fall here, we had an invasion of elm-leaf beetles, which look like miniature fireflies. They came into the attic by the thousands and into other parts of the house by the hundreds. I swept them up and destroyed them every few days, and still they came. They were a nuisance, and I also resented them because they help spread the fungus disease that has killed so many elm trees. We fought them with every means at hand. But nature herself stepped in, apparently, with some obscure but potent means of control. Since that first Fall the number of elm-leaf beetles has steadily diminished. Last Fall I saw only a few dozen of them in the house.

Our next invasion was more tolerable. During the first mild days of late Winter the ladybird beetles appeared. They were on all the window sills and they crept into the house at every opportunity. Our house has shingled outer walls, and the shingles provide ideal winter quarters for those little spotted orange beetles. When late January comes and the sun warms the shingles, the beetles crawl out to bask. I don't resent them. I welcome them, knowing that ladybird beetles are probably the best of all natural controls for aphids, sometimes called plant lice. California truckgardeners buy them by the bushel to release in their vegetable fields and keep the aphids in check. So when they first appeared here in the house I gathered up those I could catch and took them outdoors and released them, hoping they would go to work in the garden at a proper time. They did. We have had only a minimum of aphid trouble on our plants, and I credit those hordes of ladybird beetles that spend the Winter under the shingles of the house.

Our place has a number of outbuildings, a big old barn, a garage that once was the milk house, a chicken house, a small brooder house, a corn crib, and a woodshed. When we got settled in the house I took a casual census of our obvious neighbors in those outbuildings.

The garage had its normal insect population, mostly spiders and wasps. Later that Fall I found that it is also a Winter refuge for hibernating woolly-bear caterpillars, which some say can foretell the weather of the coming Winter. Incidentally, I have found them unreliable prophets, almost as untrustworthy as woodchucks, the ground hogs of legend. But they hibernate in the garage by the dozen. In the Spring they emerge in the benevolent sunlight, feast on plantain leaves, pupate into silky cocoons, and emerge as beautiful little pink-tinged yellow moths.

The garage also had two barn-swallow nests, mud structures about the size and shape of half-coconuts plastered on the sides of overhead beams. And in the old litter in the loft of the garage were several families of white-foot mice. The garage, I found, had a normal, harmless population.

The chicken house, unused for some years, had been taken over by a family of red squirrels, those hyperthyroid little bundles of indignation and energy. They came and went through a variety of knotholes in the outer walls, and I found several old squirrel nests among the heaps of litter in the corners. Those hat-size nests were jumbles of twigs, bark, dead leaves, milkweed floss, rags, a little of everything. And there was a trash heap, their kitchen refuse, fully a bushel of riddled pine and spruce cones. They had brought those cones from the woods, torn them apart to get and eat the seeds, and left them in that untidy heap. Red squirrels are not very good housekeepers.

When I went inside, half a dozen squirrels scurried, glared at me, scolded, then whisked through the knotholes and raced and thumped on the roof, still chattering angrily at my intrusion. I eventually cleaned out the place and claimed it as my own for a carpenter shop, hoping to live at peace with the squirrels. But it has been an uncertain peace, and periodically I think I should evict them. They knock paint cans from the shelves, scatter my sandpaper, gnaw paintbrushes and electric cords. And they still yell at me. I am the invader, not they. But even if I could drive them out—and, short of killing every one of them, I doubt that I could—I doubt that I would. A red squirrel in a house attic is a noisy, destructive nuisance, and a whole family of them is intolerable. But out in the old chicken house they are interesting neighbors, temperamental and unpredictable as they are. I like to have them around.

The red squirrels had rid the chicken house of almost all

other residents except spiders and mud-dauber wasps. Up to now the little red fellows have not achieved a foothold in any of the other outbuildings, though now and then I see one among the piles of firewood in the woodshed. But for some reason they have never set up housekeeping there.

The woodshed has a population of mice, most of them white-foot and deer mice—the two are not easy to tell apart without examining them in the hand. The mouse population there seems to rise and fall in direct relation to the presence or absence of rats, which move in from time to time. When the rats move in, the mice move out. Then I poison the rats and the mice come back. I prefer to have the field mice. The rats have their stronghold in the big barn, in the hay and straw that is stored there each year. I keep them in check with a selective poison in covered containers where other animals cannot get at it. Those ugly, destructive Norway rats, common all over the world, deserve no quarter.

The barn has a huge, cathedral-like loft where the hay and straw are stored. That loft is also the home for a tribe of gray squirrels. The tribe sometimes numbers as many as fifteen, sometimes drops to only four or five. It probably consists of only one family, and I suspect that as soon as the season's new litter begins to mature the older squirrels move out into the woodland just across the home pasture. The squirrels live on the corn that is stored in the corn crib near the barn. I see them there every day in the Winter, plucking the yellow kernels from the fat ears jammed against the wire mesh. Somehow they occasionally steal a whole ear, and now and then one brings an ear and climbs with it to a high crotch in the giant Norway spruce just outside my study window. There he sits and shells the corn, deftly eats the germ from each kernel, and dribbles the rest of it onto the ground beneath.

The squirrels nest on a high beam in the barn loft, a nest that looks like half a bushel of trash. I have never climbed up there to examine it, but I know that gray squirrels are no better housekeepers than their small red cousins. Like the red squirrels in the chicken house, the gray squirrels in the barn have an assortment of knotholes, gnawed to proper dimensions, through which they come and go. If they are disturbed at the corn crib they dash to the barn, swarm up its weathered old gray boards with uncanny skill, and swing through a knothole with a beautiful, arrogant flip of the tail. In Winter I marvel at their sure-footed agility on the frosty shingles of the barn's high roof, and in early Spring I watch their mating-time battles and pursuits over those dizzy heights. Now and then there are intertribal fights between the reds and grays, but not often. I have heard that in such fights the males sometimes castrate each other, but I have never seen it done. I have seen a red squirrel lose a part of his tail in a battle with a gray.

I am still amazed at the ease and skill with which all squirrels, and especially the grays, race through the big sugar maples in front of the house. I have seen one leap ten feet from limb to limb, and only once did I see one fall more than a few feet. Usually, if one falls, it catches itself on a limb below. But I saw one miss three limbs, one beneath another, and fall forty feet. It twisted in mid-air, cat-like, but failed to right itself and struck a rock. It was the only squirrel I every saw killed that way; but it was only half-grown, probably not yet fully skilled. Last Winter I saw a full-grown gray leap from a limb twenty feet to a snow-bank covered with ice thick enough to support my dog. It broke the crust in the fall, but scrambled to its feet and dashed away, apparently quite unhurt.

For some reason, the barn has never housed barn swallows. There were no swallow nests there when we came and there have been none since. The only explanation I have is that barn swallows prefer to nest where people come and go, as in my garage, though they can be annoyingly truculent when there are chicks in the nest. One year a pair of pigeons came and nested on a high beam in the barn loft. I hoped they would stay, for I like the sound of their cooing, the soft whistle of their graceful flight. I suspect that the gray squirrels drove them out. They never succeeded in raising one squab, and within a few months they left and never came back. I miss them. But the barn seems to have achieved its own balance of population, and pigeons clearly are not included in it.

From time to time there have been transient visitors in the barn, which is full of cracks and wide gaps around the big doors to the loft. One day I found a half-grown raccoon in there. Instead of bolting outdoors when it saw me, it fled to the distant recesses of the hay. I saw it there several times over the next few weeks; then it disappeared, probably gone back to the woods. Once I met a skunk there. It was as surprised as I was, and immediately assumed a posture of defense. I backed away and left it, and never saw it in the barn again. It probably was hunting mice or crickets. Or perhaps it was the skunk that had a den under the little brooder house when we came here. Two months after we moved in I saw it, sunning itself beside a hole under the foundation. It saw me too, and hurried indoors. But it evidently didn't like close neighbors, for it was gone before the first snow flew. I bade it Godspeed.

Now and then we have a cat at the barn. We keep no cats of our own, out of consideration for the birds. But there is a big black tom who belongs to a neighbor a mile away and who comes here and spends a few days at the barn every few months. He probably finds good hunting there, but after a few days he ends his visit and goes back home.

Two years ago a big white and tan cat appeared at the barn, a complete stranger and wild as a fox. Several times I saw it sunning itself on a window ledge out there, but if I appeared it took off like a streak. Through the binocular I could see that it was sleek and beautiful and apparently well fed. It stayed two weeks and then was gone. A few days after it left the barn I saw it skulking in the woods far up on the mountainside, a feral cat on the hunt. It probably was a kitten abandoned somewhere in the area by Summer vacationers. Such abandoned kittens usually are killed by other animals or die of starvation, but this one must have been of tougher fiber. It was too wild to tolerate human company, though, and it didn't return to my barn. I have never seen it since.

I took my casual census of the wild life in the outbuildings in the first few months we lived here. It was the typical population of such a country place as this. A rural house and outbuildings that have stood vacant for some time would have a different assortment, certainly a different balance, since man, a dominant factor in any such balance, has been absent. One broken window in a vacant house, for instance, will provide entry for all kinds of creatures, birds and squirrels especially. And insects, though insects need no broken windows to get inside; they find cracks and crannies, and their numbers usually vary with the weather, the number of insect predators such as bats and birds, and the time they have been free of human control.

Any country house that is structurally sound can be reclaimed by human inhabitants even if it has been unoccupied for several years. Once people move in and take charge, most of the wild creatures move out with little persuasion. They prefer their own company. Squirrels may be hard to dislodge, and so may bats. Some insects are hard to dislodge. But modern insecticides are thoroughly effective, and though I refuse to use them outdoors except in extreme cases because they kill birds and small animals, I have no compunctions against using them to rid a house of flies, wasps, ants, and other household pests. Bats, squirrels, and birds usually can be evicted and kept out by replacing broken windowpanes and closing other likely places of entry. Rats and mice can be poisoned. The house, after all, is my dwelling place, and I insist on keeping it mine.

Strange things can happen, amazing things, though, in an empty or vacant house. An acquaintance of mine left his country house for a two-months trip and came back to find a porcupine in the attic. How it got there, he still doesn't know. And I know of a young couple who went to the Summer cottage of a friend for their honeymoon. The cottage was in the woods. They left the door open one day when they went for a walk and returned to find a skunk in the kitchen. If they had retreated down the path and waited half an hour the skunk would have left the house and gone about its business. But the bridegroom was impetuous. He took down the .22 rifle from over the mantel in the living room and shot the skunk right there in the kitchen. That ended their woodland cottage honeymoon, since the skunk, as skunks often do, used its worst weapon in its dying convulsions.

Late Summer is not the best time to learn what a country dooryard and garden has in the way of trees, shrubs, and plants. But it is not the worst time, either; Midwinter is the worst time.

When we came here, all the Spring-flowering bulbs had bloomed and withered. The other early flowers had gone to seed or were hidden by later growth. The previous owners said they had planted many bulbs, squills, grape hyacinths, daffodils, tulips, lilies, that sort of flowers; but they were vague, as most people are, about where those bulbs were. "Over there," they said, "and over there somewhere," with a vague wave of the hand. We had to wait till the next April to find most of them, though I recognized tufts of grape-hyacinth leaves, like limp grass clumps, and I saw a few stiff stems of lilies through with blooming.

The common flowering plants in most country gardens were easily recognized. There were several clumps of phlox, in bud and showing color. There were hollyhocks, with weathering blooms on their tall stalks. There were day lilies and chrysanthemums. There was a bed of iris, the broad-bladed kind that probably was either the common purple or the old-fashioned red-and-yellow variety. (It turned out that both colors were there.) Flanking the front walk were twin rows of peonies in need of dividing. Eventually I moved them to the back of the flower garden, for background foliage and to clear the lawn for easier mowing.

There were lilacs, including one big clump that must have been here fifty years, it was so huge. There was a big bridal-wreath bush, typical of the country; its blossoms were long gone and now it was a huge fountain of slender stems and fine green leaves. There were two weigelas and a big clump of forsythia. Flanking the front steps were big syringa bushes in need of pruning, and there was foundation planting of yew, barberry, euonymus, and azalea.

In the edge of the flower garden was a pear tree, and beneath it was a big bed of lilies of the valley. In most country gardens the lilies of the valley will be beneath a tree or in a cool spot beside a wall or foundation. Close beside the house was the towering Norway spruce, a heroic tree that I later triangulated and found to be a hundred feet tall. Back of the house were a dozen apple trees, old trees that an orchardist would have pruned heavily. I have pruned them only casually and I have never sprayed them. They are old trees that long ago established their own balance with the natural hazards of apple trees in this area. Besides, I do not grow apples to sell. Within my plan, their primary function is to provide a magnificent display of blossoms in May, make cool shade all Summer, give me what few apples I want, and drop windfalls for wild creatures that eat windfalls. They shelter many birds, and their hollows make nesting places for bluebirds and downy woodpeckers. One year a pair of wood ducks nested in one of them. I can think of no better way to let an old apple tree make the best of its own frailties.

Someone had planted a weeping willow near the watering trough in the barnyard. When we came here it was four inches through at the butt and twenty feet high. Today it is fifty feet high and has a trunk thick as my own body. It makes a litter of leaves and dead withes every Winter which I clean up without too much complaint, because each Spring it is an amber fountain of livening branch and leaf and blossom, and all Summer long it is a whispering tower of green beauty. Orioles and robins love its swaying crown.

At one end of the big barn was an elderberry bush ten feet tall, twelve feet around. In May that bush is white with bloom and in late August it bows its head with purple fruit, some of which goes onto our pantry shelves in jelly glasses, the rest of which makes hungry birds happy. Not far from the elderberry bush was a sapling sugar maple fifteen feet high. I wondered if it should be left there. Then in late September it turned gold and orange and I knew I could never cut it down. Now it stands forty feet high and every Autumn it is magnificent.

Just across the road from the house was a row of big sugar maples, all of equal age, no doubt planted there long ago by a provident countryman. There must have been nine trees in that row to begin with, but one of them seems to have died early. For some strange reason, it was replaced by a popple, as poplars are called in this area—this one actually is a cottonwood. Today that tree stands head-and-shoulders above the maples, a giant of a tree close to five feet through at the butt. Its limbs are so brittle that every Winter storm brings down a few of them. It is untidy in Spring when it sheds long brown-red catkins, and in June when its seeds ripen it spills clouds of cottony fluff to every breeze, fluff that frosts the screens on that side of the house for several weeks. In terms of human economy, that tree is probably worthless. I wouldn't part with it for anything.

The sugar maples were tapped for years by the farmers who lived here and made their own syrup and sugar. I tapped them myself a few times and boiled down the sap in a washtub over a fireplace improvised in the backyard. Everyone who owns sugar maples and has room to do it should make syrup at least once, not only for the satisfaction of such accomplishment but to understand why maple syrup costs what it does in the market. I found that it takes at least a cord of wood to boil down the forty gallons of sap needed to make one gallon of syrup. A cord of wood and a week of fire-tending.

I cherish those maples for a variety of reasons of no commercial consequence. The Baltimore orioles that nest in them make Summer mornings rich with color and song. A swarm of wild bees is resident in one of them and probably has forty or fifty pounds of well-tanged honey there right now. I'll never know, for they can live there safe from my pilfering as long as they choose. Each Spring those maples are a glory of golden blossom, and every October they turn gold that is like no other color in the spectrum of Autumn. They shimmer and glow in the sunlight, and on a dark day they are like sunshine itself. Then the leaves come down and I am knee-deep in crisp gold as I stand beneath them and look up at November through their sky-reaching gray branches.

Beyond the road and maples is the river, with its own movement and its own life. Lakesides have their charm and personality, but after living with this river for ten years I know that my personal choice is flowing water. A river comes from somewhere, flows past my wondering eyes, and goes on to some other place. It has movement, change, and there is a sense of both time and eternity in it. The river tells me that so long as there are heights and lowlands on earth, water will continue to flow and life will persist. A river, flowing water, not only has its own life—it *is* life. I am prejudiced about rivers, and I shall have more to say about them.

Back of the house is the pastureland, the old flood plain of the river. Beyond the pastureland the mountain rises sharply. Current maps call this eminence Tom's Hill, but maps of two generations ago named it Tom's Mountain. It is a remnant of one of the older mountain chains of America and was cut down to its present size by wind and rain and frost and finally by the massive glaciers of the Ice Age. I hold to the old name, granting it mountain status and honoring the granite stubbornness with which it has stood up to the eons.

On that mountainside are pine woods and hemlock and there are stands of white pine and white and gray birch and poplar and ash. There are clumps of red oaks and white oaks, and there is a scattering of hickories. Once there were chestnut trees, and from some of the big old stumps still spring hopeful sprouts that sometimes grow as thick as my wrist before the deadly blight withers and kills them. In October those sprouts are like tongues of golden fire, telling me what the groves of chestnuts must have looked like in their Autumn glory. But the chestnut trees were gone before I came here.

On the mountainside are old stone walls, laid up by a generation of countrymen who farmed long-abandoned fields up there with plodding ox teams. There are even remnants of an old orchard high on the mountainside, now forgotten by all except the grouse and the deer. And there are springs from which brooks tumble down the mountain and flow across the pastureland to the river.

Not on my own land but only a mile down the valley is a small patch of bogland, a minor swamp created when the river changed its course several centuries ago. A small brook empties into it, and another brook of slight consequence flows out of it and down to the river's present channel. The bog itself is a few acres of ooze and muck and brush and cattails, red-wing blackbirds and muskrats and water snakes. A wonderful place, as are all boglands—a reminder that all life as we know it began in the wetlands of this earth.

So here are meadowland, wooded hillside, river and riverbanks, and bogland. Here are typical rural areas, among them the kind of places anyone can find, once he has quit the cities for a day, a week, or a lifetime. I have lived with them for some years. My day-to-day and year-to-year discoveries are neither unique nor particularly unusual. Perhaps that in itself will give them interest and even pertinence to other nature watchers.

# Chapter 2

# The Rural Roadside

A WATCHFUL *walk down any country road will provide a generous sampling of the wild life resident in that region. It will also prove that man is by no means the only traveler or the only form of life that tries to dominate its environment.*

*Whenever I am* away from home and want to get a quick idea of the native plants and obvious wild life of an area, I drive down a side road, park the car, and walk for a mile or so. I know I will get only a sampling along such a country road, but unless it has been groomed to death, that road will provide something of a cross section of the area. And, inevitably, I compare any strange roadside with my own country road and its uncultivated life.

There is nothing really exceptional about this roadside of mine, the one I know best because I have walked here almost daily for nearly ten years. It is just another country road casually lined with trees and bushes, with a few stretches of brushy fence rows, and with grass and wild plants reflecting the growth in the bordering fields and pasturelands. It has a variety of soils, a damp spot here and there, and a few rocky outcroppings. Until about eight years ago it was a dirt road, deep-rutted every muddy Spring, dusty every dry Summer. Then our local road people hardtopped it to eliminate the mud and dust; but aside from giving it an all-weather surface they changed it very little. It is still a typical country road.

Each Winter the snow is plowed from my road into long windrows, and a mixture of sand and salt is spread to minimize the ice. Each Spring that salt seeps into the roadside with the snow-melt, probably kills some plants, and certainly does no good to the roadside trees. But the salt is far less destructive than the chemicals which are used in some areas to kill roadside weeds and brush.

18

I have no intention of fighting the battle of the chemical brush-killers here, but I must say that those responsible for our local roads are wise in mowing the roadsides a few times each Summer rather than spraying them. The chemical killers destroy the roots that anchor the soil and invite costly erosion. Our old-fashioned ways here provide financial dividends in lower maintenance costs as well as preserving green roadsides properly decked in wildflowers. So the benefits are by no means all financial.

In any case, my roadside is the seedbed for most of the wildflowers native to this area as well as a host of newcomers. Today's roads are distant cousins of the old caravan routes, which were avenues of travel for plants as well as commerce. On the old routes, the caravans carried the seeds from one place to another unwittingly, sometimes in feedstuff sometimes in chaff, sometimes in mud that clung to plodding hoofs or turning wheels. Asian plants traveled all the way to Europe in this way, and European plants hitched rides far into the Orient. Our roads today are similar routes of travel. Going about the country, I am always struck by the presence of "alien" roadside plants. I have found Kansas sunflowers as far east as Indiana, as far south as Texas. I have found wild chicory of the beautiful blue blossoms almost from coast to coast. Winds might carry chicory seed that far, but nothing less than a tornado could distribute sunflower seeds so widely. A car or truck, however, may carry such seeds many hundreds of miles.

At my own roadside I have watched the spread of chicory for ten years. When I first came here there wasn't a chicory plant within a mile of my house. Today chicory is common everywhere I walk along this road. Dozens of other wildflowers are constantly being broadcast in the same way and in every part of the country. But even my roadside, where the traffic is light and primarily local, is unpredictable from year to year. I can say with reasonable certainty where I will find this species or that one, and I can guess with moderate accuracy what assortment of plants I will find, say, at the foot of the rock ledge half a mile down the road or at the moist brookside half a mile up the road. But I meet surprises every year.

This past Summer, for instance, I would never have guessed that Queen Anne's lace would spring up everywhere and mass its fluffy white blossom heads thicker than daisies. Queen Anne's lace grows at the roadside every year, but never before have I seen such an abundance of it. The previous Summer the climbing wild cucumber, which some know as wild balsam, was everywhere. Its long green stems, light green star-shaped leaves, and sparkling tufts of tiny white bloom draped almost every roadside bush and climbed countless trees. The Summer before was a bouncing Bet, or soapwort, season. That weedy member of the pink family made the roadsides pink and white from early July till November's hard frost.

None of these plants is rare along my road in any Summer, but I doubt that anyone could have predicted such abundance in any particular season. The variation from year to year is the result of many factors. One, of course, is the weather. But Queen Anne's lace normally thrives in a moderately dry season, and this past Summer was wetter and cooler than usual. Another factor is the insects. Most of my roadside flowers are insect-pollinated, and there are complex cycles in the insect world. Even less understood than insect cycles are the cycles of parasites, both those that prey on insects and those which attack plant seeds. And interrelated with these factors are the cycles in the populations of birds and small animals which feed on seeds and roots and insects. All these matters are vital in the rise and fall of plant populations, especially in such uncultivated areas as roadsides.

Every year, of course, there are such obvious and predictable wildflowers as oxeye daisies, black-eyed Susans, robin's plantain, hawkweed, the ubiquitous bouncing Bet, Queen Anne's lace, and the various goldenrods and wild asters. Along almost any rural road I can find half a dozen species of clover—the common white that is often found on lawns, the big red that is typical of cultivated pastureland, the fuzzy-blossomed rabbit's-foot clover, and both white and yellow sweet clover, which are weedy, sparse-blossomed plants. Common milkweed, with the fragrant bloom and host to Monarch butterflies, grows along most rural roads. So does dogbane, cousin of the milkweed and host to the beautiful little green-gold dogbane beetle. In fact, any roadside reflects the wildflower population of the neighboring areas, especially of the pastureland but in some degree that of the woods and, if there are damp spots, even of the margins of bogs and swamps.

I can always take a final census of my roadside in October by cleaning the burs and small stick-tights off my clothes after I have walked there. I seldom overlook the tall, spreading burdock with its magenta, thistlelike blooms in August, but in the Fall it comes home with me, or with my dog, in the form of fat, hooked-spine burs that catch on any passing object. Tick trefoil's tiny pink flowers of Summer may go unnoticed, but when its minute, triangular pods ripen they are covered with spiny hairs that cling to trouser cuffs and socks. I am usually aware of nettles, even though their small purplish flowers make no display; their sharp sting reminds me where they are. But come October and their spiny little seed cases are almost as annoying as their Summer sting. And there are several varieties of grass whose seeds have beards even sharper than the beards of a farmer's barley.

All through the Summer and early Autumn there will be common evening primroses at most roadsides with their rich yellow blossoms that grace late afternoon and evening. There may be sundrops, lesser cousins of the primroses but just as vivid yellow. In waste places there probably will be fireweed with its light magenta or pink blossoms. In my area fireweed is often called wild phlox, although it isn't even a remote cousin of the phlox family—it belongs to the evening-primrose family and has only four petals whereas all the phloxes have five. Fireweed thrives in waste places and cutover timber land, especially where the ground has been burned, and can be found well into the Arctic in dwarf form. Another four-petaled roadside wildling somewhat resembling fireweed and also locally called wild phlox is dame's rocket, a member of the mustard family. Its flowers are pink, magenta, or white. You can tell it from fireweed quite easily by examining the seed pods. Fireweed seeds are tiny and have buoyant silky floss on which they ride the wind like milkweed seed. Dame's rocket seeds have no floss and look like mustard seed.

You will also probably find giant mullein at the roadside. This mullein's big, woolly, gray-green base leaves lie dormant beneath the snow for weeks at a time, then show life at the first thaw. In Spring the plant sends up a stout stalk that by Midsummer may be seven or eight feet tall and will be tipped with a fat candle of closely packed buds. The buds open only a few at a time into small, pale yellow flowers that lure lesser moths and hungry bees. The plant is beautiful, almost classic in its symmetry of stalk and leaf. The woolly, feltlike leaves are its trademark.

There is also a lesser mullein, the moth mullein, that flourishes at the roadside. It grows only two feet high, has thin, smooth, notched leaves and somewhat larger yellow flowers than those of the giant mullein; they bloom in a loose cluster. I have occasionally found a moth mullein with white flowers, but this variation is rare. At dusk I have seen as many as a dozen moths, most of them the smaller brown and gray ones, clustered on the heads of a tuft of moth mullein, feasting on the nectar.

Related to the mulleins, and common at almost every roadside, is toadflax, more often called butter and eggs. It is a cousin of the snapdragon of our flower gardens, and its yellow-and-orange blossoms follow the snapdragon pattern.

If you are fortunate, your roadside will have bee balm, and if you are doubly fortunate it will be the crimson-flowered variety sometimes called Oswego tea. Bumblebees compete with hummingbirds for nectar at the tousle-headed blossoms. I grow a patch of it in a corner of my flower garden to make sure the hummingbirds find a visit here worth while. Bee balm is a wild bergamot, cousin of the mints and its leaves are so full of sharp-tanged fragrance that if you even brush a plant in passing you will smell of it all the way home. I usually pick a leaf or two to crush between my fingers when I pass a plant, just to have that fine fragrance around me.

There are other, less vividly colored bee balms, a pink variety and a magenta one. They, too, often grow at the roadside, but in drier places than the crimson-flowered variety. Bees and hummingbirds patronize them too, but not as hungrily. Perhaps they have less nectar. I know their leaves are less fragrant.

The earliest flower of all at most roadsides is celandine, a weedy member of the poppy family and cousin of both the May apple and the bloodroot. Celandine is one of the hardiest and commonest of roadside weeds. I have seen it in green leaf in mid-January, and by early April it is in full growth. It is often mistaken, especially in early Spring, for black mustard. The compound leaves of the two plants somewhat resemble each other. And both plants bear yellow blossoms with four petals. But celandine blooms in April and May, mustard not until June. Positive identification is easy. When the stem of a celandine plant is broken it oozes yellowish-orange juice, typical of most members of the poppy family. The juice of the mustard family of plants is colorless.

Early roadside flowers also include the wild cresses, most often the one called yellow rocket. And my road has a few anemones, rue anemones; the smaller, daintier wood anemone doesn't seem to be there at all. It may yet appear, one of these Aprils. Violets are there, of course—what rural road can endure through May without violets? There are three varieties along my road, the common violets with small, heart-shaped leaves and deep purple blooms, the marsh violet with its bigger leaves and lighter-colored blooms, and a few plants of sweet white violets in a damp spot where a brook wanders down to the road and flows through a culvert. These small white violets are the only violets I know that have a real floral fragrance. All other violets have, to me at least, only a green, woodsy smell. But the little sweet violets seem to come and go. I find them in bloom perhaps one year in three.

Coltsfoot should grow at my roadside, but I have seen only one plant. It came to bloom in early April, then disappeared and never returned. Coltsfoot is sometimes mistaken for dandelion. The blossoms are something like each other, but that of coltsfoot is a duller yellow and the blossom precedes the leaves, which never happens with the dandelion. A certain distinction between the two is the fact that the coltsfoot's stem is solid and that of the dandelion is hollow —if you never used dandelion stems as Pan's pipes and blew shrill notes through them, something was missing in your young life.

Dandelions grow at most roadsides, early and late. Until a few years ago they were along my roadside in only normal numbers; then, for some reason, they had a "population explosion." Overnight they were everywhere, in pastures, hay fields, even in cornfields. And at the roadsides, of course. One field of alfalfa a few miles from here became a vast dandelion patch. The owner plowed it up, to rid it of the infestation, but the next year they were back, thick as ever. It is a pity that dandelions, essentially attractive plants with beautiful blossoms, should be so insistent in growth that they become a pest. If they were as hard to grow as garden asters, for instance, they probably would be prized as garden flowers.

Ecologists puzzle over "population explosions" among plants and animals and even insects. From time to time someone gathers statistics and tries to discover a pattern or some involved interrelationship that will explain these things. Most of the data relate to animals, and some seem to point to involved rhythms, possibly related to sunspot cycles. There seems to be one cycle of about ten years, and within it are three lesser cycles, all of which apparently apply to lemmings, Arctic hares, even Atlantic salmon. Nobody yet knows, as far as I can learn, to what extent similar cycles apply to germs, to molds, to insects, to birds, to plants, vital though such knowledge would be to all of us. It is possible that epidemics of disease are related to such cycles. It is possible that plant diseases, which affect our food supplies, follow some of these rhythms. It could be that seed fertility and even growth of healthy plants vary within these mysterious patterns. The fact is that we don't know. All we know is that there are mysterious cycles and rhythms, and that from time to time certain germs or insects or animals or plants proliferate enormously and become, if not actual menaces to us, at least pests—a pest, after all, is something we don't want flourishing in a place where we don't want it. Like those dandelions in the alfalfa.

I have already mentioned Queen Anne's lace at the roadside. There are half a dozen other roadside members of the parsley family. The roots of some are poisonous if eaten, and the foliage of several is poisonous to animals, but none is poisonous to the touch. Caraway and sweet cicely, for instance, provide seeds common on the herb shelf and their roots are edible. Cowbane, on the other hand, is seriously poisonous if eaten by animals, as its common name implies. These wild-parsley kinfolk have loose, flat-topped clusters of small blossoms, usually dull white except in the case of the meadow parsnip whose flowers are golden yellow. And several of them grow rank, six feet tall, at most roadsides.

By late Summer you will find ironweed, Joe Pye weed, boneset, and white snakeroot at the roadside, especially in damp places. Ironweed has tufted flower heads with individual purple blossoms something like small thistle heads. Joe Pye has fluffier tufts of smaller blossoms, magenta-pink in color. Ironweed leaves, you will note, grow alternately up the stem while those of Joe Pye weed grow opposite each other. Boneset looks something like Joe Pye except that its blossoms are white. You may find boneset growing eight feet tall, Joe Pye six or seven, but ironweed seldom more than five. White snakeroot, a smaller, bushier member of the same family as Joe Pye and boneset, prefers the shade at the edge of the woodland. The others flourish in full sunlight.

The roadside census, at least as far as I am concerned, is never complete. The beginner, of course, has the whole population to explore and identify, but you will find surprises even along a roadside known for years. Only the other day I found moneywort at my roadside for the first time, though it must have been here for years. I probably had glanced at it and dismissed it as outsize partridgeberry, for both are trailing vines with round, bright green leaves growing opposite each other. But partridgeberry has tiny twin white flowers like miniature bluets—the two plants are cousins—while moneywort has bright yellow flowers as big as a nickel. Both species were in bloom this day, and when I saw this patch of moneywort I knew I had been half blind until that moment. But we all have our blind spots, our blind days.

One need not be blind to miss the peacock-blue anthers in the blossom of cranesbill, one of the wild geraniums—half the people I know have never seen them. But there they are, brilliant blue, in the center of that bright pink blossom. They aren't blue in every cranesbill flower, but if you keep looking you will eventually find a flower that has them. I have never seen blue anthers in the cranesbill's smaller cousin, herb robert, which also grows along many roadsides. Both these plants, by the way, reveal their geranium identity if you crush their leaves. They have the typical geranium odor. And the seed pods of both are long and slim, shaped a good deal like a crane's bill, pop open from the bottom when ripe, and flip the seeds away from the parent plant.

Speaking of seeds, if you find a patch of small roadside sunflowers with several plants whose flowers have no "petals," no orange fringe of outer rays, those plants are not freaks or victims of some insect which ate the petals. They are beggar-ticks. That is the way they grow. They are sunflower cousins, but their flowers have only the central part. When the flowers ripen the seeds have two thorny prongs and insist on coming home with you from your Autumn walk, beggar-ticks or stick-tights. Bur marigolds, which are also sunflower cousins and do have golden-yellow rays, like sunflowers, ripen into sharp-pronged seeds too, but they have four prongs and are not quite as sharp as beggar-ticks. They will come home with you too.

Undoubtedly you will find Jack-in-the-pulpit in some damp spot at the roadside in early Spring. You probably will notice that the spathe, the "pulpit," is all green on some plants and striped with dark purplish brown on others. They are not of different species. I have been told that the dark-striped ones are male blossoms, the all-green ones female, and this may be true sometimes. But not always. The Jack-in-the-pulpit blossom is basically bisexual but apparently is evolving slowly toward unisexuality because on some blossoms the stamens are abortive; on others the pistils are abortive. And, to further complicate matters, some plants bear both male and female blossoms, both in the same-colored spathes.

I have a theory about such blossom colors. Quite a few flowering plants have lighter-colored blossoms when they grow in full sun than when they grow in the shade. Cranesbill, for instance, and anemones. Both usually are darker when they grow in the shade, the anemones with pink veining in their white petals. Bluets show the same tendency—clear white in full sun, tinged with lavender in the shade. I always find the darker violets in deep shade. Research has shown that most plants run a slight temperature when they come to bloom and start to form seed, perhaps a parallel to the periods of "heat" in mammals. I suspect that color variations have something to do with this fertility "fever" in flowers. Darker colors absorb more warmth from the sunlight and perhaps compensate for growing in the shade. I doubt that any flower's color is there to attract insects, which apparently have little or no color vision. If attraction of insects were the purpose, why would Jack-in-the-pulpit have such striking color variations? And why would it coincide so often, both in Jacks and in other flowers, with the sun or shade in which they grow? There are still a good many botanical secrets to be learned.

Even if you could take a complete census of your roadside plants today or this year, I am sure it would be incomplete next Summer. The plants come, and they go. I have no trilliums at my roadside, for instance, though I can find them only a few miles away. One of these Springs I undoubtedly will find them here. I have no May apples, which some call mandrakes, though they too grow in my area. One of these days I probably will find them here, just as I undoubtedly will find Dutchman's-breeches and squirrel corn, lesser cousin of Dutchman's-breeches, both of which should be here. I really shouldn't say they aren't here. What I should say is that I haven't yet found them.

Every country road I know of has vines of one kind or another, and most of them have poison ivy. The beginner must learn to recognize this obnoxious plant, which I shall discuss at some length in a later chapter. Most roadsides also have Virginia creeper, which belongs to the grape family although its compound leaves are quite different from grape leaves. Some people know this vine as woodbine, but since at least four other common vines are sometimes called woodbine, I prefer the name Virginia creeper, which is its alone. It is a beautiful vine, a glory at the roadside in October with its scarlet leaves.

Wild clematis also grows at most roadsides. You will find it twining on fences and bushes, flowering in June with bright sprays of tiny white blossoms which give it another common name, virgin's bower. And bittersweet, that cruel climber with inconspicuous greenish white flowers and beautiful berrylike orange fruit, will catch your eye in the Fall. I call it cruel because of the way it chokes any tree it chooses to climb. Here in my study is a length of sapling birch with spiral grooves an inch deep caused by the hug of a bittersweet vine. You probably will also find deadly nightshade, which is known in some places as bittersweet, in the usual overlapping confusion of common names. This nightshade is a cousin of the potato and the tomato, grows both as a vine and a sprawling bush, and has small, bright purple flowers with golden-yellow centers. The flowers mature into berries that look like small, oval cherries, ruby-red and almost translucent. These berries are poisonous. Don't eat them.

If your road is bordered by a brook or river it undoubtedly will have wild grapes sprawling along the ground and climbing among the trees. Foxes love wild grapes. So do opossums. One October evening, just up the road from my house in a roadside tangle of wild grapes just come to full ripeness, I came upon a 'possum whose silvery fur was purple with grape juice from the tip of its pink snout right down to its paws. It had not only eaten its fill of grapes; it apparently had wallowed in them. Many birds like those grapes, too—robins, catbirds, jays, even flickers. They plant many grapevines in their droppings at the roadside.

Your road's trees and bushes will be typical of your area, the kind you will find in the woodlot or at the edge of the meadows. As I said earlier, I can take a sampling of any countryside's natural population by spending half an hour walking along a rural road. The newcomer to any area can profitably spend the leisure of his first week exploring the roadsides, which will give reliable clues of what to look for in the hills beyond—and without the possibility of getting lost in unfamiliar woodlands or bewildered and muddy to the knees in a strange bogland. No matter how far you wander along a country road, you can always follow it back to where you started. Or stop at a farmhouse and ask directions.

The roadside's plants, bushes, and trees also offer a sampling of your area's more common birds and small animals, since they provide both food and shelter for many of them. If you are a bird watcher, certain back roads will certainly be on your regular beat. My bird-watcher friends patrol my own road almost every day during warbler season, both Spring and Fall.

In the Spring, all kinds of birds will be nesting at your roadside—robins, catbirds, kingbirds, orioles, flycatchers, vireos, bluebirds, brown thrashers, even red-wing blackbirds where a brook flows nearby or the road borders a bog. Crows congregate in roadside poplars and loudly discuss everything under the sun. Kingbirds nesting nearby challenge the crows. Some of the best kingbird-crow aerial fights I ever saw were those I watched from the roadside. One afternoon I watched two truculent kingbirds drive a whole tribe of crows across the valley and into the shelter of the pine woods. Then, probably exhilarated by those easy victories, the kingbirds climbed high to do combat with a red-tail hawk riding a thermal up the valley. I watched for ten minutes as the kingbirds climbed and dive-bombed the big hawk, and as the hawk sideslipped and maneuvered without flapping a wing. The kingbirds didn't land a blow. Then the hawk tired of the game, flew swiftly to the next higher level, and soared in circles, disdainful of the kingbirds, which gave up and came back to watch for more crows.

In the Fall you will find the flocking flickers at the roadside, restless but putting on pre-migration fat and energy in the grapevines and berry bushes. You may even find ruffed grouse, come down from the wooded hills to feast on grapes; you are almost sure to find them if barberry bushes grow wild beside the road. If the road is bordered by a cornfield, watch for mourning doves. A flock in my area Winters in the roadside cornfields where they find a good cafeteria stocked with nubbins and other waste grain.

When the first freezing rain or sleet storm has brought out the sander trucks you will find it worth a walk along the road just to watch the birds flock in to get the sand they need in their crops to help grind their food. Sparrows and other seed-eaters are among the first patrons after the sanders have gone along my road, but I see chickadees and juncos there too, and now and then a blue jay, making it look as though he had to steal that sand. I don't know why a jay can make the most harmless action look like a felony, but he can. I have also seen whole flocks of evening grosbeaks descend on a freshly sanded Winter road and eat sand as eagerly as though it were sunflower seeds.

Some woodchucks, for reasons I shall never understand, prefer to den, or at least feed, close beside the road. Among them are individuals that have the suicidal impulse to cross the road just ahead of a hurrying car. Despite the high mortality rate, the roadside tribe of woodchucks seems to maintain its numbers. Maybe cars, in the long run, are no more lethal to them than foxes and bobcats are to their more timorous kinfolk. Chipmunks, which often live in roadside stone walls, also are too often traffic victims. And so are rabbits, especially at night when they are blinded by the lights. And skunks, which probably are lured to the roads at night to catch the mice and insects and snakes that find the lingering warmth of a macadam or concrete surface a comfort in the cool darkness. But I may say that any driver who fails to slow down for a skunk in the road will regret it. It takes weeks to sweeten a car that has run over a live skunk.

In the Fall you may see opossums traveling along the road at night, undoubtedly also lured there by the surface warmth. I see several dead opossums, traffic victims, along my road every year. The only reason fewer 'possums than rabbits die on the roads is that rabbits far outnumber 'possums, especially in the Northeast. Now and then you may see a raccoon in the road, but usually it will be at night since coons are essentially night prowlers. If they have half a chance, coons will get out of the way of a car. Last Spring, however, I found three coon kits about the size of half-grown house cats wandering at my roadside in mid-morning. They probably had been orphaned, undoubtedly were hungry, and hadn't yet learned fear of cars or human beings. I stopped the car, got out, and shooed them off the road-side, into a pasture, and over to a clump of cedars where they had a chance of survival.

Baby coons are cute as kittens and people sometimes are tempted to try to make pets of them. It can be done, though they are difficult to raise and of unpredictable temper. Their teeth are needle-sharp and they can be vicious. If they survive to full growth they still have to be watched for truculent inclinations. A female coon in heat can be harder to handle than an angry tomcat. But some people do tame them and consider them desirable pets. Some people tame skunks, too.

Squirrels, mostly grays, will be racing through the road-side trees in late Winter, especially active during mating season which in my area occurs in February. In the Fall they will always be found at any roadside that has oaks or nut trees, often so intent on the harvest that they forget the hazards of traffic. Every October I find that heedless drivers have killed two or three gray squirrels near a big hickory just down the road. This always seems unnecessary to me, for a squirrel will get out of the way of any car if given a chance.

Now and then you may see a fox at the roadside, usually in early morning or at dusk. Foxes also prowl the roadside at night, especially in chilly weather, undoubtedly because mice and other small fox-food animals are lured there by the warmth. One late May night when I was driving down a main highway not far from here my lights picked up two fox kits trying to cross the road. They were very young, not much bigger than cats, their tails still scrawny and their heads and ears looking much too big for their bodies. Probably on their first trip away from the den. They dodged the car ahead of me, then scurried safely on across. I was so intent on them that I almost hit a third one that had lagged behind till the last minute. I hit the brakes and he, too, got across in safety. I didn't see the mother, who may have been ahead, leading the family. But if she had taken them out to learn the facts of life on a highway she almost lost her whole family.

Although deer are not normally roadside animals, I see them from time to time, usually at dusk, on their way from the hemlock thickets on the mountain where they lie up for the day down to the open fields in the valley. This happens most often in early Spring and late Fall, before the leaves which provide their Summer browse have opened or after they have fallen. Then they come down to the meadows to graze.

Since deer often use the same "run" or trail, even when crossing well-traveled roads, you will see "Deer Crossing" signs even on main highways, especially in wooded areas where deer abound. Such signs mark the places where deer habitually cross the road and they should not be ignored, night or day. At night, deer are blinded by a car's lights and may lunge directly into its path. In the daytime deer may be confused by an approaching car and jump the wrong way at the wrong time. Not long ago a friend of mine driving a high-speed throughway in a wooded area suddenly saw a deer in mid-leap in front of him. The next thing that deer was right in the car, in the front-seat passenger's lap, and only good luck and skill kept the car from a disastrous crash into the ditch. The deer had come out of nowhere, it seemed, tried to leap over the speeding car, and succeeded only in clearing the hood in time to crash through the windshield. The deer's neck was broken by the impact, and the windshield was shattered.

The strangest sight of a deer I ever had on the road was one afternoon when I was on my way to the village in the car. A young doe had come down the hillside for some reason, and I had surprised her at the roadside. Instead of taking to the woods, as any sensible deer would have done, she chose to run down the road ahead of me. In the woods or open fields or topping a fence or a brushy hedge, deer are the most graceful animals I know except possibly otters and foxes; but that young doe, galloping down the hard-topped road, was as awkward as a cow, at least from behind. I idled the car and drifted along behind her, laughing, for almost half a mile before she finally had a flash of common sense. She quit the road, turned off into a meadow, and leaped the fence, her graceful self again. And I was glad that, if she had to make such a spectacle of herself, she chose to do it on a country road and ahead of a driver who wasn't hurrying.

Country roads weren't meant for swift passage. They were laid out originally for leisurely travel from farm to farm and from farm to village, and they conformed to the land itself, not to an engineer's ruler laid on a map. There is a tendency nowadays to convert too many of them into minor speedways by straightening out their curves and cutting every tree that a haphazard driver might run into. This tendency is to be deplored and resisted. We need the byways just as much as, possibly more than, the superhighways. We need the winding back roads where the driver is warned by the road itself to slow down, take it easy. We need them as a relief from the haste and tensions of the big highways where everyone seems intent on getting somewhere much too fast so he can turn around and hurry back. We need country roads where the leisurely travelers can stop and look, where the countryman can go safely on foot and know the feel of his own land. Country roads are for enjoying, and the best of that enjoyment comes to him who walks.

# Chapter 3

# Pastures and Meadows

THE FARMER *likes to think he is master of his grasslands, but if he turns his back for a season nature quietly makes them her own again. The patient explorer will find even the meadow alive with the untamed and the insistently untamable.*

*Many country places*, and practically all the farmhouses I know, are either on the edge or in the midst of meadows and pastureland. Ever since man emerged from the caves to build a shelter for his family he has chosen to live in a clearing. This must have been at least in part because it is easier there to see the approach of enemies; but it also, undoubtedly, is because the clearing has long been the symbol of man's mastery of the land. Today we reationalize these matters by saying that a farmstead set in open fields gives a sense of space and air, and if we are being practical we note that it is a convenient arrangement for the farmer. Pastureland near the barn saves time and energy for man and beast. The farmer works in his fields of corn and oats only during growing and harvest season, and what work he does in his woodlot is done in the off-season. His pastures are in use a good part of the year.

The cultivated meadow or pasture is not the most profitable place to look for wild life because it is supposed to be a field of tame grass and clover, tended and renewed by reseeding every few years. Wild plants are not welcome there, and even such wild animals as rabbits and woodchucks, which eat forage grown for domestic animals, are not encouraged. But most pastures and meadows have fence rows, difficult to trim and impossible to cultivate. In my part of the country many meadows are bordered by woodland, and the underbrush constantly tries to creep in, thus creating a brushy margin. Here and in most of New England we also have old stone walls, laid up long ago and now often fallen

34

into disorderely rows of stones, which defy the plow and the mower. All these places are havens for wild plants and offer shelter for small animals. Their seeds and berries encourage the birds. As a nature watcher I cherish these margins and old walls, though as a landowner I know that they are constantly warning me that my sovereignty over the land can be maintained only by unending work.

My pastures are all bordered by woodland and brush. A few years ago we spent several sweaty weeks reclaiming a border strip with ax and brush hook. We cut the brush, opened the soil to the sun, and encouraged the pasture grass to grow and spread. But only a few days ago I noticed that the brush is coming back, thicker than ever. Young sumac and birch and ash seedlings are as high as my head, and there is quite a stand of seedling pasture cedars and vigorous young barberry bushes. That strip should be cleaned off again. But I also noticed that meadowlarks are nesting there, and brown thrashers, and I flushed three partridges and several cottontails. The partridges were there to get the barberry berries or the birch buds, both of which are important items in their diet. I like partridges and try to encourage them. But if I fail to brush off that strip soon, that whole side of the pasture will go back to nature.

Down the road a mile or so is a field which should be an example to me as a farm owner. It is an old meadow that has been untended for about five years, as ragged-looking a plot as I know; but every time I pass there I want to stop and spend an hour just loafing and looking. A few times each season I go there and spend a few hours, and I always find something new.

It is only a small field, five or six acres, an odd tract left over in a series of farm sales some years back. Before we came here to live it had been a small pasture, but when I first saw it it was a second-rate hay field mowed every June by a farmer half a mile away. Between annual mowings it had no care; daisies, asters, and goldenrod multiplied and the original grass diminished. After a few years the farmer stopped mowing it. The hay wasn't worth his time and labor. It has lain untended since.

It lies, like my pastures, at the foot of a wooded hillside. At one end a small brook trickles down from a seep spring on the hillside and drains through a culvert under the road into a larger brook beyond. The road borders it on two sides. Since it was abandoned the brook's outlet has been partly choked and it has created a small wet area, not yet a bog but possibly one in years to come. Brush from the timbered hillside has crept down farther each year. The fence rows have spread. With the wild noose tightening, the grass, last evidence of man's domination, has been choked back toward the center of the field. Even there the grass loses ground year by year to such humble wildlings as bluets, dwarf cinquefoil, and yellow wood sorrel. In a few more years the grass will be gone and man's signature there will have all but vanished.

That field, as I said, should be an object lesson to me when I see the brush creeping down into my own pasture. But the truth is that I admire that place, in part because it is an unplanned sanctuary for many wildlings and in part because it shows what nature will do if man turns his back for a little while.

Along the upper edge of that field are the remnants of an old stone wall, behind which the woods were once contained. Today that wall is surrounded and overgrown, all but covered with Virginia creeper, wild grape, and poison ivy. And the trees have reached over the wall. Red maples grow ten feet high in the edge of the old meadow, and gray birch and sumac have sprung up as they do on any untended land. Among the birches are pasture cedars four feet high, and every year there are more and more barberry bushes, proof that the partridges appreciate this new cover.

In early Spring I can go there, to that brushy margin, and find anemones in bloom. If I search a little farther back in the old woodland I usually find hepatica, the woolly-leafed liverwort. Until two years ago I also had to go back into the woods to find wild ginger, with its heart-shaped leaves, its hidden brownish-red cups of bloom, and its strong-scented roots; but now I find that the ginger, too, has leaped the wall and grows in the edge of the field. Jack-in-the-pulpit is also there now, and for the past two years I have been able to find bloodroot of the big green leaves and the waxen-white flowers on the field side of the wall. All these plants demand a degree of shade, but not too much. They spread their leaves and open their flowers before the leaves have fully opened on the trees above them, then settle back gratefully to a Summer of shade.

Once the trees are in leaf, I don't even have to leave the road to see the bluets. Bluets, which some know as Quaker ladies, like the sun. They have taken over great patches of the grassy area, disarmingly humble plants with four-petaled white flowers less than half an inch across and borne on thread-thin stems. From a distance they look like frost on the ground, there are so many of them. Looked at closely, they often show a pale lilac tinge, the nearest thing to blue they ever achieve despite their common name.

Before the bluets have faded I can find columbines along the old stone wall, with their bluish-green foliage and their crimson-and-gold flowers. Columbines insist on leaf-moldy places and prefer the company of rocks, both of which they find there. And while I am looking for columbines, if I go down along the sluggish brook I almost certainly will find the narrow lance leaves of wild iris, which come to bud and purple bloom in late May. There are no cattails there, for they demand more of a bogland than has yet developed. Nor is there any skunk cabbage. Cattails, skunk cabbage, and other marsh plants won't move in until alders and willows take root, choke the brook, widen the area of wetland, and create a real bog. But give nature time and she will have her way with that corner. Which is another object lesson to me. If I would not have my own meadows dotted with growing bogs I must keep my brooks clear.

By the time the iris are in bloom and the bluets have gone there will be blue-eyed grass twinkling where the bluets throve, tiny blue stars with golden centers. And soon I can find, there in the sunny open space, both kinds of hawk-weed, the woolly-stemmed, rich orange-flowered variety and the clear yellow, smooth-stemmed one. The orange-flowered hawkweed is often called devil's-paintbrush. In England it is known as Grim the Collier, probably because the dark, bristly hairs on the stem reminded someone of coal-dusted beard stubble on a coal miner's face. By the time the hawk-weeds have come to bloom the whole field will be flecked with the buttery yellow of buttercups. Then will come the frost of daisies, and within two weeks after the first daisies I always see the first black-eyed Susans with their warm orange-yellow petals. Close on their heels comes the first wild carrot, Queen Anne's lace.

By then it is June and I have trouble keeping up with the wildflowers. Along the fence rows all kinds of things are happening. Those particular fence rows have few early Spring plants except dandelions and violets. For some reason the violets have made little headway out ·in the old meadow, but they thrive in the fence-row's shade and along the brook, the common meadow violet along the fence, the long-stemmed, lighter-colored marsh violet where it can have its roots moist but not continually wet. I have yet to find the little yellow violet in that field, but it will be there eventually. Only a few plants, however; the yellow violet doesn't colonize in my area as it does elsewhere. I probably shall also eventually find the big white violets. They grow in the margins of my own pastures, possibly because I once moved in a few plants and set them in the garden here at the house. I am not sure how violets spread as widely as they do, but those white violets, many of them hybrids with purple streaks on their petals, now have spread to places a quarter of a mile from the house.

Along the fence row are the typical vines, Virginia creeper, wild clematis or virgin's bower, bittersweet, wild cucumber. As yet there is no poison ivy, but it will appear soon; it grows on the stone wall just across the field and the birds eat its berries and plant them in their droppings. They have already planted a number of seedling cedars in that way.

Among the wildflowers most insistent along the fence are various members of the wild parsnip family, with their tall stems, their deeply cut compound leaves, and their large flat clusters of small white or yellow flowers. The common wild parsnip and two meadow parsnips have yellow flowers and leaves that somewhat resemble the foliage of the tame parsnips we grow in the garden. Those with white flowers, usually dull white, have a dubious reputation because they include not only sweet cicely and caraway but also poison hemlock. Poison hemlock is close kin to the plant the Greeks called hemlock, from which they brewed the poison draught with which they executed criminals and political prisoners. Socrates was put to death with the cup of hemlock. Caraway, whose seeds are used in cakes and rye bread, is rather easily mistaken for our poison hemlock. Sweet cicely's seed pods are long oval rather than round, as are those of the poison hemlock, and cicely's leaves are not as finely cut as those of the poisonous plant. The roots of the poisonous plant are particularly potent, but even the leaves have a poison content. None of these plants, however, is poisonous on contact as poison ivy is.

Milkweed also grows along the fence rows, as does dogbane. The botanists distinguish between the milkweeds and the dogbanes, though they are much alike in many ways including the white, milky juice common to both. And Monarch butterflies, which patronize few if any other plants, feed on both dogbane and milkweed. Dogbane is also the place to find the tiny, iridescent dogbane beetle, an insect only half an inch long and jewel-like in its lustrous metallic tones. I have never seen this beetle on any other plant.

There are a few plants of the orange-flowered milkweed, often known as butterfly weed and sometimes as pleurisy root. This plant's blossoms are a beautiful shade of orange, and its pods are long and slim. Incidentally, the juice of this milkweed is only slightly white or milky, quite different from that of the common milkweed or even the dogbane. Butterfly weed is unpredictable. I know a field that had a dozen plants of it several years in a row; then they all disappeared, though I know that nobody picked the blossoms or dug the roots. One year I had three plants in a corner of one of my pastures and I marked the spot hopefully. The next year there wasn't a trace of them and I haven't seen them there since. Perhaps by next summer there will be none in the fence row of this old meadow.

Common milkweed, on the other hand, can be counted on. There is one riverbank area where we have gathered young milkweed shoots for eight years, and they seem to have multiplied rather than diminished. I always pause at a milkweed patch when the plants come to blossom in July, in part because I like to smell their fragrance a few times each season and in part to look again at the milkweed's insect traps. The fragrance, almost as demanding as that of the tuberose, is so strong on a damp morning that I can smell a roadside patch while driving past in a car. The insect trap is the individual blossom, which has V-shaped slits into which a visiting insect frequently thrusts a foot, and the more the insect struggles, the tighter it is imprisoned. A bumblebee can pull itself loose, but a honey bee can't, nor can an ant. These traps serve no apparent purpose, for the milkweed is not, like the pitcher plant and the sundew, carnivorous. I sometimes wonder about these traps, which seem senseless and even cruel; then I remember that nature is neither cruel nor compassionate. Nature has no emotions, as man defines emotion.

Also in that fence row are most of the wild asters of my area, from the tiny light lavender calico aster to the big-flowered New England aster with its deep purple bloom, from the early many-flowered aster with its small white bloom to the late-flowering heath aster or Michaelmas daisy. There are about 250 species of aster in the United States, close to fifty in New England. The non-botanist who learns to identify a dozen of them is doing very well.

Close kin to the asters are the goldenrods, which are even more numerous in that old fence row and along most roadsides. At least seventy-five species of goldenrod are known in the United States, and most of them can be found in the Northeast. Like the asters, they bloom early and late. Large-leafed goldenrod blooms in my area as early as July, and so does rough-stemmed goldenrod, whose flowers bloom in loose clusters rather than in plumes; late goldenrod, whose stems have a lilac-colored "bloom" or glow, is still in blossom here well into October. Sweet goldenrod, one of the smaller species, has a strong anise scent when the leaves are crushed. White goldenrod, or silver-rod, not common in my area, has white blossoms, the only member of the family whose bloom is not some shade of yellow. Canada goldenrod grows as much as seven feet tall.

Curious about such matters, I once spent several hours counting the blossoms on several plumes of sweet goldenrod. They averaged 3,000 individual flowers to the plume. But that was only a base count, for each of those tiny flowers was made up of five to ten even tinier florets grouped in a head like the center of a daisy. Each floret has its own pistil, ovary, and pollen. So the average goldenrod plume, those I counted at least, has a minimum of 15,000 to 20,-000 individual florets, each of which is capable of producing seed.

Equally curious about Queen Anne's lace and milkweed, I did some counting with them, too. I counted several average heads of Queen Anne's lace and came out with an average of 2,450 individual florets to the head. That was about twice what I would have guessed. And I counted the seeds in three milkweed pods chosen at random. I opened these pods while they were still somewhat green, when they were just showing the first cracks of ripeness. The floss was damp, not yet fluffy, but it made a mess of the room where I was counting. Those three pods averaged only 272 seeds to the pod, only about half what I would have guessed. But the plants from which I picked those pods had from four to six or eight pods, so each plant was producing more than 1,500 seeds. I have never had the patience or the eyesight to count the separate florets on a flourishing wild aster plant, but they must run well into the thousands.

That fence row along the old meadow also has Joe Pye weed, of the tufted crimson-magenta blossom, and ironweed with its madder-purple heads of bloom, both of which come to flower in late August. And boneset, the white-flowered cousin of Joe Pye weed, which I have seen grow to a height of eight feet, but not there in the edge of that meadow. Both meadowsweet and hardhack, or steeplebush, have begun to flourish there, the meadowsweet with its loose tufts of pinkish little blooms, each like a miniature apple blossom and with a faint, delicate fragrance, the hardhack with its more tightly packed spike of deeper pink florets. Hardhack's flower spike comes to bloom from the top down, the reverse of most spike flowers. And for the past two years there have been two tall plants of goatsbeard—a cousin of both hardhack and meadowsweet—which is not too common in my area. Goatsbeard blooms in a group of spikes about the size of my finger, each spike a mass of very small yellowish white florets.

And now the sumac is spreading to that fence row. When it takes over, the whole flora will change, of course, because the sumac will create shade and drive these sun-loving plants out into the open. They will spread out, yard by yard, toward that last remnant of grass in the middle of the old meadow.

There are also the various mints. It seems incredible to me that, with the variety of mints we have growing wild—they range from catnip to bee balm, from Gill-over-the-ground to selfheal—there is only one native American among them. That is wild mint; for some reason it never acquired another common name, though it is a sturdy and persistent plant with a strong odor and flavor. All the other wild mints, as we now know them, are European natives that were brought here by early colonists for their own use as herbs. They found American soil to their liking and spread everywhere.

But the mints are not alone in having a foreign origin. The list of native wildflowers in New England, for example, is very short: milkweed, robin's plantain, cranesbill or wild geranium, steeplebush, the asters and goldenrods. That seems to cover them. The others are imports which came here with the alien settlers either by choice or by accident —the clovers, bouncing Bet, the buttercups, the daisies, hawkweed, Queen Anne's lace, chicory, dandelion, and a long, long roll of others. Some were brought as garden flowers, some as herbs, and some came as stowaways, uninvited. But here they are, and here they will be as long as green things grow.

There are a score of lesser flowering plants in that old meadow—chickweed, of course, and ground ivy and several species of cinquefoil and at least two species of oxalis. In the moist corner I always find the knot-jointed, pink-flowered smartweed, cousin of domestic buckwheat. Several cresses are also there, and the straggling wild forget-me-not with wonderfully blue little flowers. And an early-blooming wild phlox and an occasional Deptford pink. As yet there are no marsh marigolds, which demand a real bog, water around and over their roots. But if a bog develops, marsh marigolds will be there eventually.

For a time I wondered at the swiftness with which the wild plants took over that meadow. Then I saw what was happening right under my nose, within fifty yards of my own house.

A small brook flows across one corner of our vegetable garden. The brook dries up in Midsummer, but it makes that corner difficult to plow and tend. Those who lived here before we came apparently used it, but since it is a tiny plot, a triangle not more than twenty feet on a side, I wrote it off as a part of the garden. On one edge it had a few clumps of day lilies and a few ostrich ferns, nothing else.

The first Summer it grew up in a tangle of chickweed, purslane, and what we call German weed, with a few pigweeds. The next year I noticed a few violets there and a couple of Solomon's-seal plants, and before the Summer was out there were several young goldenrods and asters. At the edge of the brook there was a shoot of elderberry, a seedling.

The next time I paid any attention a stand of jewelweed was taking hold, and hedge nettles had appeared. And the elderberry shoot had become a bush six feet high. Over in one corner was a wild blackberry bush three feet high, and the ferns and day lilies had begun to fight back as the newcomers throve.

After that I lost track. That little triangle became a tangle of wildlings, fighting, leaf and stem, for root space. The Solomon's-seal shot up seven feet tall. Joe Pye and ironweed appeared. Great lobelia, with its strong, deep blue flowers, came from somewhere. Daisies and black-eyed Susans appeared. And finally I took a plant census, just to see what was there, what had come unbidden to take over that little abandoned corner. I identified forty-two species of wild flowering plants, even including two yellow meadow lilies and one wood lily. The only tame plant I found there was rhubarb, and it was having a struggle. A few years ago I dug out a clump of rhubarb that had been sulking in the garden, and I must have tossed a part of the root over into the triangle. It had taken hold and grown there, but the competition was almost too much for it. The stalks were spindly and the leaves pale and undersized. It probably will be choked out in another year or two.

That's what happens to many cultivated plants when thrown on their own in a wild environment. Not many of them have the vigor to survive, though there are notable exceptions. I have found venerable lilac bushes beside the cellar holes of houses abandoned fifty or seventy-five years ago, and now and then I find a few clumps of hollyhocks and even a clump or two of peonies there. All the day lilies along the margins of country roads are "escapes," too, which thrive on their own. Phlox is notorious for its habit of running away—and reverting to magenta in its blooms. And, to repeat, most of the wildflowers we know in America today once were tame and cultivated in garden or dooryard. They, however, have now undergone many generations of adaptation to life in the wild. Perhaps that clump of rhubarb in my abandoned triangle will prove that it, too, can survive. Perhaps I underrate it.

Most meadows and pastures, even those kept under control by an energetic farmer, are good bird habitat. I always know when Winter is near its end by watching for the robins in my home pasture. A few small flocks of robins always Winter over here, finding both food and shelter in the brush and thin woods, but when March begins to thin away I watch for the big flock of migrants that comes up the valley and scatters over the Winter-sere pasture grass. The robins arrive and stalk about the open ground, merely surveying it for an hour or so, twittering among themselves. Then they look for food, poking into every clump of grass, cocking their heads, and plunging their beaks down for worms and grubs. Sometimes they arrive before the last patches of snow are gone, and one year they came on the eve of a whirling snowstorm. But once here, they stay, and I have never know them to arrive long before the steady mild spell that signals the breakup of Winter.

While I am awaiting the robins I am watching for the red-wing blackbirds, which often get here ahead of the robins. They come, the more colorful males first, and stake out their claims in the bogland and along the riverbanks. Ten days or two weeks later their mates arrive, dressed much like sparrows, and prepare to set up housekeeping. By then I am watching for bluebirds, which I see first in the trees along the fence rows. By then, too, all the sparrows are singing. Some of the sparrows Winter here, chiefly tree and field sparrows, swamp sparrows, song sparrows, a few white-throats and fox sparrows, but they make little music before March. They find shelter in the brush and live on weed seed and dried berries.

All Winter long the little woodpeckers, the downies and their slightly larger cousins, the hairies, are at work not only in my dooryard trees but in all the fence rows and back in the woodland. Soon the flickers, the yellow-shafted woodpeckers which feed almost as much on the ground in the pastures as in the trees, will arrive. I hear them drumming on dead trees, I hear them calling, and then I see them in little flocks in the pasture, working the grass much as the robins do. Most woodpeckers fly in a series of swoops—goldfinches also fly that way, but are much smaller birds—so I can recognize a flicker in flight several hundred yards away. Flickers also reveal their identity by showing a whitish rump patch when they fly. To me they are the cotton-tails of birddom.

By the time the flickers are here I will have seen star-lings, grackles, and cowbirds in the pasture. Starlings are dirty, noisy birds in the city, but they have their virtues in the country. They eat great quantities of insects, including Japanese beetles. One year they invaded my garage through a hole a woodpecker had carved in the cornice, and I had to replace the whole cornice to be rid of them. But as long as they nest elsewhere they are welcome on my land. Grackles, with richly iridescent tones on their black feath-ers, have rusty-hinge voices; but they are beautiful birds and they, too, eat many insects.

Cowbirds flock in the pastures and meadows where cat-tle graze. Last Summer there were at least 200 in one flock here on my place. They are small, brown-headed black-birds, the males black-bodied, the females dark gray. They eat parasites and flies on the cattle and gorge on insects flushed from the grass by the cows as they move about. Domestically they are complete parasites, never nesting, never raising a chick. They lay their eggs in other birds' nests and leave the whole responsibility of hatching them to someone else. I once found a song sparrow's nest with a cowbird chick in it almost as big as the mother song spar-row. It had crowded out all but one of the sparrow's own chicks and was starving that chick to death with its big-mouthed gluttony.

The open meadowland is choice area for meadowlarks and bobolinks. Both nest in the grass. The meadowlark, with its yellow vest and black "V" of a necktie, has a long beak, a fat body, and stubby wings. In flight it is some-times mistaken for a quail by those who are not too well acquainted with either bird. The bobolink, unlike the mead-owlark, likes to live in flocks and often chooses a meadow with a brook, for it likes damp places. The male bobolink is our only land bird that is marked with black below and white above. It sings in flight.

Woodland birds are often seen in the meadow but they are not really at home there. Hawks course the meadows in daylight and owls hunt there at night, both of them look-ing for field mice and rabbits. From time to time I see a turkey buzzard—a vulture in this area—looking for carrion. One Summer day one came to my home pasture and stayed almost an hour feasting on a dead woodchuck. It ate so big a meal it had difficulty taking flight again.

As for animals in the open meadow, the daylight visitor will be lucky to see more than a rabbit or two and, near the fence row or the stone walls, a few chipmunks and gray squirrels. Now and then one will see a woodchuck, but only if the woodchuck is too busy to see him first. The hidden life there appears mostly at dusk or in the night, when the fox, the skunk, the racoon, the opossum, and various mice and voles do most of their foraging. The vole is commonly called a meadow mouse, but it is of a different species from the true mouse. Voles have short tails and small ears. And enormous appetites; a vole can eat its own weight in twenty-four hours. The meadow vole and the pine vole are the common ones in the East and Northeast. They are about the same size, three to five inches long, but the meadow vole, which prefers the open fields, is grayish-brown, and the pine vole, a woodland creature, is chestnut above and gray below. Voles are close kin to lemmings. They and bog lemmings, also found in the Northeast, are often mistaken for each other.

Also in the open meadowland but seldom seen are the shrews. A shrew looks like a small mouse with a long, tapered nose, tiny eyes, and almost invisible ears. The biggest of the shrew tribe, the short-tailed shrew, weighs only one ounce, and the smallest, the pigmy shrew, is only two inches long and weighs about the same as a dime. One species, the water shrew, has partly webbed, hairy feet and can literally run on the surface of water. In proportion to their size, shrews are more vicious than man-eating tigers. They will attack and kill a mouse several times their own weight. The short-tailed shrew's saliva contains a venom as poisonous as that of a cobra; this poison, carried into a wound by the animal's sharp, reddish-brown teeth, can paralyze a mouse in seconds. A short-tailed shrew's bite can be painful to a man but not really dangerous. But if you ever catch one alive, don't let a child play with it. As I said, however, shrews are seldom seen. In all my years of nature watching I have seen only four of them, and all of them scurried as soon as they were aware of me. They are so elusive that science still has much to learn about them except that they are very busy, very hungry little mites of life which must eat twice their own weight in food every day or they starve to death.

Deer sometimes come down to open meadows to feed, but almost always at dusk or in the night. I have seen deer in my pasture at 8 o'clock in the morning, but only on rare occasions. Those times when deer came down into the open in daylight, I have noted, were usually foggy or misty mornings, seldom when a clear, bright sun was shining. Perhaps the mist and fog give them a sense of security. I have found that deer are easier to approach in the woods on a misty or drizzly day, too, and I doubt that it is wholly because the dampness helps muffle the sound of a man's approach in the leaf-littered underbrush.

A few times I have seen red foxes come down into the open pasture in daylight. One morning about 7:30, clear and sunny, one crossed the pasture within a hundred yards of the house, taking its time, wary but in no hurry. It apparently was going somewhere and took the short cut across the pasture, for it did not stop to hunt. It watched the house, alert, but otherwise showed no fear. A friend tells me of a fox that came down into the dooryard one morning and frolicked with a shelty pup for ten minutes before it went back to the woods. I have never seen this happen. But one sunny afternoon a red fox came down into the pasture and spent fifteen minutes catfooting from one grass clump to another, hunting mice. Its actions, even to the pounce, reminded me of a cat. I watched while it stalked several grass clumps, cautious step by step, then pounced, but I could not see that it caught anything. It did catch several insects, probably grasshoppers, which were big and fat in the pasture at that time. It startled them from the grass, leaped, and caught them in mid-air with a snap of its mouth.

But the meadow is primarily a place for the plant watcher and the bird watcher. And, of course, for the person who just likes to be out in the open on a lazy, blue-sky day.

# Chapter 4

# The Woodlands

ONLY *the unobservant sees nothing but trees in a forest. Any woodland is a complex community of plant and animal life with its own laws of growth and survival. But if you would know strength and majesty and patience, welcome the company of trees.*

*From time to time* I hear someone say: "I wish I had known this country before the white man came, while it was still a vast, unbroken forest. It must have teemed with wild life."

Actually, even the Northeast was not a vast, unbroken forest when the white man arrived. There were big woods, yes, mainly oak in southern New England and white pine, hemlock, and maple in northern New England. But all the early explorers commented on the openings in the big woods, both their number and extent. Verrazano, who made an expedition from Narragansett Bay as far west as what is now central New York State in 1524, reported "open plains twenty-five or thirty leagues in extent, entirely free from trees or other hindrances." Other sixteenth-century travelers told the same story.

The fact is that the pioneers didn't have to hew their way, yard by yard, through unbroken woods all the way from the Massachusetts coast to the prairies of Iowa.

Furthermore, even the big woods had clearings. All the eastern Indians were farmers, in some degree, and they made clearings for their fields of corn, beans, and squash. As soon as they used up the natural fertility of one clearing they girdled and burned the trees and made a new cleared field. They also burned brushland to encourage grass, and they burned underbrush in the woods, partly to make hunting easier, partly to create more woods margin. The birds and animals they hunted all fed in the open or in the patches of grass and low underbrush that always

50

grow in the edges of the big forests, not in their dark, shaded, grassless depths. All animal life depends, directly or indirectly, on grass and other green forage, and such plants thrive only in sunlight. The dense shade of the primeval forest tends to starve out lesser plant life.

I remember my first visit to the big redwood forests of California, where giant trees stood so tall it dizzied me to look at their crowns. They made a canopy so dense that the occasional shaft of sunlight reaching the forest floor danced with motes like a pinhole sunbeam in a dark room. The mat of needles was a foot thick. There was no underbrush, no blade of grass. No bird sang, no rabbit hopped, no squirrel scurried. Then I came to a place where one of those forest giants had fallen a few decades before, making a gap in the high canopy and admitting a burst of sunlight. In that little opening a score of plant species had sprung up, from oxalis to manzanita brush. Birds sang there, and squirrels were busy. Then I walked on, into the dark silence of the big woods again, and again it was a place of brown silence, a deserted cathedral of giants.

We have few such virgin woodlands left today, and most of them are in remote areas. The redwoods are an exception, but even they are in limited areas. The forests we know best, those accessible to most of us, are relatively young and full of clearings. In Connecticut, for example, a survey made in the mid-1940's showed that 90 per cent of the forest was less than sixty years old. This is a cutover land. But it certainly is not without woods, young though they are. In 1860, only 27 per cent of Connecticut was wooded—probably less than half, perhaps only a third, of the wooded area in this state when the white man came. But by 1910 the Connecticut woodlands had expanded to cover 45 per cent of the land area. And by 1955, 63 per cent of the state was in forest again. This despite the vast increase in population and the sprawling spread of cities and their suburbs.

Other parts of New England never were as extensively cleared as Connecticut once was. Maine, for instance, never had more than 25 per cent of its area cleared. And today, despite all the tree-cutting of the past, three quarters of New England is in timber, probably not a great deal less than was wooded when the white men arrived.

I can read the human history of New England whenever I walk in the woods in my area. Nearly every woodland I explore, even on sharp mountainsides, has a network of old stone walls, most of them now tumbled into serpentine stone piles. Those walls were not laid up by woodcutters taking out saw logs or firewood or wood for charcoal. They were built by farmers who had cut the primeval trees and were waging New England's endless war with the stony freight brought here by the ancient glaciers. They cleared the stones from their fields, year after year, and built them into walls, not only to mark boundaries but to clear the way for the plow. On my own mountainside are half a dozen such wall-enclosed fields, now grown up to trees forty or fifty years old, fields that haven't been tilled since the days of oxen. Those fields were abandoned long ago. Now they are a part of the woodland which covers the whole mountainside.

My woods, like most of those of southern and central New England, is a mixture of trees, white pines, hemlocks, oaks, white ash, shagbark hickory, and birch primarily. There is little beech in my woods, and there aren't as many maples up there as I would wish. And there is more gray birch and less white birch than I would choose to have. For the most part, it is an old-field tree stand that has been cut over several times and is still in the process of maturing as a woodland. It would provide a certain amount of saw-timber, I suppose, but not enough to tempt me to invite the loggers in. The farmer who owned this place fifty years ago did a certain amount of logging there, and he cut the lumber of the house I live in on that mountainside. I still find thirty-inch stumps of old chestnut up there, stubbornly defying time; beams, rafters, and the interior trim of the house came from the trees that grew there. The sheathing and other lumber for the house came from white pines whose stumps have now rotted and disappeared. But the pines are coming back, and with them the hemlocks. The chestnuts, of course, are gone.

The best stands of pines are in two old hay fields up there. In both of those fields there are several rugged old pines, patriarchs and parents, in all probability, of most of the pines on the mountainside. They probably were left standing, as was the custom, to provide shade and shelter for farm animals which were pastured in those fields. Look around in any stand of young pines and you probably will find such a parent tree or its stump.

Pines thrive on old pastureland and hay fields, areas with thick turf. Seeds from the parent tree work down through the grass, find a place to root, and shoot up quickly in the warmth of full sun. In a few years the seedlings are as tall as a man and have begun to shade and smother the grass and weeds. A mat of needles accumulates and makes it even more difficult for other plants to get started, and the thickening shade discourages those that manage a roothold. Within fifteen years the old pasture is an almost pure stand of pine with little or no undergrowth.

As the pines grow, their dense shade kills their own lower limbs. More light and space appear beneath them. Storm and blight bring down a tree here and there and the sun can reach the ground again. Patches of brush spring up in such openings, and soon there is a determined growth of gray birch, ash, maple, fighting each other for space and growing room. But pine seedlings, which need a few years of light and elbowroom to get started, seldom make headway in such openings and almost never in the pine woods themselves. In the deep shade one finds only the lesser, shade-tolerant plants such as Christmas ferns, partridge-berry, lady-slipper, and such shade-demanding parasites as Indian pipe and false beechdrops. Out along the margins, where there is more sunlight and more room, one finds columbine and cranesbill and toothwort and Canada Mayflower, the false lily of the valley. Sometimes one finds carpets of ground pine and ground cedar there and reaching back into the deep shade; these are very ancient ones which have now declined to the status of creepers and must settle for the crumbs of woodland existence. More often, though, they are found in the hardwood forests where they have sunlight, weak though it is, from leaf-fall till opening-bud time in April and May.

As the pines approach maturity, in fifty to seventy-five years, their growth slows. Growth, of course, varies with the soil and conditions of climate, but in a favorable situation a white pine in thirty years will attain a trunk two feet in diameter and sixty feet in height. Under good conditions, a white pine fifty years old will be at least a hundred feet tall, and some very old pines run up to 150 or 175 feet in height. They are the giants of their kind, however, and few mature white-pine woodlands today run much over 125 feet.

By the time the pines have reached this stage of maturity, more and more of them will be victims of storm or disease, and more and more openings will appear in the woodland. The underbrush in these gaps spreads and the deciduous trees take firm hold. The pines begin to lose ground. The next phase will belong to the hardwoods, which are crowding them year by year. But meanwhile another pine woods has been springing up in another old pasture or meadow, seeded by some old patriarch, perhaps a tree in the doomed pine woods itself, since pine seeds are winged and can travel on the wind for a considerable distance. I am speaking now of the white pine and the pitch pine, principal pines of our woods in the Northeast; in the West and Southwest are pines with wingless, nutlike seeds, notably the piñon pines, whose seeds look like small brown beans and are the choice fare of squirrels and discriminating people.

I can spot the old meadows and pastures on my mountainside by the white pine woods, even though the walls have tumbled or been carted away. But the hardwood forests, which cover the greater part of these hills—and make October a particular glory of color—are less an index to the farmer's tenure than to the activity of the woodcutter. The native woodlands here, and in much of the Northeast, were cut by successive generations to clear fields, for firewood and lumber, for charcoal, and to fuel the early woodburning railroad locomotives. Often they cut every tree big enough to make a board or a stick of firewood. The devastated woodlands invited erosion. Contrary to common belief, most of New England's barren hillsides were not farmed to death; they were robbed of their forest cover, left open to wind, rain, and frost, and their soil and fertility simply eroded away.

The last great harvest of white pine in New England was, roughly, from 1890 to 1925. The loggers cut not only the pines but any hardwoods that had sprung up in the openings in the pine woods; they cut clean, in logging language —took all the usable trees. But they left a fire-inviting tangle of slash and trimmings; and where fires swept, the hills were soon eroded down to bedrock and the woods were slow in coming back. Elsewhere, hardwood sprout thickets sprang up in a few years. Hardwoods sprout from their stumps. Of the native conifers, only pitch pine will renew itself from the stump; once a white pine or hemlock is cut, the roots die and that tree is gone forever. But many of the hardwood stump lands became sprout thickets, then new hardwood forests, with oak, maple, beech, ash, hickory, birch.

The terms "hardwood" and "softwood" are confusing. They are lumbermen's terms, now taken over by foresters despite their ambiguity. To the lumberman, any cone-bearing tree, pine, spruce, hemlock, etc., is a softwood. Broad-leafed trees, oak, maple, beech, hickory, even poplar and birch, are all hardwoods. The distinction is arbitrary. Yellow pine, for instance, though it is as hard as maple, is a softwood. And birch and poplar, each as soft as white pine, are hardwoods. To me, this doesn't make sense; but argument over it is futile.

Oak, beech, sugar maple, and white birch like a heavy, fertile soil. But I notice that all of them make out on my own mountainside, which in many places has thin soil and is persistently rocky. I know, however, that they do best in places where there was a thick earlier growth of gray birch and quick-growth underbrush that built up a thick mat of leafmold with their leaves and fallen branches. In the thinnest-soil places the gray birches still predominate, building up that mat of leafmold. They are weedy, quick-growth trees that come down by the dozen in Winter storms, rot in a season or two, and sprout generously from the root. Ten years of gray-birch growth will create enough soil to nurture oaks and maples, so they have an important place in the evolution of any woodland.

The primitive oak forest—oak and chestnut, really, and even including a good deal of beech; they are all of the same botanical family—originally covered the whole coast of Massachusetts and most of Rhode Island and Connecticut and extended from there south and west. North of the oak-chestnut woodlands was the hemlock-white pine area, which had large groves of northern hardwoods, mostly birch and maple, scattered through it; this area extended into

southern Maine and covered the southern half of New
Hampshire and Vermont. North from there the woods were
primarily spruce and northern hardwoods. To a degree,
those areas persist today, with a good deal of overlapping.
Hemlock, for example, grows abundantly in southern Connecticut where there is protection from severe wind and
blazing Summer sun. And where the soil is somewhat fertile
and moist, especially on north slopes facing swamps, the
spruce-hardwood type of woods will often be found in
southern Vermont and New Hampshire and even in Massachusetts, normally the hemlock-white pine area.

The really old oak forests have all been destroyed, primarily because their area happened to be that part of the
Northeast which was first settled and became most densely
populated. Actually, in terms of geological environment,
the oak forests shouldn't have been here in the Northeast to
begin with. The climate is too cold and too damp. The oaks
belong in the more temperate Appalachians. But apparently they migrated northward several thousand years ago,
just after the last great ice sheet melted, when the climate
was warmer than it has been in recent centuries. Somehow
the oaks came to New England, throve, and made a slow
adaptation to weather changes as they came. If, as some
believe, we are now in a long-range warming trend again,
perhaps the oaks that have persisted here will move still farther northward in the next few centuries.

The hardwood forest seldom makes as dense a canopy
as the conifers do, and because the hardwoods shed their
leaves in the Fall they allow six or seven months of sunlight to reach the forest floor. So most hardwood forests
have a growth of underbrush and even a considerable population of lesser trees. My own woods are pretty well
mixed as a result of repeated cutting in the past, but even
there I find a familiar pattern, a pattern that persists in
most of the hardwood forests I know, especially in the maple or birch woods. For instance, there is sassafras, of the
pungent root and twig, and sleek-barked hornbeam and
weedy chokecherry with an occasional big bird cherry.
There is a scattering of oak and shagbark hickory. Here
and there are white ash, usually in clumps and shooting up
to claim their share of the sunlight. And flowering dogwood
persists, never much of a tree but wonderfully beautiful in

May with white blossoms that make the lower woodland look as though it were full of white butterflies.

Among the bushes I usually find hazel and laurel and spicebush and various viburnums. And the hardwood forest floor, with its dappling sunlight and deep mull of leafmold, is almost always rich with such wildflowers as hepatica, bloodroot, columbine, wild geranium, Jack-in-the-pulpit, anemone, moccasin flower. Partridgeberry grows there, even in deep shade, and occasionally I still find trailing arbutus, though I would not tell anyone except my wife where to find it, and I whisper it to her.

But this is true only of mixed hardwood forests or of woods primarily of maple or birch. I have never seen a real forest of ash or hickory, for instance, or of elm for that matter. Those trees seem never to colonize extensively, as maples, birch, and oaks sometimes do. They grow in groves or in clumps or individually, seldom covering more than an acre or two with their own seedlings.

When you find an oak woods you will find limited undergrowth and few of the lesser trees. Not far from where I live is a patch of oak woods only about twenty acres in extent where not another tree grows except out at the margin, where there is a fringe of young ash and maple. The reason is rather simple. Oak leaves are tough, leathery, and full of tannin. They decay slowly. Earthworms, which soon reduce the softer, sweeter leaves of most other hardwoods to leafmold, dislike oak leaves. So the oak leaves form a thick, fibrous layer on the floor of the oak woods where other trees cannot get a roothold and even few bushes except blueberries thrive. Relatively few flowers can grow in the oak-leaf mat, either. In oak woods I find among the Spring flowers only goldthread, starflower, some partridgeberry, and, most common of all, big patches of Canada Mayflower, which some call wild lily of the valley. These flowers can tolerate the acid soil of the oak leaves and manage to find a roothold in the tough mat.

On some of the mountainsides and other uplands of the Northeast you will find large patches of blueberry bushes. If you look back in local records almost invariably you will find that those blueberry patches were, a generation or two ago, oak woods. When the oaks were cut, usually for lumber or charcoal, the blueberries already had a foothold, and with the trees gone the berries throve. Dig into the soil and you may find it toughly matted with the fibers of those old oak leaves, which still haven't completely rotted away.

To find the real wealth of Spring flowers in the woodland, go to maple or birch woods or mixed woods such as mine. In such a place the softer leaves have leavened those of the occasional oak and the processes of decay and earthworm energy have built a deep, fertile mull. Typical of such places is a spot on my own hillside where there are several clumps of white birch, half a dozen sugar maples, a big shagbark hickory, and a small grove of white ash at the margin. A brook, hurrying down the hillside in its own gully, spreads a small fan of misty falls among the ash trees, then leisures off across the open pasture beyond.

That woodland patch has deep leafmold, is on a slope facing the southeast, and gets moisture from the brook and its mist. The sun is broken only by bare branches from mid-October till mid-May. The combination of sunlight and rotting leaf litter warms the soil early, and when I go there in early April I find hepatica in full bloom and anemones waving on their hair-thin stems. By mid-April the bloodroot leaves appear and the first lanceheads of Jack-in-the-pulpit are in sight. Before May arrives I find violets in bloom there, wild ginger leaves thrusting up. Nearby are the light green leaves of the lovely little showy orchis, looking deceptively like Canada Mayflower leaves except that the orchis leaves are thicker and have no stems. The orchis, by the way, comes to bloom when my apple trees first open blossom, never varying that schedule more than a day or two.

All these flowers appear early, hurry into leaf, and blossom. They get their season's work done before the tree leaves have spread a full canopy. And only a few of them continue in leaf long after they are in full shade. You can mark a patch of Jack-in-the-pulpit in May, go back in July and find almost no trace of it. You won't recognize those Jacks again until late September, when the closely clumped berries, hidden in the undergrowth of grass all Summer, have turned an eye-catching lacquer-red. Bloodroot and wild ginger simply vanish by the end of June; they retreat into the root, as do the anemones, which I seldom find after June.

Identification of trees is not really difficult if you use your eyes, your common sense, and a good handbook. Some of the willows still baffle me, but I get some consolation in knowing that they baffle others, too; willows, like sunfish, crossbreed and produce hybrids by the dozen. When I find a big willow with dark brown bark and narrow, rather dull leaves I mark it down as a black willow; when I see a somewhat smaller willow with broader leaves that have a distinct shine I tag it as a shining or glossy willow; and when I see a shrubby willow with smooth, greenish bark I know it is one of the pussy willows, especially if it grows at the edge of a bog. All willows like wet places and all have silvery catkins, but the catkins of the pussy willow are bigger than those of the others. The really big pussy willows that you can get at the florist's in early Spring are produced on cultivated, hybrid trees or bushes; the wild ones are seldom more than half that big.

Aspens, poplars, and cottonwoods belong to the poplar family and are all called "popples" in New England. All have rather thick, heart-shaped leaves with long, limber stems; they whisper as the leaves catch every passing breeze and flutter against each other. Aspens and poplars usually grow with tall, tapering central trunks and without major branching; cottonwoods branch freely and fork from the main stem. The beginner may confuse aspens and poplars with birches. They all belong to the same big botanical family, but there are distinct differences in their bark. The beginner also tends to mistake the lesser gray birch and the big white birch, which look much alike especially when young. But the gray birch's bark has a dirty white look and the white birch's bark is a clean white. And gray birches are always small trees, seldom as much as eight inches through, whereas the white birch is a big, magnificent tree, sometimes three feet in trunk diameter. Whether you can tell them apart as young trees or not, if you find a white-bark birch more than a foot through you can be sure it isn't a gray birch.

There are also other birches, including the black or cherry birch, which has reddish-brown bark much like that on a tame cherry tree and leaves like a cherry. I often pluck a twig of it to chew; the twigs and roots contain the essence used to flavor old-time birch beer. I find black birch on the hillside, almost never on a riverbank. Down along the water, with their roots in wet soil, I find the two biggest birches of all, red or river birch and yellow or swamp birch. They too have leaves like a cherry tree, lance-shaped. Red birch has cinnamon-red bark and the smooth bark of yellow birch is tinged with yellow and tends to peel in ragged strips.

Who does not know the common maple leaf? The two most common maples of the Northeast are the sugar maple and the red or swamp maple. They look much alike in Summer and Winter but are readily told apart in Spring and Fall. The sugar maple's color is yellow—its flowers are greenish-yellow in April, and in October its leaves usually turn rich, golden yellow. The swamp maple's color is red—its flowers are a deep wine-red, and in the Fall its leaves turn equally red; they provide the vivid flame of color that runs across the countryside, that glorious contrast to the gold of the sugar maple. Swamp maples like wet soil; sugar maples prefer dry soil. But one can't be dogmatic, especially about the red maple. One Summer day a few years ago I was upon my own mountainside with a friend who is inclined to make pronouncements. We came to a good-size maple that I said was a red maple. He said: "It can't be. Not growing up here." I was sure it was, but I let him argue while I searched the grass beneath it. In a few minutes I showed him a small handful of winged maple seeds that had been overlooked by squirrels and chipmunks. Every seed was tinged with red, as red maple seeds always are; sugar maple seeds ripen to a yellowish tan. I showed them to my friend, who still held out until he had found a few of those red seeds for himself.

Two lesser maples of the uplands interest me because their common names, moosewood and elkwood, are reminiscent of pioneer days when moose and elk still roamed New England. Neither of these is more than a large shrub, seldom twenty-five feet high. Moosewood, sometimes called striped maple, has smooth bark striped light and dark gray up and down the trunk. It bears greenish-yellow blossoms and keys that dangle in a tassel on long stems. Elkwood, or mountain maple, has uniform dark gray bark, flowers late with tiny white blossoms in erect spikes, and bears the smallest of all maple keys. I find moosewood in the shade on high, rocky places, and I always find elkwood in a misty, rocky ravine where a brook's spray cools the air.

One other maple, though common almost everywhere in the United States, fools many beginners. There is one just down my road, close by a clump of black and white ash trees. Not long ago a newcomer to the country, proud of his newly achieved ability to tell one species of ash from another, pointed to that tree and puzzled: "What kind of ash is that?" I had to tell him it wasn't an ash at all but a maple, an ash-leaf maple more commonly known as a box elder. His confusion was understandable, for the compound leaves, three or five to a stem, look like deeply notched ash leaves, lance-shaped and not at all like the familiar maple leaf. But the tree bears its seed in the typical maple keys, which cling to it all Summer and well into the Winter. Box-elder sap, by the way, makes a special syrup and the whitest of all maple sugar, but the yield is low and practically nobody makes it any more. Syrup and sugar can also be made from birch sap and ash sap, but it is dark in color, rather bitter in taste. It once was made and used in backwoods medicine.

There are fifty-odd oaks native to North America and most of them can be found somewhere in the East. Fewer than half of them occur in the woods I know best, and I doubt that the amateur, unless he makes a special study of oaks, will ever identify as many as twenty-five species. The typical lobed oak leaf is one index but by no means infallible, since several rather common oaks have leaves like those of the beech or chestnut. But any tree that bears acorns, no matter what the shape of its leaves, is an oak. Even the evergreen live oaks of Florida and California bear acorns. So do the willow oaks of the South, though their leaves may be mistaken for the long, slim leaves of the glossy willow.

Nearly all oaks fall into two major divisions which the beginner can easily recognize, white oaks and black oaks. Those in the broad white-oak division have leaves with rounded lobes and their acorns mature and fall every Autumn. Those in the black-oak division have sharp-tipped leaf lobes and their acorns, which require two years to mature, cling to the branches all Winter.

When we first came to this farm I found several beech-leafed oaks on my mountainside and thought I had chestnut oaks, which are rather rare in this area. Then I found a few of their acorns, which were small, round, and not too bitter to the taste. Chestnut-oak acorns are almost twice as big, egg-shaped, and puckery with tannin. Then I learned that the chinquapin oak, for some strange reason, grows in this part of the Housatonic valley though it is rare elsewhere in New England. Mine were chinquapins, even more unusual than the chestnut oaks I thought I had. Which proves that you can't draw hard and fast rules about where you will find a particular tree. The one rule-of-thumb those chinquapins followed was that they like damp soil—they were growing near a seep spring.

The elms are traditionally New England trees, but I have seen elm-lined streams in Iowa, elm-bordered streets in Kansas, and elm groves in Illinois. There are three species here in the Northeast, and I have all of them here on my place —the familiar American elm of classic wineglass shape, the slippery elm of stream banks and lowland areas, and the rock elm of stony hillsides. I sometimes wonder where the Baltimore orioles would hang their nests if we had no more elms. It seems to me that two of every three oriole nests I have ever seen were slung high in the limber tips of tall elm trees.

Botanically speaking, the pine family includes spruces, hemlocks, firs, and cedars as well as pines—which in a sense excuses those who call all evergreens "pines." But in non-technical language a pine is a cone-bearing evergreen whose needles—with one exception, the single-leaf pine, which grows only in the deserts of the Southwest—occur in clusters of two or more. Spruce, hemlock, and fir needles grow singly, and the cedars have overlapping scalelike leaves instead of needles.

The white pine is king of them all in my lexicon, though in the North the crown goes to the spruce and in the West it goes to the fir, with the hemlock rated at least as crown prince. The white pine is the grand tree of the Northeast, beautiful, stately, and eminently useful. Its needles grow in clusters of five, making it unmistakable. They are four or five inches long, soft and flexible to the touch. The cones are long and slim, sometimes eight inches long, and hang downward. The seeds ripen and fall the first season, but the empty cones sometimes remain on the tree all Winter.

The pitch pine's needles are as long as those of the white pine, but they come in clusters of three and are stiff to the touch. This is the only eastern pine with a growth of needles along its main stem. The egg-shaped cones are seldom more than three inches long, are prickly, occur in clusters, and cling to the branches for years. When I see a ragged-looking pine loaded with old cones I set it down as a pitch pine before I even count the needles in a cluster.

The red pine is sometimes called the Norway pine, though it is native to America. Its five-inch needles are as soft and flexible as those of the white pine but they occur in pairs. Its cones also come in pairs, without stems, on opposite sides of the branch, and have no prickles. The red pine is essentially a North-woods tree, but it grows as far south as central Pennsylvania and west into Minnesota.

The beginner sometimes confuses the red pine and the jack pine, which is sometimes called scrub or gray pine. I don't know why. The jack pine is a smaller tree to start with, and often grows in sandy soil and rocky places. Its needles also grow in pairs, but they are short and stiff, less than two inches long. Its cones are egg-shaped and persist on the branches for years, but they stand upright, never in clusters or on the sides of the branches. The scrub pine of Long Island and the New Jersey "barrens" resembles the jack pine of my area in many ways but is a different species botanically.

Many Americans know spruces and firs only as Christmas trees, since those two species provide the bulk of small, cut trees marketed every holiday season. Both are essentially northern trees, uncommon in my area and from here south. Spruce needles are square in cross-section and grow all around the twig, giving it a bottle-brush effect. Fir needles are flattened and grow on the sides of the twig, giving it the look of a feather. Spruce cones hang down from the branch and fir cones stand erect. When I see a stand of balsam firs in northern New England, with their dark green color, their symmetrical shapes, and their pungent fragrance, I think they are the most beautiful of all conifers. But some people give the award to the spruces. I wouldn't quarrel with them; all evergreens are beautiful.

I am also partial to the hemlock, perhaps because it likes my mountainside's soil, and thrives here. The hemlock's needles grow like those of the fir, on opposite sides of the branch, and the whole effect is feathery. But hemlock cones are small, only about half an inch long, light brown, and papery to the touch. If you are uncertain whether a tree is a fir or a hemlock, drill a hole in the bark of the trunk with a pocket knife. If it is a hemlock you will strike a vivid red layer close beneath the brown outer bark. If the red layer is missing, the tree is a fir.

We have two common cedars here in the Northeast, the red and the white. We call the red cedar "pasture cedar" and use it for fence posts. It is the common one, the one that sprouts in pasture margins everywhere. But in the woods I also find white cedars, which are supposed to grow only down on the coastal plain. How the white cedars got here, I don't know, but they are unmistakable. All cedars have green, flakelike overlapping leaves, but the red cedar also has tiny, needle-sharp thorns along the twigs, and the white cedars have no thorns. And in the Fall the red cedars bear purple-blue berries a quarter of an inch in diameter, while the white cedar bears tiny, tan, papery cones like miniature hemlock cones. In gathering Christmas greens we always choose white cedar boughs rather than those from red cedar; the green is fresher and they have none of those tiny, pestery thorns to annoy the fingers.

But I had no intention of taking a census of the woodland. I went wandering among the trees and found a host of friends, as any woodland wanderer will after a few excursions. And I have scarcely mentioned the birds and animals of the woods.

As I said earlier, birds and animals usually prefer the margins of the woodlands rather than the depths of the forests. They live where they can find food and even those we call predators, the flesh-eaters, subsist on the grass-eaters and the leaf-eaters. The bear, the lynx, and the bobcat follow the deer, the rabbit, and the mouse, and deer, rabbits, and mice usually feed where there is grass and brushy browse, along the margins of the woodland. In Winter the deer retreat to the evergreen thickets for both shelter and food. I find them among the cedars and hemlocks when the snow lies deep. Squirrels probably outnumber all other woodland creatures except mice and voles. Squirrels prefer oak woods, with their wealth of acorns, or mixed hardwood forests with the varied nuts; but they also patronize the pine woods and feast on the seeds in the cones.

Porcupines have become a woodland nuisance and a forester's problem since we killed off the fisher, the porcupine's principal enemy, and put a bounty on the bobcat, another of its persistent foes. In Spring and Summer the porcupine feeds on lesser vegetation at the woodland margin, but in Winter it eats bark, the vital cambium layer, and destroys valuable timber. The problem of the porcupine, one of the least prolific of all animals—it bears only one young a year—is an eloquent example of man's persistent shortsightedness in many matters of conservation.

Foxes seldom prowl the big woods except in passing; the mice and rabbits that make up most of their fare live in the margins and open meadows. Skunks, too, are primarily margin and meadow foragers, though they may den in the woods. Raccoons usually den in big, hollow trees, but most of their hunting and foraging is done in the more open areas and along the banks of brooks and streams. Coons usually, but by no means always, wash their food before they eat it. I've known them to spend a whole night in a cornfield half a mile from the nearest water, eating like mad and never drinking a drop or washing a mouthful.

I find relatively few birds in the big, deep woods. Big owls live there, and now and then a colony of crows. Jays often live in an oak woods and compete with the squirrels for acorns. Woodpeckers nest and feed in the woods. I find that hairy and downy woodpeckers and flickers prefer to nest in dead hardwood trees, but that the big pileated woodpecker will nest in either hardwoods or pines, and in dead trees or live ones, wherever he can find an opening and start chiseling.

The smaller woodpeckers enlarge old knotholes in dead trees or cut round holes, but the crimson-crested pileated fellow, big as a crow and with the power of a small jackhammer in his neck and beak, cuts oblong holes, sometimes three inches across and five or six inches long. They are so big that owls and wood ducks sometimes appropriate them for nesting places. Last year a pileated woodpecker spent several weeks cutting big, oblong cavities in a ten-inch birch just over the hill from my house. He cut eight such holes, for some reason I never understood, and so weakened the tree that a windy rainstorm took down its whole top. Then the big woodpecker went to work on the tall stump, as though he wanted to destroy it right down to the roots. But usually the pileated bird works on dead trees. It even uses certain dead trees as signal posts. For several weeks this past Summer two pileated woodpeckers perched in dead popples just across the river from my house and hammered out echoing messages, or maybe challenges, to each other several times a day.

The thrushes, of course, are birds of the woodland. Some of them, notably the wood thrush, will come down into the open and even nest near an occupied house; and the robin seems to think suburban lawns and tree-lined streets were deeded to him long ago. But the hermit thrush and the veery, and the olive-backed thrush in northern areas, are die-hards who cling to the depths of the woods, nest there, feed there, and sing their wonderful melodies there. I hear the wood thrush from my house, morning and evening, all Summer, and now and then I hear a veery; but if I would hear the hermit thrush or see any of them I must get well back from the road and into the solitude of the forest, and even then I must keep my eyes and ears alert to find them.

In the Summer I always find chickadees in the thin woods, and when I go up to the thickets of hemlock and cedar in the Winter they fly around me, twitter as though welcoming a visitor, and accompany me on my walk. I often find Wintering-over robins there, following their thrush habits of woodland life and feeding on the cedar berries. And the cardinals, which came and stayed this far north only in the past five or six years, whistle and flash their brilliant color at me in the tallest of the hardwood trees.

Always, Summer and Winter, I find ruffed grouse in the woods, most often in the hardwoods where berries are more plentiful than among the pines, but occasionally feeding on wintergreen or partridgeberry under the thick canopy of the conifers. If I visit a stand of wild barberry I usually flush partridges, and often I find them in black birches or wild apple trees, where they feed on the leaf buds.

All birds, as all animals, can be found where they can find food. Learn what they eat, seek out the places where it grows, and you will usually find the birds there.

The woods are both pleasant and interesting in Summer, but they are a challenge in the Winter if one would know one tree from another. A black oak is not difficult to tell from a white oak when they are in leaf, but the test of knowledge comes in bare-limbed December. It is easy to distinguish a sugar maple from a red maple in April or October, but they are hard to distinguish when all the leaves have fallen.

I have found that I need some knowledge of what I call tree fingerprints in the Winter—the color, texture, and pattern of the bark. There are obvious ones. Shagbark hickory has loose, shaggy strips on its bark. Beech bark is sleek and gray. Sugar maple's bark has flakes and plates, and swamp maple bark is somewhat smoother. But I have been baffled for a time by the resemblance of a bird cherry's bark to that of a black birch, and black oak and white oak both have bark with similar marks and ridges. I have even been puzzled by the similarity of the bark on a white ash, a slippery elm, and a box elder. The shape of the tree, the way it branches, and the place it grows often help in Winter identification. But just to make a Winter walk interesting, the bark on a sapling never looks like the bark on an older tree of the same species. Trees, like children, need a few years for their features to consolidate.

One could spend a lifetime in the woods and not know all there is to learn. I have spent ten years with my own woods and still know only its outlines, its simpler identities and relationships and truths.

# Chapter 5

# The Bog
# and the Swamp

THE PONDS *and the wetlands are a world unto themselves. The adventurer there, be he novice or veteran, will be aware of ancient beginnings and insistent change. There he will see those subtle interrelationships of life which the specialist calls ecology.*

*I shall never* get over the feeling that bogs and swamps are primitive places, a vestige of prehistoric ages. Swamp muck has the feel and look, even the smell, of land and life evolving; and the life I find in the bogland, both plant and animal, has an ancient and faraway look, like life from another age.

This is not wholly imaginary. When land first appeared on this earth it was marshland newly lifted from the depths of the primeval seas. Those marshes were the refuge of the first amphibians and the cradle of the first animals that learned to walk the earth. In much more recent times, when the great ice sheets were melting back whence they came, vast swamps were created by the melt, to simmer under a perennial blanket of mist and grow up into jungles of plant life creeping northward again after the icebound centuries. Life has always gained its first foothold in the wetlands, which even today mark land and life in transition.

In late Winter I walk down my road to a bogland area and look for skunk cabbage, the earliest sign of Spring. There are older plants and more primitive ones even in my area—ground cedar, running pine, scouring rushes, for example—but when I see the big purple-striped green horns of skunk cabbage thrusting up through the frozen muck, often through ice and snow as well, I have the feeling that they are the grandfathers of all times. Those horn-shaped hoods are close kin to the spathe of Jack-in-the-pulpit, also one of the arum family, but they have a far more ancient look about them. And the clublike spadix set with small flesh-colored flowers, which will be revealed inside as soon as the hood begins to open, exudes no honeyed, sweet-scented bid for the attention of bees. The bees are still Winter-bound, so the skunk cabbage flowers have the odor of carrion, to attract the hardy flies that have been living on the decaying flesh of animals that were Winter-killed. In every way, the skunk cabbage is far different from the swamp violet that will eventually come to blossom nearby. To me it is a primitive.

As Spring moves in, at this small bogland, the big cabbagelike leaves will unfurl, sometimes two feet across, in vivid green display. Break a stem or crush a leaf and the juice is rank with the skunky, oniony odor that gives the plant its common name. By then I will begin to see in the murky water the young blades of cattail and sweet flag and the various bur reeds, all like giant, primitive grasses. When the cattail comes to blossom in June, that blossom will be strange, too—a long, cylindrical spike set at the top of a tall stem, the upper half all stamens which spill a wealth of yellow pollen on the lower half, all pistils and ovaries. And this lower half will mature by September into a fat frankfurter of tightly packed brown fluff and minute seeds. The sweet flag will come to bloom with a slim thumb of yellowish-green florets, and the bur reeds will put forth brownish-white tufts of fuzzy bloom that eventually mature into thorny little seed balls like miniature pineapples. Ancient-looking and exotic, all of them.

Here and there tussocks lift their heads out of the water and on them grow Jacks-in-the-pulpit and arrow-leafed Sagittaria and water plantain. And, if I search for them, properly booted against the muck and murky water, I can find several varieties of orchid, from the little snake-mouth Pogonia to the beautiful yellow lady-slipper. Ancients all, and strange ones in root or leaf or blossom, or in all three.

It is in the bog that the Spring peepers, the Hylas, come out of muddy hibernation and creep up the bush stems and cry their Spring song, one of the oldest songs on earth. The peepers, only about one inch across, smaller than a twenty-five-cent piece, are actually tree toads, and the tip of each toe has a tiny adhesive disc with which the peeper can cling to bushes, reeds, even to a windowpane, as one did here at my house one April evening. The peepers usually begin to call soon after the first red-wing blackbirds arrive. I have never seen one in daylight, but when they are calling in the dusk it is quite easy to find one on the margin of a bog by using a flashlight and following the sound to its maker. This has its difficulties, of course, for the peeper's call often has a ventriloquous effect; but peepers congregate in large numbers and the searcher needs only be patient and persistent to find one.

Not long after the peepers begin to call they, as well as the dry-land toads and the sleek-skinned frogs, lay their eggs, making the water slimy with the gelatinous egg masses. By May that water will teem with tadpoles hatched from those eggs. And by then it will also teem with hungry minnows that eat tadpoles; and water snakes will be there to eat tadpoles and minnows without discrimination. These northern water snakes are harmless, but in the Deep South such bogs and swamps are the home of the cottonmouth, a pit viper and virulently poisonous.

Frogs, toads, serpents, turtles—ancients, every one of them. And ancient too are the occasional salamander I see there and the sluggish mud puppy, so primitive it can breathe through its gills, its mouth, or its skin.

Even the insects of the wetland have a primitive look: Dragonflies, lineal descendants of fossils a hundred million years old and possibly among the earliest flying creatures; and damsel flies, their close cousins—at rest, the dragonfly holds its wings outspread but the damsel fly folds its wings over its back. Giant moths which, like all their kind, are in turn egg and worm and encased mummy and moth again. Fireflies, with their still mysterious inner fire. Caddis flies and mosquitoes, whose larvae are as committed to life in the water as are fish. Water striders, which skate on the water as easily as long-legged children skate on ice. And all the strange aquatic insects such as back swimmers and water boatmen and water scorpions.

And the swampland birds—show me a more primitive-looking bird than the heron, with its stilt legs, its long, serpentine neck, its darting head and stiletto beak. Or the kingfisher, with stubby wings, rackety voice, truculent crest, and fantastic bifocal eyes for seeing under water as well as in the air. Or the fat, uptilted bittern, a veritable caricature of a bird; or the woodcock, all beak and no tail.

Even the angry-looking coot, with its long legs and paddle-fitted toes.

One late Spring evening I sat on a grassy bank of this small bogland for an hour at dusk, hoping to see a water shrew. The water shrew is smaller than a mouse and, because it is so tiny and has feet covered with long, buoyant hairs, can literally walk on water. Violets were in bloom on the dry bank where I sat, and red-wing blackbirds were making their evening clamor. A great blue heron had dropped in from the sky and stood four feet tall in a shallow spot, staring at me suspiciously, the black plumes on his white head like grotesque ears. An American bittern had come out of the cattail tangle onto a tussock and alternately stared at me with beady eyes and thrust his long beak at the sky where the first stars would soon be out. I hoped to hear the bittern utter that "plum puddin'" sound characteristic of his kind, but he just stood there, silent, not even probing the muck for food.

No water shrew appeared. A muskrat swam out of the tangle into open water, his wake like long, silvery whiskers V-ing out from his nose, and either saw me or got a whiff of my scent. He dived in panic. But the water was shallow. He stood on his head in the mud, hind feet frantic, for a long moment before he completed a wet somersault and swam madly back into the swamp.

Dusk crept in, and the mucky smell, the deepening shadows, the eerie look of the stilt-legged heron, made my skin prickle. I was sitting beside an ancient swamp, not a little pasture-margin bogland, and it was two hundred million years ago. If I sat there just ten minutes longer a sixty-foot brontosaurus right out of the Jurassic Age would come lumbering into sight.

Swamps do that to me, particularly at dusk.

Actually, the bogland is a fascinating place, whether it is a backwater left when a river changes its course, as is that little swamp I know best, or one of those big lowland swamps once typical of the Midwest and still typical of the Deep South. Beavers made a good many of the swamps in the Northeast, to begin with; but the beavers vanished and where they have come back they are now either a novelty or a nuisance to most people. And swamps today are too commonly considered wasteland, to be drained and "reclaimed." In our passion for "reclamation" we do all kinds of ultimately foolish things. We drain the swamps, lower the water table, create floods, rob waterfowl of their natural habitat, and glibly call it progress. But that's not a battle to be waged in this book. There are better arenas.

Any bogland, as I was saying, is a fascinating place primarily because it is essentially primitive and because it inevitably resists the taming hand of man. The plow cannot reach its soil and the man with an ax can reach its trees and brush only when Winter and ice have given him footing. Usually there is better timberland elsewhere for his harvest, anyway. The result is a natural tangle, marsh and muck and brush and undergrowth, humid and mosquito-infested in Summer, blazing with color in the Fall, full of competing life in the Spring.

If I want to know which birds are Wintering over in my area, I go to the bogland. There, in the shelter of the brush, I will find the robins and the occasional bluebird that didn't go South. If there is food to be had anywhere, they will find it in the depths of the swamp. I have even found a flock of cowbirds in the alder thickets there in January, though I had thought they were provident enough to migrate. There I have seen flocks of goldfinches, looking deceptively like sparrows in their Winter plumage. The goldfinches find thistles and ironweed and dozens of other food plants in the Winter swamp. The robins feed there on sumac berries, among other things, and may find a few worms and larvae in the frosty muck. And when the first breath of Spring touches the land, I always find the outriders of the great migration of blackbirds, rusties and redwings primarily, in the bogland.

In Midwinter I often go to the swamp to see the ice, which takes forms there that I find nowhere else. The thick muck, in a deep freeze, heaves and almost seems to writhe, and when I look beneath a mat of dead leaves I usually find a mass of ice crystals like stalagmites in a limestone cave. They sometimes stand six inches tall, ice spikes big as lead pencils. I lift the ice from a little hollow, an old footstep perhaps. It is glassy smooth on the upper surface, but its under side is a mass of icy stalactites, crystalline spikes pointed downward. Then, perhaps during the January thaw, comes a mild day or two, and the bogland is full of puddles, the air over it steamy. The warmth is not only from the sun; it is from the earth as well, where the dead vegetation is simmering in the heat of its own decay. The whole bog is a kind of elemental hotbed. I think that if I were a frog I should choose the mud of such a place for my place of hibernation. It is not what I would call a warm Winter bed, but it is certainly warmer than a wind-swept hillside.

Warmth of this degree, however, is of little concern to the hibernators there, the frogs, the toads, the turtles, and the snakes. They are all cold-blooded, primitive in our lexicon. The frogs, the toads, and the turtles burrow into the mud to hibernate. The snakes crawl into holes or some-times into mud or loose soil, often a number of them to-gether. Wherever they go, they escape the Winter cold of the open air. Their bodily processes slow down. Body tem-perature diminishes to a few degrees above that of the sur-rounding earth. Breathing almost ceases, the heartbeat falls to so deliberate a rate that it is hard to find, and the inert body lives on its stored fat. The human problem of main-taining body heat in the high 90's in the face of zero weather is completely avoided.

Another kind of hibernation occurs here, too—the hiber-nation of the tree, the bush, the vine, and the bulb or tu-ber. We seldom think of plant life as hibernating in this way, but the process is much the same as with the hiber-nating animal. Life processes are slowed down or almost suspended. The plant has withdrawn its vital juices into the root or bulb. On trees and bush the latent buds, formed during the mild days of Autumn, are there on the branch and twig, somewhat protected by scales and wax but other-wise taking the weather as it comes. By late February or early March, as soon as the days turn faintly mild and the daylight approaches the length of night, sap begins to rise, especially in the trees of the maple family. Buds begin to quicken imperceptibly. I see this change in the swampland in the color particularly of the red-osier dogwood. This bush's smooth-barked stems are of a ruddy color the year around, but when this quickening begins those stems glow almost blood-red. It is as though red and living blood were rising just there beneath their bark. The sap which actually is rising is as colorless as the maple sap from which syrup and sugar are made, faintly amber, but its presence does something quite wonderful to the color of those red-osier dogwood stems. The same thing is happening in the willows of the swampland, but the result is amber, not red. Willow stems, both of the brush and of the bigger trees, liven and brighten and glow with the color of late Summer honey. The big weeping willow out beside my garage becomes a towering amber fountain, every long, slim withe aglow. The dead look of Winter is gone.

And then Spring comes to the swamp.

I have said that the skunk cabbage is the earliest sign of Spring there, and that is true. But skunk cabbage is really a promise of Spring rather than Spring itself. The Spring peepers are the voice of Spring, the absolute certainty that Winter has lost its grip, though I have known a six-inch snowfall after the first peepers began to call. But when I go to the swamp and see the first pussy willow out of its bud scales, I know that the turn has come.

I often find pussy willow in bloom in March. Willows are unisexual trees, bearing either male or female blossoms but not both on the same tree. The "pussy" is the male catkin and, like most willow blossoms, it appears before the leaves appear. The tree is small, relatively, actually a shrub and seldom as much as twenty-five feet high. March comes and I begin to watch the willows on the margin of the swamp. One mild day I see that the brownish scales on the fat buds have begun to part, and if the mildness continues the silvery gray catkins appear in another day or two. The twigs are covered with them and glow in the sunlight. At first the "pussies" are smaller around than a lead pencil, but they grow quickly. If the weather turns chill they simply wait, as though protected by their fur coats. That "fur" is as soft to the touch as a real kitten's fur. In botanical fact, however, it consists of fine, hairlike stamens. As soon as the rather inconspicuous catkins open on the female trees, these male stamens produce pollen. The silver "pussies" turn gold with the pollen, then lose their silvery look and become bristly and yellowish green. Before all the pollen has drifted away, the first of the leaf buds have begun to open. The "pussies" are all through.

Even before the willows are in full leaf, the marsh marigolds are leafed out and showing flower buds. The marsh marigold is really a big buttercup that likes wet feet. In New England marsh marigolds are often called cowslips, probably because careless observers long ago thought they saw a resemblance to English cowslips, which really are primulas.

By mid-May the swamp is full of flowers and bees. Violets are everywhere, especially on the moist margins. Dogtooth violets, those lovely yellow, star-shaped lilies which went into every rural May basket in my youth, are absent from my swamp, but they are common forty miles south of here. Wild forget-me-nots do bloom here, on leggy stems, their roots in the edge of the water. I am always surprised to see how many bees patronize those tiny, sky-blue blossoms, which would seem too small to merit much attention. Also at the water's edge grows the wild blue phlox. This phlox also grows in the woodland where the shade is thin and there is moisture for the roots. And before May is out I find the larger blue flag, a wild iris, in bloom. I had thought this iris demanded muck and water over its roots, but when I transplanted one into my dryland flower garden it throve. In the bog, this iris grows quite tall, sometimes almost three feet. A lesser iris, the slender blue flag, with narrower leaves and smaller flowers, also grows there, but sparsely. While the iris are in bloom, cranesbill (the wild geranium) dapples the drier banks with its rose-colored blossoms, and sweet fern and sensitive fern grow lush.

By early June the trees and shrubs of the bogland are in bloom. The dogwood shrubs, especially the red-osier which was so conspicuous when Spring was getting a first foothold, have flattened clusters of dull white blossoms that make you think of miniature clusters of elderberry bloom, which comes a few weeks later. And while the dogwood is in bloom the chokecherries open their fuzzy, fat, drooping clusters of white flowers. You can always tell when chokecherry is in bloom by listening for the bee-hum. Bees love it, swarm to it.

Meanwhile most of the water plants have come to blossom without attracting the attention of anyone except bees and other flying insects. Their blossoms, for the most part, are inconspicuous, often pale green or yellowish white. The more colorful swamp blossoms come later in the season, Midsummer or even August. But I always watch for the vervain, especially the so-called blue vervain, which is not blue at all, but deep purple. And for the great lobelia, which is truly blue and spectacular with a showy stalk of flowers sometimes three feet tall. It completely overshadows the water lobelia, which comes to bloom about the same time but whose flowers are small and sparse and their color disappointing after one has seen the great lobelia. Water lobelia grows in the water, not on the moist bank, and its thick, straplike leaves are at the base of the stem, submerged. Only the flower stalk appears above the water.

As the season pushes toward Fall, the vervain begins to fade and the composites take over. Ironweed shoots up with its tall, weedy stems and long, lance-shaped leaves, and heads into a cluster of purple flowers that look like the bachelor's buttons in my garden except that the ironweed flowers have no outer petals, just that central tuft. Boneset and Joe Pye weed have also grown tall and rank. A youngster who helped me measure one stalk of boneset announced its height as six feet and thirty-two inches. Boneset blooms in terminal tufts of small, white, fuzzy flowers. Joe Pye's blossoms, also at the tip of the stalk, are much like those of boneset except that they are a warm magenta-pink, something like the color of field thistle heads but a shade redder. I always find all these flowers on the damp margins, never in the water itself. And on those damp margins I always find an assortment of dry-land plants grown to unusual size in the rich fertility of the mucky soil—asters, goldenrods, milkweeds, dogbane. And the ubiquitous bouncing Bet, which flowers early and persists late, well after the first light frost.

By mid-September almost any swampland will begin to show signs of the season's end. The bur-reed seed balls lose their green, the cattails are turning a rich red-brown, the conelike seed cases of the alder brush are ripening. The chokecherries show a first flush of color in their leaves; their cherries ripened in late August and flocks of birds have been gorging on them for days, birds from the meadow and woodland as well as those which were at home in the swamp all Summer. Robins are there in flocks, and I see more flickers than I would have expected. Catbirds make a noisy holiday of it, quarreling among themselves as well as with everyone else.

The Jacks-in-the-pulpit, out of sight in the tall grass all Summer, are revealed now by their clusters of red berries. The false spikenard, which grew four feet high, now droops, borne down by the weight of its terminal cluster of berries, just a bit smaller than peas, which were yellowish white speckled with brown, then turned ruby-red. Those berries are edible, rather sweet to the taste, and aromatic. Solomon's-seal, the species called "great," has its berries too, twin berries that look like small Concord grapes both in shape and color, at the base of each leaf. The Solomon's-seal grows as much as eight feet tall in the swamp, with long, lance-shaped, wavy green leaves, a beautiful plant.

The color touches the chokecherry leaves. Then it begins to mark the leaves of the dogwood brush, not as vivid as the deep wine color of the flowering dogwood of the hillside but a warm red just the same. The red-osier dogwood berries ripened in August, first to dull white, then to lead gray, and the birds ate most of them. The stems of the fruit clusters still are on the bushes, stiff-fingered little hands pointing upward, red as cherries.

My swamp has no tamaracks, but many New England swamps do have them. The tamarack is the only conifer that sheds all its needles in the Fall. It is a beautiful tree, tall and tapering, and in the Spring its dress of brand-new needles is a delicate light green, almost misty in effect. The color deepens into Summer, but by late September it begins to change to tan, a special golden tan that has a kind of glow. A grove of tamaracks in full Fall color is like a cluster of giant candle flames without the red of fire, only that warm yellow-gold color. Then the needles fall and the trees stand stark all Winter.

My swamp does have swamp maples, which were all crimson when they came to bloom in late April and which in October are crimson again. There are few colors in the woodland that can equal the reds of the swamp maples. At a certain stage, the swamp is like a gigantic red bonfire, magnificent. The swamp also is host to the ash-leafed maple, the box elder. This tree makes no great Autumn show, its leaves crisping into a lifeless tan and soon drifting down; but its seed tufts give it special distinction. It bears keys, like other maples, except that on the box elder those keys are borne in generous clusters, like coarse tassels. They have been inconspicuous, the color of the leaves, all Summer. Now they turn a warm tan, a better color than the leaves ever achieve, and when the leaves fall the tree is still decked out in those tassels of seed keys. Several box elders in my swamp were still full of those tufts of keys last December. Winter birds appreciate them, and I have seen squirrels harvesting them, for their small but meaty kernels.

The leaves turn. Then the Fall rains come, and the wind. The leaves come down. The swamp water is covered with the color that shaded it, and for a few days the swamp is like a great, variegated patchwork quilt. Then the water begins to leach the color and the leaves slowly sink to the mucky bottom. The grass has been sered by the first hard frosts. The cattails stand for a little while, their brittle leaves making a papery rustle in the wind, their tall stalks top-heavy with the fat fluff-heads. Then the wind whips the leaves, bends them down, and the cattail beds are a stark forest of those seed stalks. Muskrats harvest roots and bring down the stalks here and there; field mice and chipmunks, leaping from dry tussock to tussock, gather the fluff for their Winter nests, and late birds open other heads, still standing, and leave them in tatters to the Winter wind.

The swamp falls quiet. The frogs have hibernated, burrowed into the muck. The turtles have made their own Winter quarters in the muck. When the last of the asters and goldenrod were gone, the bees quit coming, their season's work completed. The water snakes, robbed of energy by the Autumn chill, have burrowed in for the Winter's sleep. Last November, however, I saw a four-foot water snake in a pool at the swamp, still more or less active. The air temperature that day was in the 20's, and I thought every snake for miles around would have been safely hibernated. But this one was active enough to note my presence and swim swiftly away, back into the cattail tangle, when I tossed a stick at him to prove that he really was alive.

By November there will be scums of ice on the pools in the swamp. The muskrats will have their Winter quarters completed and most of the harvest in. I probably won't see a muskrat, though I have on occasion seen one swimming under the clear ice on a bitter day in January. The ice, of course, seals most of the cold away from the water and the muck of the swamp's bottom. And the muskrat is well dressed for Winter weather. But muskrats usually stay close to home through the Winter months. They build three types of structures besides a burrow in the bank. The biggest is the lodge, used as living quarters in Winter and as birthing room and nursery in Spring. It is a dome sometimes five feet across, built of roots, reeds, and mud in water two feet or so deep. It has an inner chamber well above water level, no outside exit except into the water, and when its foot-thick walls freeze it is a fortress. Nearby will be several feeding shelters, each like a miniature lodge and built largely of edible material with a thick mud coating overhead. The muskrats can take food there to eat or eat the roots that went into the walls. And along the muskrat's everyday travelways under water there will be a number of push-ups, built after the bog freezes over. Natural bubble holes are enlarged to about four inches in diameter and the muskrats bring roots and other vegetation and thrust it through the ice, upward, building heaps as big as a man's hat on the ice. These are breathing holes, where a rat can come up for air and, if he chooses, climb out onto the ice and have a snack while safely hidden from danger overhead. The muskrat is a practical fellow; he makes his shelters edible.

The cold will deepen. The ice will thicken. Snow will come. When I go to the swamp in January I shall see only the leafless trees and bushes, the brown and graceful curve of the goldenrod stems, the stiff ranks of dead cattail stems. The tussocks will be like big warts on the swamp's white face and the muskrat structures will be smooth, symmetrical mounds in the snow. In the snow I will see only a few tracks, mostly of animals that seldom visit the swamp except in Winter. The muskrats, wise and provident, have no need to be abroad, and the other swamp folk are asleep.

There probably will be the tracks of a fox, come down from the hills in search of a meal, perhaps at one of the muskrats' push-ups, if some muskrat is less than usually wary. There will be the lacy track of a field mouse, probably a white-foot, out for air and a bite of breakfast. There will be the seemingly aimless track of a rabbit, a cottontail just wandering but alert for the first sign of fox or hungry owl. If the rabbit has been unwary for a few moments, I will find the notice of his death written in the snow—a few spatters of blood, a few tufts of gray fur, the mark of an owl's wings as it struck from the air or the prints of a fox stalking, then pouncing. The story of life and death, written on that blank sheet of Winter.

Chickadees may speak to me from a brush patch. There probably will be a flock of juncos, to go winging away on a gusty wind. There certainly will be tree sparrows and goldfinches, harvesting goldenrod seed and shriveled berries. If I am fortunate I may see the flock of robins that Winters here in the valley. And if I am particularly favored a cardinal will whistle from the wooded hillside. I will answer him. We will whistle back and forth, and soon I will see a flash of red coming my way. He will come and perch high in a Winter-naked swamp maple and gladden my heart.

If the insistent reclamation men had their way, the time might come when there would be no more swamps or bogs. If that time comes I hope I am not here to see it.

# Chapter 6

# Flowing Waters

*IF YOU would know any land, know its streams, its living waters. A brook or a river is a valley articulate and in ever-changing motion; its story is the story of the earth and one of the major forces that shaped it and clothed and populated and made it good.*

*I was once asked* by a morose man from the city: "What makes anyone think a brook or a river is something special? What are they but water, muddy water, running downhill?"

I wanted to ask if he had never seen the Potomac or the Ohio or the Mississippi; if he had never sat for an hour and watched the Hudson, fouled as it is, moving majestically through New York City's own dooryard. I wanted to ask if he had never stood beside a brook and listened to it at dawn or walked beside it on a June afternoon. I wanted to tell him about brooks and rivers, but it would have taken me an hour to say the things that a brook or river can tell a willing listener in five minutes. I said: "Perhaps one must live with running water to understand."

Any river is really the summation of a whole valley. It shapes not only the land but the life and even the culture of that valley. The trees that grow on its banks and all the greenness there may be common elsewhere but they still are special to that river. So are the birds, the insects, the animals that live along that river's banks. And the river has its own swarming life, its fish, its amphibians, its reptiles. To think of any river as nothing but water is to ignore the greater part of it.

If I would trace the story of mankind I must start at the ocean, mother of all life, and travel up a river. I will come to a place eventually where the river forks, and by following either fork I will come to a brook. Walking beside that brook I will finally climb a hillside and find a source spring. There, beside that spring on a wooded hillside, I can look out over the land and see how man, though warm-blooded and terrestrial, followed the flowing waters of this earth to his own present destiny.

Man is far removed from his aquatic and amphibian beginnings, but he can no more do without water than can a fish or a frog. Air is his element, but his own body, his corporeal being, is more than 70-per-cent water, which must be constantly replenished. In the beginning, man lived beside the sweet water simply to slake his daily thirst. Then he learned that he could travel from place to place on a floating log. His ingenuity made a raft of two logs and he became a traveler. When he had refined the raft into a boat he became an explorer, with means of transportation well beyond the length of his own stride. Water became not only his daily drink but his highway. And eventually, when he had combined four paddles into a waterwheel, water became his power, his industry.

The first tribal village was beside a stream. When villages became cities, they too were beside the rivers. When the first men ventured across the vast, salty seas they departed from river-mouth docks and sought river-mouth landings on alien shores. When their harbor cities became crowded they moved upstream. And when the farmer chose new land he looked for springs and brooks, the sustaining sweet water, and for a river that would power his gristmill and float his produce to market.

Then man discovered coal and harnessed steam and laid iron rails and dug deep wells for water. And he dumped his trash, his garbage, and his sewage into the rivers, which he thought he no longer needed as sweet, flowing water. The polluted rivers poisoned him and beleaguered him with flood and challenged his wisdom and his skills. And man, who could send a rocket around the moon and dissect the atom, who could diagram the universe and weigh the sun, still couldn't live a week without a drink of fresh water.

I was thinking of these things this morning as I sat for an hour on the bank of the Housatonic River which flows past my own house. And I was thinking of the springs on the mountainside and the brooks that flow from them to join the river. I was remembering the high plains of my boyhood, which were so long unsettled and little used because live water is so scarce there, where the only rivers I knew were the shallow, meandering Platte fifty miles to the north and the marshy, oxbowed Arkansas 150 miles to the south. I was remembering my first trip across eastern Utah, a barren land with scattered sage and bunch grass its only vegetation. Then I saw what I was sure must be a mirage, for it looked like a line of tall, green trees. It was no mirage. It was the towering cottonwoods that flank the Colorado River as it winds across the desert toward its spectacular canyons to the south. I stopped for an hour in the cottonwood shade, listening to the clamor of red-wing and yellow-headed blackbirds and marveling that a river could bring such cool, sweet change in the midst of the desert.

The Housatonic, like so many New England streams, is relatively short and uncomplicated as a river. It rises near Pittsfield, Massachusetts and flows generally southward about 150 miles across western Massachusetts and Connecticut to Long Island Sound. It has only three tributaries that are even called rivers, and two of those are no more than good-sized brooks. It is heavily polluted with sewage and industrial waste in its upper reaches, relatively clean through its middle course, and a sluggish, polluted stream once more in its lower forty or fifty miles.

Here where I know it best it is nominally clean, largely because the upstream pollution has been ameliorated by miles of intricate and sunlit wandering in the broad valley just to the north. It has a slow current here, in part because there once was a low power dam half a mile below my house. That dam maintained several feet of water in what was then a big marsh just up the valley from here. Men who were boys at that time tell me, with glowing eyes, about the number and size of black bass they caught in that backwater. But the hurricane of 1938 brought a flood that washed out one end of the dam. The hydroelectric plant was removed and the dam never repaired. The river dropped four or five feet, the big marsh soon drained, and now that legendary fishpond is a thicket of swamp maple and alder brush with a brook winding through it. And my section of the river, though still ten or twelve feet deep in places, is almost as placid as a millpond most of the time, though just below the old dam it surges into rapids and soon becomes a hurrying, white-water mountain stream. A heavy rain upstream or a quick snow-melt in

March can raise the river level several feet overnight and set the current boiling. It is a river of uncertain moods.

Even where the farm fields come down to it, the river is lined with trees. That is the natural state of a riverbank. The trees here are typical eastern trees. There are a few willows, but not as many as seem to line the rivers of the Midwest. Most of them are the typical black willows of the East. And there is willow brush, much of it wild pussy willow and undistinguished except in early Spring when the silvery catkins appear. Just down the river is a grove of popples; they are American aspens, with tall, tapering central trunks and slim and scattered branches. Their leaves, like those of the quaking aspens of the western mountains, whisper in every breeze. There are a good many elms, mostly white elms, the traditional trees of the New England "common" and characteristic of riverbanks throughout the Northeast. Here and there is a slippery elm, with somewhat larger leaves, deeper-furrowed bark, and broader-winged seeds. There are a few white birches, though those big birches usually grow on higher, drier ground. And there are many basswood trees.

The basswood is known in Europe, and often in America, as the linden. The American species grows taller, has a broader crown, and its leaves are larger than those of the European linden. Basswood blossoms are unique. They are small, creamy white, and come in small clusters on long, drooping stems. Those stems spring from long, narrow, leaflike green wings quite unlike the tree's large heart-shaped leaves. The blossoms are so fragrant they make the whole riverbank sweet in June, and they are so rich in nectar that it drips like sticky mist. You can hear when the basswoods are in bloom, for all the bees of the countryside are busy in the trees. Basswood flowers make excellent honey.

There are a few oaks along the river, mostly the familiar white oaks of the East but now and then a northern red oak, which really belongs on higher ground. There may be swamp white oak somewhere along my river, but I have never found it. I live on the northern edge of the normal range of this big, beech-leafed oak, but the chinquapin oak grows here, as I mentioned in a previous chapter, though we are out of its usual range. I may have mistaken a small swamp white oak for a chinquapin.

There are ash trees along the river, thickets of them here and there growing so close they are tall and spindly, as well as an occasional big, spreading tree. I can understand why anyone confuses the three species we have here, white ash, black ash, and red or river ash. All three grow to the same shape, all have bark much alike, and all have the same pattern of compound leaves. Black ash leaves usually occur in a nine-leaflet pattern, four pairs and a terminal leaflet on each stem. But both white ash and red ash have, usually, only seven leaflets, three pairs and a terminal one. Until I got it through my head that red ash prefers the wet soil of a riverbank or swamp margin and white ash prefers higher, drier ground, I often mistook one for the other. Black ash, incidentally, is also a wet-soil tree. So now when I see a seven-leaf ash on the riverbank I know it probably is a red ash, and a seven-leafer on high ground usually is a white ash. All ash wood, by the way, makes good fuel for the fireplace, especially while it is still green. There is an old saying in my area: "Ash green is wood fit for a queen."

Just to add to this ash-tree confusion, there is also the tree commonly known as mountain ash, which grows wild in the Northeast but which is also used in ornamental planting because of its showy bunches of bright orange berries in the Autumn. This tree really isn't an ash at all; it belongs to the same family as the apple, even though its compound leaves look much like those of the real ash. In England it is known as the rowan tree. The seeds of the real ash trees look something like half of a maple key, though the vane is longer, narrower, and not curved.

Also along my river, and most rivers of eastern America, is the sycamore, sometimes called plane tree or buttonwood. You can easily spot a sycamore by its smooth brown bark which peels off in large sheets and reveals cream-colored or soft greenish-tan fresh bark beneath. A big old sycamore sometimes looks as though someone had daubed it with splashes of dirty whitewash. The leaves look a good deal like the familiar maple leaf, but its fruit comes in the form of rough-surfaced balls an inch or more in diameter which turn light brown in the Fall and cling to the branches all Winter. I think of them as buttons for some Paul Bunyan's mackinaw, and possibly those who first called the tree "buttonwood" had the same notion.

The shrubs and bushes along my riverbank include bush dogwood, viburnum, alder, shadbush, and sumac. There are three kinds of bush dogwood—red-osier, round-leafed, and silky cornel, which is also known as kinnikinnik. And that name, kinnikinnik, calls for a moment's explanation.

Kinnikinnik is an Algonquian word meaning "mixture" and was used for the blend of dried bark and leaves, with or without tobacco added, which was smoked by both Indians and whites in the early days. Because the mixture was rolled between the palms to reduce it to a proper texture for a pipe bowl, French voyageurs called it *bois roulé*, rolled wood, indicating that the kinnikinnik the Frenchmen knew was mostly made of bark. One simple blend consisted of dried sumac leaves and dried inner bark of one of the bush dogwoods, probably the silky cornel. Hence the name kinnikinnik for this shrub. Sometimes the blend also included willow leaves, arrowwood leaves, and bearberry leaves. The red bearberry is also sometimes called kinnikinnik. I have smoked several blends of kinnikinnik and must report that I prefer tobacco in my pipe.

None of the bush dogwoods grows more than six or eight feet high, and all have typical dogwood leaves, toothless, with parallel veins, and growing opposite each other on the stem. Red-osier and silky cornel stems are maroon, but round-leaf dogwood stems are green. If it seems important to be sure whether a red-stemmed bush dogwood is red-osier or silky cornel, slit the stem and look at the pith. If the pith is reddish-brown, the twig is from silky cornel. If the pith is white, it is red-osier. All three of these dogwoods come to flower in June with flattened clusters of small, white, four-petaled flowers that mature into loose clusters of whitish or bluish-gray berries about a quarter of an inch in diameter. Those berries are not poisonous, but they are not really palatable either, though most birds eat them.

The viburnums range from straight-stemmed arrowwood to the pimbina—often called high-bush cranberry though it is unrelated to the true cranberry—and the pithy-stemmed elderberry. Various of the straight-stemmed viburnums are called arrowwood. They all have roughly heart-shaped leaves, and tradition says the Indians used their stems as arrow shafts. That I doubt. But small boys cut them now and then and use them for homemade arrows.

In the Fall I watch for several of the viburnums, and for various reasons. The maple-shaped leaves of dockmackie turn a rare purple and add a surprising grace note to the October color. The pimbina's leaves, also maple-shaped, turn maple-red and orange. And the nannyberry has grape-colored berries that shrivel and look and taste like raisins; for this reason, the bush is sometimes called wild raisin. But the birds like those berries, so I seldom find many.

Every countryman and most country visitors know the elderberry, which to me is as beautiful as most cultivated shrubs with its big, flat-topped clusters of tiny white flowers in June and its heavy heads of little purple berries in August. The oversweet fruit makes good wine or jelly—and stains fingers and clothing like ink. Birds like elderberries so much that they flock to the bushes when the fruit is ripe and sometimes break the brittle branches with their weight. Elderberry stems are full of soft white pith which can easily be pushed out to make tubes. Old-timers used them as spiles when gathering sap from maple trees. And country boys made popguns from them and used them as stems for corncob pipes in which they smoked dried sumac leaves out behind the barn.

The names "elder" and "alder" are confusing, but the elderberry belongs to the viburnum family and the alders are kin of the birches. Both like damp soil, which is why they grow along my river. Alders make thickets along most riverbanks and in the edges of swamps, sometimes growing fifteen feet high. In late Fall or Winter they can baffle the beginner because they have seed cases that look like miniature spruce cones. But in the Spring they bear flowers in the form of dangling catkins sometimes three inches long and eye-catching with their purple and yellow coloring.

Come mid-April and the shadblow blooms in the riverside woods like tall spurts of shimmering white mist among the leafless trees. I first knew shadblow in the high mountains of southwestern Colorado, which simply proves how broad is the range of this cousin of the apple. But I knew it there as serviceberry. In the Northeast it gets the name shadblow or shadbush because it comes to blossom when the shad come up the streams to spawn—or did come when the streams were habitable for shad, not heavily polluted. It blossoms in tufts of small, white, long-petaled flowers before the leaves appear. In June those blossoms mature into bluish-purple fruits that look like fat rose haws and have a pleasantly sweet taste. Many birds and all kinds of animals, from bears to chipmunks, relish those berries. Here on my riverbank the shadbush grows as a tall, straggly shrub or slim tree fifteen feet tall, with leaves much like apple leaves.

Sumac grows everywhere, in damp soil and dry, high and low. In the Northeast we have three common species, staghorn, smooth, and dwarf, but even the dwarf sumac often grows as big as the other two except when the staghorn becomes a twenty-foot tree, as it does halfway up my mountainside. All three varieties grow here along the river, sometimes mingling in the same patch. If it is important to know them by name, remember that staghorn sumac has very fuzzy branches and stems, smooth sumac lacks the fuzz, and dwarf sumac has narrow green "wings" along the leaf stems. All of them bear fruit in fat, cone-shaped clusters, and the fruit of all three is deep red when ripe. This clustered fruit and its red color are points to remember if you live or prowl where poison sumac may be growing—poison sumac fruit comes in loose bunches and ripens greenish-white or lead-gray. Poison sumac, which acts like poison ivy on contact with the skin and is to be avoided, is rather rare in the Northeast and usually is found only in swampland near the coast. I shall have more to say about poison sumac and other poisonous plants in another chapter.

There are vines along all rivers. In my area the most common ones are wild grape and Virginia creeper. The grapes here are mostly the tiny river grapes, the fruit about the diameter of a lead pencil and borne in clusters like Concord grapes. The vines run everywhere, along the ground, over the bushes, and up the trees, snares for unwary feet. Old vines are sometimes two inches through and tough as ropes, and I have seen them dangling from branches forty feet above the ground. Many northeastern river valleys have fox grapes, which bear bigger fruit. The fox grape was the wild ancestor of the Concord and other American varieties of tame grape.

Virginia creeper is a cousin of the grape and climbs by means of tendrils like those of the grape. Its fruit is much like that of the river grape but even smaller, ripens in loose clusters, and is edible but not worth tasting. Virginia creeper climbs even more vigorously than wild grape and for some reason seems to thrive on standing dead trees. I have seen a sixty-foot dead poplar festooned with Virginia creeper all the way to the top. Such a tree is a spectacular tower of flame in late September, for the Virginia creeper's five-part compound leaves turn an especially brilliant scarlet.

There is little poison ivy along my part of the river, for which I am grateful. Most river banks abound with this obnoxious plant, which I shall discuss later with the other poisonous plants. We do have bittersweet, with its bright orange berries in tan husks, and we have deadly nightshade with its bright green leaves, small purple and gold blossoms, and poisonous, waxy-looking red berries. And we have patches of wild raspberry, the red-stemmed black-cap, whose small black berries are tedious to pick but wonderfully sweet and tasty. The long, slender canes of the black-cap are not as viciously thorned as the heavier canes of wild blackberries, which also grow along my riverbank, but they can be painful to bare arms or legs. Many places have the wild red raspberries, but there are few along my riverbanks.

The wildflowers along any river will be representative of the area's meadows, woodlands, and bogs, since there are no wildflowers really peculiar to a riverbank. My river has its dry banks where asters and goldenrod grow lush. It has places where fireweed makes big splashes of magenta-pink in July and August. It has shallow backwaters where marsh marigolds flourish in the Spring and cattails stand stiff and fat-thumbed all Winter. It has a hundred places where milkweed lures the Monarch butterflies and releases its clouds of silk-buoyed seeds in September.

One place along the banks has a great patch of dwarf phlox, magnificent in May, and just ashore from a certain cove I can always find the biggest, darkest, longest-stemmed violets I find anywhere. Vervain likes the marginal mud and turns the area purple in late Summer. There are certain moist banks where we gather yellow rocket for greens every Spring and where the wild ducks feed all Summer. And nearby are bloodroot, anemones, and Jack-in-the-pulpit.

Along the river near my house is an especially lush growth of scouring rushes and horsetails, related plants that reach back in lineage all the way to the Paleozoic era, perhaps 300 million years ago. Both species are quite common on riverbanks and pond margins, but the horsetails are so adaptable that they sometimes grow in the slag and cinders of a railroad roadbed, and I have seen them pushing up through the thin layer of macadam on a suburban side street. Scouring rushes grow in long, tapering cane-like stems, leafless and three to six feet in height, stiff, dark green, and segmented in sections like the joints of a fisherman's bamboo fly rod. They are brash to the touch and are strengthened by tiny siliceous particles that make them abrasive. Pioneers used them to scour pots and pans; hence their common name. The horsetails are a lighter, vivid green and are shaped like miniature pines, with whorls of branches with scalelike leaves. They sometimes grow four feet high on my riverbank and they, too, are brash to the touch. They wither down over Winter—the scouring rushes don't—and put forth new growth each Spring. Before that growth starts I always find the spore heads, thumblike shoots six or eight inches tall, sometimes tan, sometimes flesh-colored. Their only function is to produce spores, and when the spores ripen they wither and the green plants appear.

In the marshland forests which produced the Coal Age there were ancestors of these horsetails that grew sixty feet high. They looked almost exactly like these miniatures on my riverbank. So when I walk among the horsetails today I am, in a sense, walking with the dinosaurs. All time has done to these ancient plants is dwarf them.

I like to know a river not only from its banks but from out on the river itself, where I can feel its currents and see the way the water responds to its channel. I also like to fish. So we have a small boat that I can paddle or row or fit with a small outboard motor. In that boat I have explored the river, prowled upstream to a place where the shallows strand me except in time of flood. In that way I know the river from early April to December.

In April the water is still high with snow-melt and Spring rain, roiled and strong of current. Then I can explore the backwaters and the brooks, which have become minor estuaries. By July the river has become a sluggish, turbid stream with muddy banks where little, yellow-freckled spotted turtles sun themselves and herons stare suspiciously.

By October the stream has cleared and the trees have begun to turn color. Catbirds and jays are busy at the grapevines, squirrels are racing in the treetops, the pileated woodpeckers are drumming on dead trees out of sheer exuberance. The sky is deep blue; the wine of swamp maple and amber of popple are spilled in vast reflections, like pigment floating on the water. October is the time to make a long, leisurely trip on any river if you would know how beautiful it can be. Then the Autumn rains come, bringing down the leaves, and the river flows with a variegation of color that is unbelievable.

December comes, and ice. At first the ice fringes the river, brittle lace along each bank, and the river's water is black in contrast. The cold deepens and one morning I look out and see the river iced over, bank to bank. The ice looks black but really is crystal clear and takes its color from the dark water underneath. A few more days of insistent cold thickens the ice and it looks gray, now masking the dark water beneath. Then the snow comes and my river is a pristine white highway happily free of all wheeled traffic.

The ice will come and go—we say it takes three freeze-ups and three go-outs to make a Winter here—and finally will come the last break-up. The ice will all go out on the surging current of early Spring. And the first mergansers, which some call shelldrakes, will arrive. They are beautiful birds, particularly the males, with their red-orange beaks, dark green heads, and striking contrast of black and white wings and body. The females are drab by comparison, with ruddy heads and bodies striped and speckled in shades of brown and gray with only a little white. We have two species, the common American mergansers and the hooded mergansers. Their colors are much the same, but the hooded ones have long feathers on the head that can be lifted into a spectacular crest. All mergansers are swift of flight, good swimmers, and leave me breathless with their long-distance dives. Now and then I see a pair of them riding an ice floe in March. I wish they stayed here to nest, but they go on north, into Vermont and New Hampshire and on into Canada.

After the mergansers come the ducks; mostly blacks in my area but with an occasional pair of mallards. And wood ducks, those colorful little fellows that are always a delight to the eye. The blacks, the mallards, and the wood ducks nest along the river. Blacks and mallards build nests much alike, in the low brush or tall reeds, close to the ground, sometimes on the ground, making a deep cup of grass and reeds and lining it with down and feathers. The nests are always close by the water and hard to find unless you flush the brooding mother off her eggs. Usually she will stay there until you are within a few feet of her. One afternoon, prowling through the alder brush looking for a patch of yellow lady-slipper, I was almost struck in the face by a black duck as she flew off the nest. I don't know whether she was trying to frighten me off or what, but my instinctive dodge saved my glasses though her wings slapped me on the head as she rocketed past. And there, in plain sight, not four feet in front of me, was her nest, a roughly matted cup of reeds and stems, lined with soft gray down. In it were eight pale buff eggs with a slight greenish cast, the size of small hen's eggs but, like all duck eggs, disproportionately long.

The wood ducks nest in hollow trees and are the only ducks I know that perch in trees. Mergansers also sometimes nest in hollow trees, but I have never seen one perch on a limb. Wood ducks often appropriate the tree holes that pileated woodpeckers have cut. One year a pair of them nested in a hollow limb of an old apple tree beside my barn. I have heard of them nesting on a haystack and even in the loose hay in a farmer's barn loft. Kindhearted people sometimes put up nest boxes on poles in the edge of a bogland and wood ducks happily use them.

After the ducks come, Spring is here. It may throw a cold tantrum or two, but there is no stopping the season. I get my boat into the water and survey the Winter changes in the river, thinking of fishing expeditions.

I have no notion of telling anyone where or how to fish. Rivers, as well as fishermen, are insistently individual. And fish—who can read the mind of a fish? But there are basic rules we follow. One of the first is to explore the river early and see what Winter and Spring freshets have done to our familiar coves, deep holes, backwaters, shallows, and snagtangles. After that we have to learn by experience, and some things we have to learn all over again every year.

I now am primarily a still fisherman, though I troll from time to time. I have whipped my trout streams in years past and like to think I can still "read" a brook, and I have cast plugs, bugs, and minnows at ten thousand bass in lake and pond. Now I prefer to sit in a boat and do my fishing the lazy way, with time to think and listen and just quietly become a part of the landscape. I fish for fish, but I also fish to learn what is going on out there on the river. Many an evening we have gone out on the pretext of catching breakfast and spent an hour watching the swallows put on an aerial circus over the water. Or listening to the whippoorwills. Or watching the moon rise. And many a Summer morning we have got up before dawn to go fishing, actually to drink vacuum coffee and eat sandwiches while the mist rises and the sun comes up and every bird along the river sings as though this were the first dawn that ever was. Any time that fishing becomes nothing but fish, the fisherman has missed the real point of life.

But fish are a good excuse. We have more or less the usual assortment of fish one finds in any river of the Northeast. Because the river is fed by many brooks there are trout, mostly browns which tolerate warm water, but occasionally a few brookies. The brookies haunt the colder water at or near the mouth of a brook. The brown trout often are in the deeper parts of the river.

We have perch, yellow perch. Some years we catch more perch than anything else except rock bass and sunfish. Rockies and sunnies like the warm, shallow water and the rockies, as their name implies, like a rocky bottom. Sunfish like the shallows where the sun has made the water tepid; we find them in great numbers in shallow coves and backwaters and sometimes I fish for them with a fly rod, just for fun. They give me a brief, hard fight on light tackle. Rock bass will sometimes do the same thing, but at other times they wouldn't rise to a fly for anyone.

There are a few pickerel, the Eastern pickerel, which we get now and then by fishing among the tangled roots where a shore has washed to the foot of the trees. They make bony eating, but they are fighters and fun to catch.

Aside from the trout, the black bass, both large-mouth and small-mouth, are the choice game fish in the river. The large-mouths like warmer, shallower water than the small-mouths. We occasionally get a large-mouth in a quiet cove where the water is less than three feet deep. They like weedy water, sedgy places, and old stumps and logs. For small-mouths I usually look for a raft of driftwood in a deep, cool backwater. If I drift a bait or lure down deep in such a shaded place I sometimes get worthwhile action. As often as not I get an old lunker of a rock bass, though, and fight him briefly to the net and try again.

Someone dumped shiners into the river years ago, as careless fishermen do in other rivers, and they bred and multiplied. Now we have what we call silver carp. They are sometimes fifteen inches long, take a worm like a trout, and fight like mad—for one minute, then quit. They are trash fish. So are suckers, some of which are eighteen inches long and put up a struggle worthy of a big brook trout. I reserve special curses for those big brookies which turn out, after a fierce fight, to be suckers when I get them to the boat. Catfood!

And there are bullheads, small yellow-bellied brown catfish. Bullheads feed on muddy bottoms and bite best in the evening; some fishermen come to the river at dusk and catch bullheads by lantern light far into the evening. If skinned and soaked in salt water, bullheads make palatable fare when fried, but I think they have a muddy taste. When I catch one I throw it back, remembering the big, sweet-fleshed channel "cats" I caught as a small boy in the streams of Nebraska. All catfish have long, sharp spines on their dorsal and pectoral fins and can inflict painful wounds on unwary fishermen. They should be handled with care.

For bait we use almost everything, from garden worms to plugs, from grasshoppers to artificial flies, but we usually come back to worms for serious fishing. Most of the time we use bait rods, but now and then I want more action and use a fly rod, even with bait.

We have found that in the Spring or Fall all kinds of fish, even sunfish, can be caught in either sun or shade. In the Summer most fish except sunnies seem to prefer shaded water. Early morning and late afternoon are the best times for Summer fishing, though we have struck a school of hungry yellow perch in sunny water at 2 o'clock on a hot July afternoon. Perch, by the way, run in schools. Catch one and you probably can catch more in the same place. We sometimes drift down the river, slow-trolling with a small spoon ahead of a big worm until a perch strikes.

Then we anchor and fish, usually with luck. We have found some of our choice perch holes that way, places that looked so unpromising we would have passed them by.

The brooks on my place are not fishing water. They tend to dwindle to trickles by Midsummer. They are pleasant places to know, however, with the music of their rapids and insignificant falls and with their wealth of ferns and wildflowers along the cool, shady banks. The bigger brooks have these same virtues, but because they have more water and a steadier flow the year round they are often good trout streams. Trout fishing in the East, however, is too often a matter of catching tame, fishery-raised trout that have been dumped into the streams only a few weeks before. And most of the accessible brooks are so heavily fished that solitude, an essential ingredient of enjoyable fishing, is almost impossible. But if you can find a back-country brook that hasn't been fished to death, it may be worth casting a few flies.

Most eastern brooks that have trout have brownies, brookies, or rainbows, or some combination of them. All trout usually feed upstream, so the lure or bait should be drifted down to them.

Brook trout usually lie behind an obstruction, a big rock, a log, a sandbar. They also like the quiet water at the foot of a swift rapids. Since they lie deep as a rule, they take bait and wet flies better than dry flies.

Rainbows will usually be out in the fast, heavy water in the middle of the brook.

Brownies often lie between the brookies and the rainbows, between the strong current close to shore and the swift water in midstream. Brownies as well as brookies like back-eddies.

During hot weather all trout tend to retreat to deep, cool, preferably shaded pools from about 9 in the morning till 5 or so in the afternoon. They do most of their feeding morning and evening. In Spring and Fall and on cool, overcast Summer days, however, they are often moving about all day. But I have seen active trout which were constantly feeding ignore every fly in my book and sneer at worms. I don't know why. I doubt that anyone knows.

But, as I said before, any stream is more than water or fish. And, with exceptions that I can count on the fingers of one hand, the fish I caught are secondary memories of all the brooks and rivers I have ever fished.

There was the late August afternoon when the fish were as sleepy as I was. I let the boat drift into a slack eddy near the bank where it hung almost motionless and I sat there, on the verge of a nap, in the dappled shade. A motion on the bank caught my half-opened eye and I glanced up and saw a half-grown red fox trot up the game path on the bank and pause to look at me, not more than a fly rod's length away. His dark eyes stared, his big ears cupped, his little black nose quivered. He had been panting, dog-like, and his ribs still throbbed. Apparently he got no man-smell, nothing to frighten him, for he sat down and watched me, simply curious, puppy-curious. He sat there several ninutes, then opened his mouth and yawned and I thought he might lie down right there and take a nap with me. I am sure he considered it. But something on up that game trail demanded his attention. He went on, unhurried, with no sense of danger from me. He had been so close to me that I could hear his breath as he panted.

One full-moon evening my wife and I had been up the river in the boat and were drifting down, sitting quietly, watching and participating in the half-light world. The current carried the boat close by a small island, and at the downstream end we saw a big raccoon and four kits on the narrow mud flat at the island's lower end. Their silvery fur glistened in the moonlight; their black-masked faces and ringed tails were sharply contrasted black and white, beautiful. The mother was digging fresh-water mussels at the water's edge. She held one in her paws, forced it open with her uncannily adept "fingers." The kits scrambled for the morsel inside. Then the mother saw the boat, sat back on her haunches, hissed, and the kits simply vanished, flashed into the underbrush just behind them. The mother stood there, facing us, defiant, as we slowly drifted past, not twenty feet away. And the blue-black mussel shells she had opened before we came lay shimmering, opalescent, in the moonlight. She was still there when I looked back.

There was the day we saw the otters. Several times I had seen what I dismissed as an unusually large, light-colored muskrat swimming near the far bank where the current had undermined a maze of tree roots. But something about that rat made me wonder. I wanted a closer look. So we went up and sat on the bank opposite those roots, binoculars in hand, and waited. And the "muskrat" appeared, not a muskrat at all, but an otter. It came out from among the roots, swam about for a few minutes, then swam directly across the river toward us. We watched with the glasses until it was within twenty feet of our bank. I lowered the glasses to watch without them, and it must have seen my motion. It dived, and it looked five feet long as it looped up and over, sleek, sinuous, the epitome of grace in the water. Actually, it probably was somewhat less than three feet long. It swam under water across the river and appeared near the roots again. There a second otter, the mate, appeared just for a moment. They must have had a den in the bank behind those roots, perhaps an old muskrat den, and probably had a litter of cubs. Later, when the cubs should have been out and swimming, I looked for an otter slide on every steep bank nearby, but never found one. Otters, particularly when they have growing cubs, are very playful and take special delight in coasting down a bank into the water, belly-flopping on their sleek, wet fur like small boys coasting in the Winter. They even use snow slides of their own in Winter, whisking down an icy bank into the frigid water. But our otters had disappeared before Winter. They probably moved on, to another part of the river or to another stream, for otters are travelers, unlike mink which will stay in the same stream or swamp for years unless they are trapped to extinction. I have never seen mink in my part of the river, though from time to time I hear reports of them. I suspect such reports, for none of the trappers I know catches mink here any more.

Every Summer comes a day—usually two or three days —when we know it is useless to go fishing. But we often go out in the boat, just the same, simply to marvel at the incredible fecundity of nature. Those are the days when the May flies emerge. The scientific name of the May fly is *Ephemera,* and it couldn't be more apt. In their larval and nymph stages, these astonishing little insects live in the mud or under water for at least a year, sometimes for two or even three years, but when they finally molt into winged creatures they have a very brief life, some of them only a few hours, some a day or two. This life span is still in some dispute, and one researcher has kept winged May flies alive several weeks. But in the open they appear to emerge with wings, fly for a few hours in what seems to the human observers to be absolute ecstasy, and die. They don't eat, but they mate, on the wing, and they lay eggs. There are a number of species, but all look much alike to the naked eye, all indulge in ecstatic flight, and all have brief lives.

We never know when the day of the May flies will come, but we do know when it is here. The water is alive with the nymphs, tiny creatures even smaller than mosquito larvae. They come to the surface, swimming madly, and seem to dapple the water, make it almost dance. Fish swarm, breaking the surface, even leaping, as they feed, for these nymphs are a special treat. Within minutes after the swarming nymphs appear there is a host of what look like tiny gray-white moths. What has happened is that the nymphs have molted, there on the water's surface, and the winged May flies have taken to the air. But this change is not yet complete. These new creatures have still another molt to undergo, which makes them unique among the insects. They flutter ashore or to the overhanging bushes, rest there briefly, and molt once more. And then the true May flies surge back into the air as though in exultant triumph. Often we see the nymphs on the water in mid-morning, see the first winged stage flutter ashore by noon, and by late afternoon see the mad dance of fully adult May flies, like shimmering clouds. They swirl, sweep upward, surge here and there, like mist caught in a whimsical breeze. I have had them sweep around my head in such a swarm that I had to hold my nose to keep from breathing them in. In the last hours of daylight I have seen them climb high and catch the rays of the sun after it has set and look like a silver cloud, twinkling and ever changing. If it happens to be a moonlit night, they can look like a shower of gold dust in the air, their filmy wings reflecting the moonlight.

That evening we watch the screens and close the doors tightly, and we put on no outside lights. May flies are strongly phototropic, can't resist light. One such evening we had to go out and, out of habit, I left the porch light on. When we returned a few hours later the whole porch floor was white with May flies and the globe on the porch light was full to the brim with their bodies, thousands of them dead on the altar of an incandescent lamp. The next morning after the first flight of the May flies the river is still boiling with feeding fish, for millions of May flies have died during the night and fallen into the water. The stream sometimes is gray with them in the eddies. A couple of days and it is all over, the flight finished, the brief life of the May flies ended for another year. But we know there is little use fishing for another week. The fish are replete, gorged on May-fly larvae and winged May flies. But for a few days before the flight and for several weeks afterward the fish, the bass and trout particularly, will rise to such dry flies as the Gray Drake, which imitates the May fly.

There are other insects of which we are well aware. In Spring there are midges, black and biting little pests, and there are black flies, scourge of the North woods but no more plentiful here than mosquitoes. There are the big, spotted deer flies, which bite like tigers. There are the colorful but harmless dragonflies and damsel flies. There are, on occasion, small swarms of Monarch butterflies over the river, undoubtedly lured to its banks by the fields of milkweed that grow here and there.

The river, any river, is all these things, all these forms of life. But it still is essentially water, flowing water. That is its ultimate lure for me. Water and wind are the freest of all the elements around us, the least tamed. We dam rivers and pollute them, we try to confine them in dikes, and we shunt brooks one way or another to reclaim a field or pasture, but we never really subdue flowing water. Water will have its own way eventually.

And the age-old lure of flowing water entrances us from the time we set toy waterwheels in a draining gutter until we sit beside a river, rheumatic in joint and old and frail in body, and see the parable of life in the seaward flow. As long as there are hills upon this earth there will be brooks and rivers, and as long as there is human life there will be men to watch verdant Spring come to those rivers and their valleys, lush Summer come to the humid river bottoms, Fall sweep color like flame and flow like pigment, Winter snow and ice mask but never halt the flow of living water.

What makes a brook or river so special? It is useless to try to answer the question, for he who asks it will never understand the answer. Rivers and brooks are special simply because they *are* brooks, and they *are* rivers.

## Chapter 7

# The Miniature World

**TANTALIZINGLY** near at hand, just beyond the curve of a lens, is another world, infinitely varied and filled with amazing beauty. The man with a hand-glass in his pocket has the key to discovery of a whole new universe even though he never leaves his own backyard.

*Just beyond the world* of the obvious lies another world, the world of the miniature, with brand-new vistas for the confined or the lazy nature watcher. It is the world just beyond the reach of normal vision. I catch glimpses of it often, but with my naked eyes I can see only enough of it to tantalize me. With a pocket-size magnifying glass I can enter it as though I were walking into a Lilliput world.

I first discovered this world's fascination many years ago. I had discarded a broken flashlight but saved the crude, molded-glass lens, being a magpie sort of person. I put it into my pocket, felt it there when I went outdoors a little later, and wondered how good it would be as a burning glass. I tried it, scorched a hole in a dead leaf, and then happened to see a head of lawn clover blossom through it. Suddenly that tuft of everyday clover was a whole bouquet of flowers. I studied it for ten minutes through that crude lens, of no more than four power, and had my first glimpse of what a good glass might reveal.

Impatient to see more, I took the lens from my camera. The difference between that fine lens and the bit of molded glass from the flashlight was as dawn and midday. I spent an hour exploring with it. But the camera lens, made for quite another purpose, was not really satisfactory. So I went to an optical store and bought my first hand lens. It happened to be a Scelsi Doublet of ten power, a pair of polished three-quarter-inch lenses set in a one-inch aluminum barrel and pivoted in a housing to protect the lens. I still have that glass, which to me seems ideal. Also available are pocket glasses with dual lenses which can be used separately or combined for a variety of magnifications. Either type is excellent.

With such a glass one can start anywhere, but I would start in the dooryard with a head of white clover, just as I did long ago. Focus the glass on that little tuft of bloom and you will see that it really is a closely packed bunch of what appear to be half-opened sweet peas. The individual florets are only about a quarter of an inch long, but under the glass they look ten times that big. The petals are smooth, not ruffled as in a sweet pea, and the whole flower is simplified. The petals are clear, creamy white, and beautifully curved. Staring through the glass, you seem to hold an exotic corsage in your hand. Remove the glass, blink your eyes to clear them, and it is only a head of white clover again, quite insignificant. But for a little while you were there in that other world, seeing it in the proportions you might if you were the size of a rabbit.

Pluck a head of red clover, the kind that farmers plant in hay fields and that escapes to roadsides almost everywhere. This is at least twice as big as the clover head from the lawn, and to the naked eye it looks magenta-pink. Under the glass it is another bunch of sweet peas, these with pink petals closely lined with hair-fine markings of deep crimson. These petals, too, are not ruffled, but simple, smooth, and beautifully curved. The outer one stands like a tall, curved Spanish comb behind the inner petals, which are shaped something like twin pink clam shells. They guard the stamens and ovary, which can be seen through the narrow slit between the shell-petals. That inner sanctuary contains the pollen and the nectar. To reach it, and insect must force the guardian shell-petals apart. Neither honey bees nor butterflies are strong enough to do this readily. It takes a bumblebee to do that. So the bumblebees are the agents of pollination for red clover, as the Australians learned when they first tried to grow this plant. It grew well enough in Australian soil, but it failed to produce seed. Australia had no native bumblebees. When American bumblebees were imported and turned loose over the clover fields, the problem was solved. The bumblebees pollinated the clover and became welcome and successful immigrants.

Looking through the glass at a head of red clover one can understand why.

The roadside will provide several other clovers for examination under the glass, since clover is widespread and has a great variety of forms. Beside my road I find the fuzzy little heads of rabbit-foot clover, the tiny yellow heads of hop clover, and both white and yellow sweet clover, which grows tall, has only a few leaves, and bears its blossoms singly up the stem. Now and then I also find a bushy, full-foliaged clover of the sweet-clover type which has purple flowers. It is alfalfa, escaped from some nearby hay field. All the clover florets are substantially the same shape, that approximation of the sweet pea. Other members of the clover family in my area include vetch, patridge pea, and tick trefoil, whose little seed pods break into tiny triangular stick-tights when they ripen. In any Autumn walk I come home with some of those trefoil pods clinging to my clothes with their minute hairy hooks.

Before going farther afield, pick a dandelion blossom. If your lawn is like mine there will be a few dandelions in bloom from April till November, though they pass their urgency of bloom by mid-June. When I look at a dandelion head through the glass I get the feeling that I am looking at a particularly beautiful quilled dahlia or a brand-new type of golden chrysanthemum. But the glass also reveals a maze of green-yellow stamens among the golden petals, hair-thin and each with a two-pronged tip, the prongs curving downward like the traditional horns of a goat. There are hundreds of these stamens, as many as there are petals. Actually, what we think of as petals are individual florets, for the dandelion is one of the composite family, the members of which bear their blossoms in compact communities that we think of as single flowers.

It takes patience and steady fingers, but one can remove a single floret from a dandelion head and under the glass see that it is a tube that flattens out into a single strap-like petal; and out of that tube rises the greenish, prong-tipped stamen. It takes a stronger glass than my ten-power to see, but down in that tube lies the ovary from which the seed will eventually mature. And clinging to the base of that floret-tube are the beginnings of the silky hairs that will become the airy fluff of the ripe dandelion head, the fluff on which the seed will ride the air. All this is packed in a floret less than three-quarter inch long and smaller in diameter than a common pin. Some of it can be seen under the ten-power glass.

Pause at the edge of the garden and find a flower of that ubiquitous member of the pink family, common chickweed. It should be easy to find because chickweed is in bloom, even in New England, almost every month of the year. That is why it is so difficult to get rid of. Chickweed produces seed before most other plants have wakened in the Spring and long after they have closed shop for the year in the Fall.

The chickweed blossom is only about a quarter inch across, and to the naked eye it appears to have ten white petals backed by five long, pointed green sepals. Under the glass it looks big as a daisy, and those milky white petals number only five, as they should in any member of the pink family; but each one is slit almost to the base, as are the much larger flowers of another roadside weed of the same family, the bladder campion. At the base of each chickweed petal stand two stamens, their shafts thin as hairs and faintly greenish-white. At the stamen tips are the anthers, looking like lead-gray eggs lying on their sides, precariously balanced. In the center of the blossom is the ovary, faintly grooved in five sections, and from the top of its pineapple-shaped fatness rises the five-pronged style, curved back fountainlike. So here is a perfect flower, in all ways typical of the rule-of-five that prevails in the pink family. Five petals, ten stamens, a five-part ovary with a five-pronged style, all set in a five-sepal base. And the whole of it only a quarter inch across.

Out at the roadside one probably can find the bladder campion just mentioned, which blooms from June through August. The flower is much like the chickweed blossom, though large enough to see all details clearly with the naked eye. The campion, however, hides its ovary and styles in a fat green "bladder" the size of a boy's marble just beneath the petals. It takes an insistent bee to force its way in to reach the nectar there and pollinize the flower. Another of the pinks, the little crimson-petaled Deptford pink, should be somewhere at the roadside, too. A glass will reveal some of its details, but it can be appreciated with the naked eye.

And bouncing Bet, sometimes called soapwort, certainly will be growing not far away. Bouncing Bet grows everywhere and blooms even after first frost. Its typical pink-family flowers are about an inch across, come in clusters at the top of the plant, and are white tinged with pink or lavender. Chickweed is blood-cousin of all these, but it takes a glass to prove it unless the observer has far better eyesight than I have.

The roadside or the edge of the meadow will provide a head of Queen Anne's lace, or wild carrot. The fluffy, flat-topped head of white is obviously complex but doesn't seem mysterious. When one looks at it through the glass, however, the aspect changes. The foamy-looking cluster is made up of dozens of individual clusters, and each small cluster consists of a miniature of the whole head, which consists literally of a whole bouquet of small white blossoms. Single out one of those individual florets. It has five milky white petals, each notched like the mitten leaf of a sassafras tree. I have examined these florets many times and have yet to find any order or system in which the clefts in those miniature petals are arranged. They seem to be wholly at random, some to the right, some to the left. From the base of each petal rises a single stamen, its pollen-bearing anther cinnamon-brown. In the center of the flower is the ovary, a frosty white bead with twin stigmas sticking straight up. All this is in an individual floret less than one-eighth inch across. Incidentally, the "ruby" that is supposed to be in the center of each head is sometimes missing and sometimes appears double. It is a deep red floret shaped exactly like the white florets of the head, even to the lobed petals.

The casual eye sees only that lacy head of white bloom. The ruby blossom usually found in the center may require a second look, but still with the unaided eye. Those cinnamon-brown stamen tips, though, those notched and curled petals, those twin-pronged ovaries, are practically secret. I never see them until I look through the glass.

Go farther afield, into the meadow, and find a daisy, the common oxeye daisy of the field with its egg-yellow center and its fringe of white rays or petals. Here again is a whole community of individual florets, for the daisy too is a composite. That yellow center is a close-packed mass of tight yellow tube-flowers, each complete with ovary and stamens.

The white "petals" around the edge are also individual flowers, each with a single long, straplike white petal. These ray flowers, however, have no stamens, only ovaries and pistils. They are female flowers, not bisexual as are the florets that make up the yellow center.

Choose any of the composites, a sunflower, an aster, a hawkweed, a chickory, and the same arrangement holds true—a mass of individual florets forming the center, a fringe of ray flowers with long petals forming the blossom's so-called petals.

Remarkable among the composites, to me at least, are the goldenrods. Examine a plume of goldenrod and you see that it is a whole community of minute flowers arranged along the branching stems at the tip of the plant. But that only begins to describe the goldenrod plume. Each of those individual blossoms is itself a composite flower, like a daisy. Every one of those tiny floral tufts, in most instances less than a quarter inch across, is itself a whole community of florets. Here, indeed, one must use the glass to begin to see the secrets, for there are mysteries within mysteries, florets within florets. Pluck one of those minute flowers, as they seem to be—there may be fifty or more to a single goldenrod spray—and examine it under the glass. It has ray petals like those of a daisy, perhaps only four or five, perhaps as many as nine. Those ray petals, just like the white petals of a daisy, enclose a head of even smaller individual florets like the yellow center of a daisy. And here is a place where the ten-power glass is inadequate. It can only hint at the detail, the astonishing order and organization of those individual florets, each of which is a slight fraction of an inch long and smaller in diameter than a pin. Each one has stamens and an ovary, and the stamens produce pollen and the ovaries produce seed.

Incidentally, goldenrod pollen almost never produces hay fever. That allergy usually is caused by wind-blown pollen, such as that from ragweed and various grasses. The pollen of goldenrod is sticky, almost never carried by the wind. Unless one deliberately sniffs a plume of goldenrod held close to the nose, it is most unlikely that one will get the pollen where it might cause trouble. Even an allergic person can walk through a whole field of goldenrod and escape trouble if he doesn't lean over and sniff the blossoms.

But a hay field in bloom or a roadside patch of ragweed in bloom should be avoided by susceptible persons.

The miniatures among the flowers, which invite the pocket lens, are everywhere. For instance, common plantain, which invades lawns and paths as well as garden borders, comes to blossom in what looks like a faintly gray-green thumb on a long, slim stem, the whole head half the diameter of a lead pencil. Seen under the glass it is a compact mass of buds with scattered greenish-white four-petaled flowers. The peppergrass plant that grows at the edges of my garden bears tiny white flowers at the tips of its stems, flowers that mature into the peppery little flat seeds I sometimes pluck and chew for their tang. Even the bristly, fat green head on the common pigweed that flourishes in waste places everywhere is a mass of green blossoms that can be examined under the glass.

And don't pass up that garden weed called purslane. Country folk have long known it as pussley. It grows in my garden, no matter how I try to be rid of it, and I have yet to see a garden that didn't have a few plants of it somewhere around. Go to the garden in June, or any Summer week thereafter, and pluck a sprig of purslane. Look at the branch tips. There, hidden in the rosette of fleshy green leaves, you will see a fleck of golden yellow no bigger than a pinhead. That is the purslane blossom. It opens only in the morning sunshine. Under the glass it is seen as a greenish-yellow cup composed of five petals, each twin-loved. It may have anywhere from seven to twelve stamens, each with tiny, glistening orange beads of pollen on its tip. A green style rises from the ovary at the blossom's center and forks into five curved golden branches. All this in a space so small that it can be, and often is, hidden under a small drop of dew.

I fight the purslane in the garden all Summer long. But every morning when I see those golden flecks of miniature blossom I think of the portulaca in one corner of the flower garden, spreading its colorful, velvety petals to the sun. They are cousins, and I cherish the one, try in vain to be rid of the other. The only time I see any beauty in the purslane is when I look at those tiny golden cups through the ten-power glass.

Various grasses are rewarding to the person with a

pocket glass, especially when they come to blossom—with caution, of course, if one is subject to hay fever. Grass flowers are simplified to the essential elements. Because grasses are pollinated by the wind rather than by insects, their blossoms have no petals. They consist of pollen-bearing stamens and ovaries with styles that are usually feathery to catch the almost invisible pollen. These stamens and ovaries are shielded somewhat by greenish bracts called glumes. If you would see flowers in utmost simplicity, look at the grass on your own lawn when it comes to head and blossom. The ten-power glass will show you how uncomplicated a flower can be.

I like to use the glass in April and May on trees and bushes as they open their flower buds. For every tree that has big, showy flowers such as the magnolia or the tulip tree, there are a hundred with inconspicuous blossoms with secrets for the glass to reveal. The poplars, the birches, and the aspens flower in catkins, as do the willows. Those catkins are of both sexes, sometimes on the same tree, sometimes on different trees. The male catkins, which produce the pollen, are the more conspicuous, sometimes four or five inches long and looking something like big caterpillars. The female catkins are much smaller and often have to be sought out. Under the glass, the male catkins can be seen as closely massed stamens which, as they mature, produce anthers at their tips and then pollen on the anthers. Stamens and anthers are of various shapes, varying with the species of the tree. The female catkins are little more than tufts of ovaries, each with its styles to catch the pollen. And again there is variety in the shape and color of ovaries and styles. The diversity of nature in shaping such essentially simple elements as stamens and ovaries, anthers and styles, is almost incredible. I marvel every Spring when I examine them with a glass, and I never set out for an hour's look without spending at least twice that long.

When the maples come to blossom, not long after the poplars have hung out their catkins, they too invite close inspection. Maple flowers are very small, but they bloom in clusters. When they have petals, the petals are minute but they always come in fives. If there are no petals, the calyx is five-parted. The stamens are nearly always long, so long they make the flower tuft resemble a tassel. The flowers of sugar maples are greenish-yellow, those of swamp maples a deep, rich crimson. All are beautiful under the glass. Most maples come to bloom before the leaves appear.

Even the flowering dogwood invites a look with the glass. What we think of as the big white petals of the dogwood flower are not petals but bracts, leaflike elements that in the dogwood are white or, in some species, pink. The true flowers of the dogwood are only about a quarter inch across and are clustered at the center of those four white bracts. Each of these florets has four green sepals and four greenish-white petals, with the ovary and style in the center and stamens around the ovary. The glass reveals this clearly. This floral structure becomes obvious when the flowers have faded and the big white bracts are gone. Then each flower has become a green berry, making a berry cluster at the center of what we called the dogwood "flower." Those berries mature into the familiar oval, lacquer-red dogwood berries of September, which are choice fare of the squirrels and any number of birds.

All members of the apple family, from the pasture rose to the apple tree, from the wild strawberry to the tall meadowsweet, are fair game for the man with a pocket lens, as are spirea and bridal wreath, common shrubs on suburban and country lawns. The flowers of all of them follow the rose's rule of five—five green sepals, five petals, and a wealth of stamens arranged in circles around the multiple ovary. The ovary may be complex, as in the strawberry, or relatively simple, as in the apple where it is only five-part, again following that rule of five. Cut an apple crosswise and you can see that five-part, star-shaped center, each part with its seed and all enclosed in the fibrous vanes that make up what we call the core of the apple. Under the glass the tiny individual flowers in a spike of meadowsweet bloom can be seen as close kin in almost every way to the big, spicy apple blossom. I am forever fascinated by the varying shapes of the anthers, at the stamen tips, in all the rose family's blossoms.

If one wants to enter a field that can lead to the semi-microscopic, one can also examine pollen under the ten-power glass. In size, the individual grains range from the diameter of a pin down to that of a pinpoint. And they come in almost every conceivable shape, from minute spheres to barrels, ovals, and drums. But the study of pollen calls for infinite patience and higher magnification. The pocket lens can only make one wish for a miscroscope with which to excursion into that vast, tantalizing world.

Still another world at least partially accessible to the pocket lens is that of the mosses and lichens, some varieties of which grow in almost every woodland and, indeed, even in places where no other form of plant life exists. Lichens really demand the use of a miscroscope for more than casual study, but the ten-power glass will reveal many interesting things about them. There are at least 2,000 kinds of lichen in America—some set the number considerably higher —but perhaps a dozen of them can be recognized by the amateur who is willing to learn a few fundamentals. Lichens never grow in cities or any area where fumes contaminate the air, but they can be found in rural woodlands and even on rocks in nearly any rural dooryard. They are familiar to mountain climbers, of course, because they are the only form of plant life that grows on high, cold peaks. They are the dominant form of plant life in Greenland and other such frigid areas. The reindeer moss of the Far North is a lichen. So is Old Man's Beard, the gray-green hairlike growth on trees in the damp, cold spruce woods of the North. (Florida moss, which resembles Old Man's Beard and grows on live oaks in the South, is not a lichen. It is a member of the pineapple family of plants, incredible as that seems, and is an epiphyte, a plant that lives on and in the air without need of roots in the soil.)

Lichens are really a dual form of life, algae and fungi linked so closely that they appear to be a single plant. This complex partnership is called symbiosis, in which the algae manufacture the food and the fungi absorb the essential moisture. Neither can grow without the presence of the other. The algae in the partnership are closely related to those that grow as maplike green stains on tree trunks, and the fungi are related to the molds.

The most common lichens are of one of two forms, one crustlike, the other coral-like. The crust forms resemble fragments of leaves cemented to the surface of a rock. Some are lobed and ruffled, somewhat like lettuce leaves, and range in color from gray-green to red-green. Some are flat, smooth, and dark green above, sooty black beneath.

On some islands off the Maine coast the yellow wall lichen, which is closely attached to the rocks, is so plentiful that the island cliffs are almost golden in appearance. Here in the hills of New England a species called Cladonia covers rocky ledges and barren patches with a faintly green-gray coral-like growth. One species of Cladonia also grows on old stumps and rotting logs and sends up little fingers, gray stalks, bearing brilliant red tips which are the plant's reproductive organs. This species is called Scarlet-Crested Cladonia.

The mosses are altogether different from the lichens, though they often grow side by side. Mosses are very old plants, still primitive in many ways, and their life cycle is more like that of the ferns than of any other plants. They reproduce by spores, as the ferns do, and again like the ferns the moss spores produce plants quite different from the parent which in time send up both male and female organs and produce sperm and egg cells which unite and grow into the familiar spore-producing moss plants again. So there are two kinds of plants in every moss clump, those which grow spores and those which produce the egg and sperm cells.

Moss foliage varies from species to species, but the really spectacular distinction is in the spore heads. This phase of moss life is revealed in fascinating detail by the pocket lens.

The spore heads are borne on thread-thin stems that often are only a fraction of an inch tall and seldom are more than an inch. The spore head itself is a capsule which is seldom as large in diameter as a kitchen match and often is nearer the size of a common pin. The capsule assumes various forms, each peculiar to the species. The capsule of the Crisped Ulota, for instance, a species that grows on trees, is like a wide-mouthed urn. That of Webera moss, which grows on the soil, is a gently twisted horn. That of the Edenton, a brilliant yellow-green moss with flattened foliage, is shaped like a curved cow horn. Some mosses have bell-shaped capsules, some are like crook-necked gourds, some are like ridged balls or eggs. And, to repeat, all are minute.

These spore capsules or pods have lids or caps which drop off when the spores are ripe and ready to disperse. Once the lid has been cast off, the lip of the spore pod can be seen to have a fringe of teeth, sometimes only four, sometimes as many as sixty-four, but invariably in multiples of four. These teeth scatter the spores as they are spilled out by the wind or by a passing bird or animal. The stems on which the pods are borne are like hair-thin springs, and they jerk back and forth, showering the spores. The teeth on the rim of the pod swell up, fold over, and close the pod in damp weather, protecting the spores. When the rain or mist passes, they shrink and open the pod again.

Many of these details can be seen under the ten-power lens. I can count the teeth on some of the spore capsules, but not all of them. If I want to study a specimen, I bring home a tuft of moss and put it under a strong light here in my study, where there is neither wind nor shadow to set the filament waving or distract my eye. But half an hour spent seated beside a patch of moss in the edge of the woods, peering through that pocket lens, is always time well spent.

Moss, unlike the lichens, has no prejudice toward cities and contaminated air. Several species can be found in most urban areas if one knows where to look. I have taken more than a passing look at the moss in Trinity Churchyard, on lower Broadway in Manhattan, and I have found several species growing along the Hudson River waterfront, even on some of the old piers there. But mosses thrive better in the clean air of the country, and one can always find several species in old fields, on patches of thin soil at the roadside, in the thin soil on ledges of rocks, or on tree trunks or fallen logs in almost any damp, cool woodland.

In country or city there is still another world that invites the hand lens. That is the insect world. Flies, wasps, bees, beetles, mosquitoes, moths, and butterflies can be found almost anywhere.

The ten-power glass will reveal the structure of a housefly's wing, for instance, or the head and remarkable mouth parts of that ubiquitous pest. It will even make understandable the fly's ability to walk up a pane of glass or across the ceiling by showing the tiny pads on the fly's foot, which somewhat resemble buttons of foam rubber. Or catch a honey bee and look at the hind leg and see the hairy area called the pollen basket, with which the bee carries pollen from blossom to hive. Look at the foreleg, with the "comb" the bee uses to clean and groom its antennae.

I am always fascinated by the heads of insects, especially by their eyes. Insects have two compound eyes, each consisting of a cluster of individual eye cells. These cells are almost always hexagonal in shape and are fitted together like the cells in a honeycomb. Most insects also have simple eyes of one cell each. The grasshopper, for instance, has three of these simple eyes on its forehead between the two big compound eyes. Through the glass the shape of the individual cells in the compound eyes can be seen in most insects.

Katydids and other members of the cricket family make their characteristic sounds by running a "scraper" on the lower surface of one forewing over a "file" on the other forewing. Under the glass both the toothed "file" and the "scraper" can be examined. So can the long, flexible antennae of all members of the cricket family. And speaking of antennae, look at the next mosquito you can catch. If the antennae are relatively short and smooth, the mosquito is a female. If they are long and feathery, the mosquito is a male. Only the females bite or sting. Male mosquitoes gather in swarms along my river in late Summer, create a loud evening hum, and sometimes die by the hundred on my front porch. But even when they are present in clouds we are seldom bitten. There seem to be few females in such swarms. The males apparently gather in clouds, hum a kind of swan song, and die in a sort of communal immolation.

The antennae of moths and butterflies can be examined without a lens, but under the glass one can see details, particularly of the moth antennae, that are most interesting. It is a general rule that butterflies have simple antennae, hairlike and thickened at the tip, and that moths have feathery antennae, some of them looking like the wing feathers of a bird. But even more interesting, and demanding of the lens, are the scales that cover the wings of all moths and butterflies. These scales rub off on the fingers like dust when you handle a butterfly or moth. In some species the scales are too small to be examined under the ten-power lens, but in most of them the shape and color can readily be seen. Butterfly scales are shaped like long rectangles with one end gently notched, sometimes with one notch, sometimes with as many as three. The scales on a moth's wings are always long and narrow, sometimes pointed, sometimes so finely divided that they appear fringed at the tip. When scales are scuffed off, the basic wing is revealed as a veined, transparent sheet like the wing of a fly or wasp. The scales provide the color. They also strengthen the wing, since they lie in an overlapping pattern like shingles on a house roof.

I get particular pleasure, as well as a kind of satisfaction, from searching out and examining the eggs of moths and butterflies, which are laid in clusters and masses, varying with the species, on leaves and twigs. These eggs have only one purpose, to perpetuate the species. They will hatch into caterpillars which will follow the intricate lepidopterian cycle, caterpillar, pupa, butterfly, egg, and caterpillar once more. That is the reason for those eggs. And in that light they need be no more than a fertilized life germ surrounded by a film of albuminous substance and encased in some kind of covering that will protect the germ from cold or drought. The logical shape is a sphere or an ovoid, and the color is of little consequence, except to conceal them.

But when I examine the eggs of the lepidoptera I find all shapes, many colors, and elaborate designs of color and texture. Some are shaped like barrels, some are cones, some perfect hemispheres, some like cheeses, some like turbans. And on the surface of these shapes are designs, ridges, lines, grooves, even geometric patterns. Some of the eggs look like tiny, carved gems. Besides these patterns, there are colored dots and colored lines, some of them microscopic, all of them arranged in symmetrical patterns. And the colors range from red to blue, from gold to green, from brown to brilliant yellow. The only uniformity I find is in the fact that the eggs of each species are always the same, in shape, in color, in decoration.

Human logic, scientific logic, would say that the colors are for either protection or attention. Protection or attention from what? Under my glass, those eggs are spectacular. I can't imagine an insect or any bird that could overlook them. And the attention of another bird or insect would certainly be destructive. And in terms of scientific logic, those grooves and ridges should be lines of cleavage, where the egg would open when it hatched. But that isn't the way it happens. Ridges, grooves, and colored markings disappear before the eggs hatch, and when the egg does hatch it simply opens, more or less at random.

I am left with no reason for those decorative markings and beautiful shapes, no plausible, logical reason. And somehow that delights me. The egg of a butterfly or a moth defies all the human utilitarian concepts. It is an egg, and it serves to perpetuate the species. But it is also an infinitesimal thing of beauty which needs no reason for being beautiful. It simply is. And that defiance of man's insistence on mechanical meanings is worth many times the cost of that ten-power glass, many times the hours I have spent squinting through it at butterfly eggs. It renews my faith in nature and convinces me that there are limits to scientific understanding.

# Chapter 8

# An Assemblage
# of Animals

EVERYTHING *that moves on this earth leaves
its tracks somewhere. The countryman
reads the messages written by his animal
neighbors in dust or mud or snow. And
sometimes, if he is patient, he gets to know
them by becoming a part of the dawn, the
dusk, or the night.*

*Animal watching* is mostly a matter of tracks left in the dust, the mud, or the snow. Snow is the blank page on which you will find the tracks of most animals, though the prints themselves are often better in mud. After the Winter's first snow I always go out to see what new neighbors I have and what the old, familiar ones have been up to.

Around the outbuildings there always are mouse tracks, the tracks of deer mice or white-foot mice. These little wild mice not only look much alike but their tracks are identical, fine, lacelike trails in which the individual footprints are only half an inch long. Sometimes you will find a central thread of a tail mark, since these little round-eared fellows have tails as long as their bodies. There will also be vole tracks. Voles, often called meadow mice, keep more to the open than the mice do. Their tracks are much like mouse tracks except that the footprints will overlap; mouse prints almost never do. And voles, with shorter tails, seldom leave tail marks.

To find mouse and vole tracks, look at exposed grass clumps and weed stems. Both mice and voles feed on grass seed and weed seed. A goldenrod stem may have a scattering of fine, dark chaff on the snow beneath it, proving that the mouse or vole has dined there. If the snow is more than a inch or so deep, the tracks may suddenly vanish, as though the track-maker had taken wing. Actually, the reverse is true. The mouse, or more often the vole, has gone under the snow, dug a tunnel, and filled it in behind him. Voles, and sometimes mice, make a whole labyrinth of passageways under the snow. When the snow melts you can see these runways, like a network on the ground. In the runways you may find an occasional tuft of grass or fine weed stems big as a child's fist, marking a temporary bedroom or the remains of a Winter harvest.

Next most numerous, in my area at least, are the gray squirrels. Between my big barn, where the squirrels live, and the corn crib, where they feed all Winter, I am sure to find a maze of their tracks. Normally the gray squirrel travels by leaps, and in the snow you will find the footprints closely bunched. As with most leaping animals, the tracks of the hind feet are somewhat ahead of the forefeet; and as with most climbers, the toes will be splayed. The squirrel prints are much like those of the mice, but larger, the hind foot about two inches long, the forefoot less than an inch. If the snow is more than a few inches deep the prints will be in a kind of squinched hole with the bunched tracks at the bottom. But you will seldom find a tail mark. The squirrel carries its long tail high. When in a hurry, the gray squirrel may leap four or five feet at a time.

The tracks of the red squirrel are much like those of the gray squirrel but about one fourth smaller. And the red squirrel's leaps are seldom more than three feet long. The flying squirrel's tracks are almost identical with those of the red squirrel, but if you can find where the flying squirrel landed on its glide down from the nest-tree you will see the body mark as well as the footprints, and often the edge of the "wings," or glide membranes, will show as parentheses connecting the fore and hind feet on each side. If you live in a fox-squirrel area you will find fox-squirrel tracks almost identical with those of the gray squirrels.

If it is the first snow of Winter or one late in the Spring you probably will find chipmunk tracks. This will be the Eastern chipmunk, if you live anywhere east of Nebraska. The chipmunk's tracks are like those of the squirrels, but only about half the size of a red squirrel's tracks. Chipmunks seldom venture far from a safe retreat, a den in an old stone wall for instance, when there is snow on the ground, and such forays are usually to gather weed seed or withered berries to supplement the Winter diet. In the North, chipmunks hibernate. In my area they seem to rouse from time to time, especially during warm spells, and come out of their dens for air. Still farther south they are out and active much of the Winter.

After taking a census of the mice, squirrels, and chipmunks, look for rabbits. You can find rabbit tracks almost anywhere, even in the edge of the city. I have seen cottontail tracks in New York City's Central Park. Rabbits are almost as ubiquitous as mice.

Is there anyone who doesn't know what a rabbit track looks like? There are those two prints of the hind feet, long ovals about four inches apart, and behind them a few inches are the almost round prints of the forefeet, usually with the left foot an inch or so behind the right one. Like all leapers, the rabbit overreaches his forefeet with his hind ones, making tracks that seem to point the wrong way.

Here in the Northeast we have two species of these small rabbits, the Eastern cottontail and the New England cottontail. Few casual observers, even few rabbit hunters, know them apart. The Eastern cottontail is grayish-brown, the New England cottontail reddish-brown. The Eastern is a trace the larger and has somewhat longer ears. But their tracks cannot be told apart. You will see the Eastern cottontail more often in daylight, since it feeds in early morning and late afternoon. The New England cottontail prefers to feed at night and usually lives in thicker cover. Most of the rabbits killed by automobiles on the roads at night, in my area at least, are the reddish-brown New England cottontails.

The rabbits usually have been all over my place. As I follow their tracks I see their whimsical approach to life, for they start here and go yonder, they nibble at a Brussels sprout stalk still standing in the vegetable garden, search for a carrot I missed in the Fall harvest, taste the frozen stems in the parsnip row. They wander through the flower garden, come to stare at the house, scuttle back to the pasture or to the warren they maintain under the big chicken house.

There are other rabbits here, the snowshoe rabbits or varying hares, but I have to go into the woods far up on the mountain to find their tracks. There aren't many of them in my area, for I live on the southern fringe of their normal range, which doesn't extend much below southern Massachusetts and central New York State.

Snowshoe rabbit tracks are arranged like those of the cottontail but they are considerably larger. The hare has big feet and they are generously furred. In a sense, this hare's feet are snowshoes that enable him to travel on snow that would bury a cottontail to the ears. The snowshoe rabbit's hind footprint may be six inches long and two inches across. Because it is so hairy, the print is fuzzy, not clear-cut. And the snowshoe, like all big hares, can leap a considerable distance, ten feet at a jump if he is in a hurry. For real leaps, though, the Western jack rabbit takes the prize. I have measured jack-rabbit leaps of close to twenty feet.

Next I look for the tracks of raccoons, and the most likely place to look is near water—a brook, a riverbank, or the shores of a pond. Coons like to wash their food before eating it, though they do not always do so, by any means.

A coon's forefeet leave prints like those of a miniature human hand, complete with a long thumb. This print may be close to three inches long if the one who left it was a big buck coon. The tracks of the hind feet are like miniatures of a baby's foot except that the toes are longer and thinner and the whole foot is long and slender. The hind foot may be four inches long. The coon walks like a dog, so the prints are staggered, forefeet in front, as they should be.

I expect to find coon tracks at the compost heap or at my dog's food pan. Being full of curiosity, the coon probably will have made a circle of the house. If there is a garbage pail, he is sure to have investigated it, and unless the lid is tightly locked he probably will have taken it off, inspected the contents, maybe have scattered those contents all around. A coon is clever enough to open almost any garbage pail unless it has a special latch. The coon's feet are so adept and the coon's wits are so keen that it is often difficult to keep one in a cage with an ordinary fastening. Tame raccoons have even managed to open simple padlocks.

Quite possibly there has been an opossum among the night's visitors. The 'possum's forefeet leave prints like small human hands with the fingers and thumb widespread. The hind feet are shaped something like a monkey's hand, with the thumb far back. At a glance, the 'possum's feet would seem much better adapted for manual dexterity than those of a raccoon, but the fact is that the 'possum is one of the most inept and dim-witted of all animals and the raccoon is one of the most clever and adept. The individual prints of a 'possum's feet are about two inches long, and they are in the same order, forefeet in front, as those of a coon. If a 'possum has been around he will have wandered almost as aimlessly as a cottontail, but he almost certainly will have visited the compost heap. 'Possums eat almost anything live or dead, animal, vegetable, or insect.

To my mind, the opossum has no business north of Virginia. But there are a good many of them here in New England and throughout most of the eastern half of the United States, even in Maine. The opossum is a kind of living fossil, a holdover from the remote past. It is the only marsupial we have in the United States. The gestation period is less than two weeks and the young are born as little more than fetal entities, so small that fifteen of them can be put in an ordinary tablespoon, smaller than honey bees. The mother helps these primitive babies into her abdominal pouch where each one attaches itself to a mammary teat. They remain there two or three months, then emerge and live with the mother the rest of the Summer and Fall. They are mature the following Spring.

Despite its warm coat, the 'possum is not really fit to live in a cold climate. Its ears often get frostbitten and sometimes its tail is so severely frozen that part of it sloughs off. This makes life even more difficult because the opossum uses its tail as a fifth foot in climbing.

Every Winter I see an occasional 'possum wandering about in the snow, seeming to resent the cold but not knowing what to do or where to go. For several Winters in a row I saw one, possibly the same one, in my road. It would sit in the snow at the roadside, holding up one naked, cold-red paw after another, its long, pink-tipped nose half frozen, its eyes watering, the picture of utter misery. Time after time I stopped the car and shooed this creature out of the road and into a clump of pines where it might find food and shelter. But each time it came back to the road, like a miserable beggar who didn't know enough to go in out of the cold. Some 'possums take shelter in a hallow tree or a den someone else has made among the rocks and sleep out an especially cold spell, but this one had no such wise instincts. Finally it disappeared. Probably a fox came along and put it out of its misery.

There are porcupines in my woods, but I have never seen either the animal or its tracks near the house. Porcupines are also stupid beasts, but not quite as dim-witted as opossums. The porcupine's tracks are rather fuzzy because the feet are very hairy. The feet are three inches or more long, and the prints of the hind feet overlap those of the front feet. The animal usually leaves a tail mark, a gently waving streak in the snow like the mark that might have been made by dragging a small pine bough. If the tracks are clear enough they will show four toes on the forefeet, five on the hind feet.

Porcupines live on buds, leaves, and other green stuff in Spring and Summer, but in the Winter they eat bark. They take up quarters in a grove of pines, poplars, maples, or other choice trees, climb part way up a big tree, chip off the outer bark, and settle down to eat the vital cambium layer. They girdle one tree after another and kill the tops. They are an expensive nuisance in the woods.

At best, porcupines are thorny propositions, though they never attack man or beast. They can't really "shoot" their quills, but when they lash their tails they often fling a few loose quills several feet. Their chief defense is those bristling quills, which are needle-sharp, barbed, and most difficult to remove from the flesh. Any dog who has had a porcupine encounter needs help. My dog once had to have a vet remove thirty-two quills from his mouth. Wild cats have been found dead from the effect of porcupine quills. Wild cats sometimes kill porcupines, and occasionally a fox kills one. The fisher, a weasel-like animals which has now been virtually eliminated from most of our timberland, was once the most effective control for porcupines. Fortunately, porcupines reproduce slowly, bearing only one young at a time and only once a year.

I find foxes the most interesting animals of all to trail in the snow. The red fox is the most common in the Northeast, though the gray fox is a resident in all but the Plains States and the far Northwest. We have both species where I live and over much of New England. The red fox has a white tip to its tail and is a warm reddish-brown. The gray fox is salt-and-pepper gray and his tail is black-tipped. The tracks of the two are virtually identical. They look very much like the tracks of a large house cat. But if you find a particularly clear print you will see the mark of claws on a fox foot and no claws on a cat foot. Foxes have fixed claws, like a dog's. A cat's claws are retractable. Unlike a dog, a fox walks with one foot almost precisely behind another, so that the tracks make a straight line, not a twin line of staggered prints.

Foxes occasionally come down to my house, as they do to most country places. During the Fall and Winter we often hear them barking in the nearby pasture, and one night one barked directly under the windows of the sleeping porch. His tracks were there the next morning, showing that he had gone around the house, investigated the paths and outbuildings, visited the compost heap, then had returned to his hunting in the pasture. Sometimes I find where a fox has caught a field mouse, a meadow vole, or a cottontail. There may be the marks of a brief struggle by the rabbit, but where a mouse or vole has been killed there are only the marks of the fox's pounce and a tiny drop or two of blood to prove the kill.

The most surprising fox escapade I ever followed out was at the railroad track which crosses my land. It is a stub line on which a short freight train is run every other day, so on odd days the snow lies untouched on the rails. One morning after a four-inch snowfall I found fox tracks between the rails and followed them for a few hundred yards. Then the fox, prankish as a small boy, climbed onto one rail and tried to walk it. The prints were clear as day on the rail, still covered with the pristine snow. Mr. Fox walked that rail about twenty yards, then lost his balance and fell off. He climbed back on and that time walked the rail close to a hundred yards before he fell off again. Once more he got back on, and that time he mastered the trick. He walked several hundred yards before he deliberately stepped off—no slip that time—and walked away, apparently satisfied with his skill and tired of the trick. Then I, of course, had to try it myself. I couldn't walk that snow-clad rail more than fifteen yards before I lost my balance.

The skunk is another common night visitor to the country dooryard, nearly always the common striped skunk, since the Eastern spotted skunk, or polecat, is, despite its name, not common in the East. Its range is the South-Central part of the United States. The common skunk's forefeet leave a print something like that of a very small dog, but the hind foot's print resembles that of a miniature human foot about two and a half inches long. Claw marks are often visible on the forefoot prints, almost never visible on the hind foot prints.

The skunk is not quite as deliberate as the porcupine, but it is not accustomed to make way for anyone, man or beast. It eats a little of everything, insects, snakes, mice, birds, eggs, vegetable matter. It often raids compost heaps and garbage heaps, probably not so much for the waste food as for grubs and other vermin that live there. Skunks usually live in dens, often those abandoned by woodchucks or foxes, but occasionally they take up residence under farm buildings. I understand that a skunk can be discouraged from living in such quarters by liberally salting the place with moth balls; apparently skunks don't like the odor. If left to their own devices, skunks are good citizens and helpful country neighbors. They eat great numbers of insects, grubs and such pests, as well as mice and other vermin. But they do insist on being treated with respect.

And there are the deer. The white-tail or Virginia deer is most numerous of the three common species and is found in wooded areas all over the country except some parts of the West. The white-tail is tawny in Summer, bluish-gray in Winter, and reveals the dazzling white underside of its tail in flight. The somewhat larger mule deer of the Mountain West keeps its black-tipped tail down in flight. The Pacific Coast's black-tail deer runs with its tail either up or down. Moose and elk are related members of the family. Moose are now found only in our northern-border states, Maine to Idaho, and in Canada. Elk, once native to much of wooded America, now are found in the Mountain West; the largest of all, the Roosevelt or Olympic elk, live in the dense rain forests of Oregon. Most of us who live in the East, the South, or the Midwest will see only white-tail deer.

Deer need woodland and brushy cover. They often came down to open fields and meadows at dusk and during the night to feed, but during daylit hours they almost always hide away in the woods. I find their tracks in my pastures after every snowfall, and in early Winter I find where they have been down to my apple trees for windfalls. Now and then in the Winter they visit my vegetable garden to see what can be salvaged there.

A deer's hoofprints are much like those of a cow or

sheep, the cloven hoofs leaving separate marks which to-gether form a long oval. In any herd there will be does, fawns, and at least one big buck, so if a herd has visited me I will find tracks of various sizes. Those of the average doe are about three inches long at most, those of a fawn may be only half that big, and the biggest tracks of all will be those of a buck. Four-inch tracks would be those of a large buck. No matter what the size, the tracks of a doe tend to be broader in proportion to length than those of a buck. With sharp eyes, you may find deer tracks in a pasture after a rain. In my pastures the cows have trodden out a num-ber of paths, and when I go out after a rainy night, even in Summer, I frequently find deer slots, as the tracks are called, in those muddy paths. And all Summer long I find deer droppings in the pasture, dark brown pellets some-thing like rabbit droppings but elongated and half an inch long, twice as big as rabbit pellets. Game trails often thread the woods and many of them are used by deer. I find deer tracks in such trails in my woods in Summer dust, Au-tumn mud, and Winter snow. In Winter I nearly always find their tracks among the cedars and hemlocks. In places their browsing keeps the cedars trimmed to the trunk six or seven feet from the ground, as high as they can reach standing on their hind legs.

Reading tracks in the snow calls for your detective skills, but it really is something like reading history—you are try-ing to piece together, from the evidence, who were there and what they did, perhaps why they did it. It all hap-pened before you got there. But there are ways to see the animals themselves and watch them in action. I have two methods, both of which call for patience. One may be called the Still Wait.

The Still Wait is most likely to be successful at dawn. I get up at least half an hour before daylight and go to a chosen spot in the edge of the woods. I have several such stands—three on the mountainside, two at the edge of the pasture, two on the riverbank. None of them has special blinds or hiding places. This type of nature watching re-quires no concealment. The only necessities are that one get there early and remain quiet. The best time is from the first streak of dawn till full daylight. By the time the sun is fully up the best possibilities usually are over.

For such a wait I dress comfortably and, if the weather is chill, take an extra jacket for warmth. I prefer dull-colored clothing, preferably browns or greens, but I have had success wearing a light tan windbreaker, old blue dungarees, and a red cap. The degree of color is more important than the color itself, since nearly all animals lack color vision. The world they see is all blacks and whites and grays, like the world recorded on black-and-white camera film.

I have found that chances for success are best when it is misty or foggy. Even a light drizzle helps, though it makes uncomfortable waiting for the watcher. I don't know whether the animals get a sense of safety and concealment in fog and mist, but I do know that the dampness helps muffle the crack and rustle of any normally awkward human being's passage through brush and woodland.

Early one morning I went to a stand in the thin brush at the edge of the pasture just as the birds in the tall trees were starting their pre-daylight songs. All Spring and well into Summer the songbirds make a loud celebration in that last dim half hour before sunrise. Then they fall silent for a time, only to resume their chorus in even greater volume when the sun actually rises.

When I took my stand—it actually was a seat on an old stump—a blue jay squawked at me, indignant at being roused, and two song sparrows twittered questioningly and a chickadee somewhere nearby *chick-chick-chicked* at me, then said *Chickadee-dee-dee* and was silent. The treetop birds sang, two crows down the valley cawed, and slowly the light increased. The chickadee returned and perched on a twig within three feet of me and twittered as though talking to itself. A catbird came from somewhere and said *Nyaa, Nyaa* and peered at me. A fox sparrow glided down into the dead leaves at my feet and began to scratch for breakfast, busy as a mother hen in the barnyard.

I had hoped to see deer, but none came. Instead, a cottontail appeared from the underbrush, flopped its ears, scratched its nose with a long hind foot, and stared at me. It nibbled at a tuft of grass and stared again, jaw waggling, nose twitching, as though wondering if that big stump in dungarees was there yesterday. It blinked at me and hopped over and sniffed the toe of my boot, nosed the cuff of my dungarees, then turned and hopped off a little way. It came back, nosed my boot again, tasted a violet leaf and spat it out, seemingly undecided whether to be suspicious or not. Then it went away, the fox sparrow came back, and the chickadee perched on my shoulder and whistled twice and flew off. A white-foot mouse appeared at a seedling maple only a foot high, stood on its hind legs, revealing its snow-white belly, and sniffed the air. The mouse had no interest in me.

Still no deer came. But suddenly a red fox was standing there, not ten feet from me. I don't know where he came from. I didn't see him come. He was simply there, his tail a plume, snow-tipped, his red fur almost frosty with mist, one forefoot lifted, both ears alert, black nose wriggling to catch my scent. Some shift in the air currents must have taken my scent to him, for he hunched slightly, then leaped over the nearest bush and was gone, as silently as he had come, without even the whisper of a leaf.

The birds in the treetops were silent. A touch of a breeze shook down a light rain of the night's mist from the leaves overhead. It pattered around me. Then the first rays of the sun struck the hillside and the birds sang again, a great chorus, a veritable hallelujah to sunrise. The new day had begun. The mists shimmered and swirled above the pasture, smokelike. My Still Wait was over. No deer would come now. But I had seen a fox, had looked him in the eye and seen the way his nose wriggled and the way the night mist frosted his nut-red fur.

Another time when I took a dawn stand in the brush at the edge of the pasture a fox walked out of the woods not fifteen feet away and for fifteen minutes showed me how a fox hunts mice in the meadow grass. He caught two mice before a shift in the air took my scent to him. Then he vanished like a shadow.

And one dawn I watched a doe come down to a clearing in the woods with her two fawns, still in their dappled coats. She grazed for ten minutes within fifteen yards of me, and the fawns played like lambs, butted their mother, nosed the grass, still too young to eat it. One of them took a few sucks at the mother's dugs, but obviously wasn't hungry. She walked away and left it. Then she caught my human scent, stiffened, snorted, and stamped her forefeet. The snort was a hoarse, coughing sound almost like the bark of a gray fox. It was the alarm signal, and the fawns didn't wait to ask questions. They leaped for cover and were gone into the brush. The doe stood there, defiant, till they were out of sight. Then she snorted again and was off, graceful as a swallow.

If you try the Still Wait there will be times when the birds jeer at you and even the rabbits will stay away. But even those times will not be wasted. You will have been in the open to watch the new day come. You will have been well repaid.

My other method of watching animals in action requires somewhat less patience but even more discretion. It is a harmless kind of jack-lighting which happens to be illegal in some states. If it is frowned on by the law in your state, skip the rest of this chapter. In any case, find out before you try it, or you may be arrested. It happens to be legal in my state, so I take a powerful flashlight and go out into my pasture in the full darkness of late evening. Sometimes I sit and wait in the darkness, sometimes I walk slowly and quietly, swinging the light here and there until it picks up the glow of reflected eyes. Once I see that gleam, I can spotlight the animal.

Animals that hunt or feed at night have eyes specially adapated to night vision. Inside their eyeballs is a reflective layer that traps light and sends it through the visual area a second time, thus multiplying the acuity of night vision. This "reflector" in the eyeballs creates the eye-shine when a strong light strikes the animal's eyes at night. Now and then I read about someone seeing an animal's eyes "gleaming like coals" in total darkness. This is sheer poppycock. No animal's eyes gleam except by reflecting a strong light.

In my home pasture, within a few hundred yards of the house, I have in this way watched skunks, opossums, foxes, raccoons, deer. I seldom see a rabbit. I don't know why. Now and then I see a wolf spider, the only spider I know with reflective eyes. This spider's eyes under the light look like two pinhead-size rubies in the grass.

Most of the animal eyes glow some shade of red, though there is quite a variation. The opossum's eyes often look orange or orange-red. The skunk's eyes sometimes glow amber, but I have never seen an annoyed or disturbed skunk whose eyes were not fiery red. Deer eyes are definitely red, though I have heard men say they have seen them green. I never have. A raccoon's eyes are clean, clear red.

I understand that an African lion's eyes reflect a golden yellow color, that those of a zebra show silver, and that an alligator's eyes look pinkish-orange under the light. And I have been told that a timber wolf's eyes reflect silvery green. I have never had the chance to prove this, but I know that my own dog's eyes usually gleam a silvery turquoise blue. When he is angry or excited, though, my dog's eyes reflect a distinct reddish color. I suspect that there may be a similar change in the eye-reflection of other animals. I noted, just above, the change in a skunk's eyes. Perhaps my friends who say they have seen deer's eyes reflect green were reporting such a phenomenon.

One night, returning home late in the car, I saw two fiery red eyes in the road just beyond my garage. They were a foot and a half apart, and I wondered what huge beast was standing there, head down and ready to charge. I eased the car toward the eyes, wary. And finally saw, not a huge animal, but two birds! Two whippoorwills were sitting in the road, facing each other. My car's lights were reflected from one eye of each bird. I was quite sure, from their markings, that they were whippoorwhills; then they flew into a nearby tree and began to call, and there was no mistaking them. That is the only time I ever saw the eye-shine of a whippoorwill, but I know that most night birds have reflective eyes. I once spotlighted a screech owl, and its eyes were a bright ruby red, even redder than those of the whippoorwills.

The only way most people will ever see flying squirrels, except as pets in a cage, is by night-lighting them, and even then it probably will be an accident unless one knows a hollow tree where a pair of these shy little nocturnal animals is nesting. Or unless one maintains a bird feeder on a window sill and stocks it with nutmeats and lives near a woodland. Flying squirrels often visit such feeding stations at night and can be watched from indoors with the illumination from a flashlight.

The flying squirrel is about the size of the common red squirrel but is olive-brown above and white below and, like all nocturnal animals, has large, prominent eyes. Flying squirrels don't really fly; they glide on loose folds of skin along the sides from wrist to ankle, which can be stretched taut into air foils. If they launch themselves from a tall tree, they can glide well over a hundred feet. They live in hollows in trees, often in old woodpecker holes. Sometimes they invade attics, but when they do they are usually better tenants than either red or gray squirrels, though they do scurry about at night. In the woods, if you find a dead tree with a number of woodpecker holes in it, you may provoke a flying squirrel to rouse and poke out an inquisitive head by knocking on the tree.

In thin woods at night, if you see a shadow that seems to glide from a treetop into your spotlight's beam and through it, you may very well have had a glimpse of a flying squirrel. If you are quick enough you may be able to follow it with the light and watch it for a few minutes as it scurries about on the ground. The flying squirrel's big eyes are reflective and show red in the light. If you find a tree with a nest of them you can spend an hour watching the squirrels come and go in the light, quite unperturbed by it.

There are two hazards to watching animals by spotlight. One involves skunks, which usually do not mind the light but now and then resent it. One night I spotted a skunk in a bad mood and not ten feet from me. It was as startled as I was, and a startled skunk immediately assumes a posture of defense. I backed slowly away, keeping the light on the skunk, and I escaped unhappy consequences. When you catch a skunk in the light, use caution, especially at close quarters. Avoid quick or noisy motions. Keep the light on the skunk. It may baffle and partially blind him, and it enables you to see where he is and what he is doing. A skunk can send a jet of spray ten or twelve feet, even farther if the wind is right. And skunks have a habit of shooting first, without waiting to see who is friend and who is foe. Especially at night.

The other hazard is the law, even in states where such harmless spotlighting is legal. State troopers, game wardens, and most farmers are suspicious of all prowlers with flashlights, especially in deer country. Poachers often kill deer with the use of jack-lights, which blind the deer long enough for the poacher to get two or three shots. Killing deer by the use of spotlights is illegal and punishable by heavy fines in most states.

Even if you plan to do harmless jack-light watching on

your own land it is wise to tell your neighbors, the game warden, and the state troopers what you are up to. Otherwise you may find yourself surrounded by a posse. The legal authorities in my area know that I am often out in my own pastures with a powerful flashlight, and my neighbors are tolerant of my strange behavior, but last year a state trooper newly assigned to this area caught me red-handed one dark night. Or thought he did. Actually, we were both embarrassed until I proved my identity and told him what I was doing. Then he spent ten minutes watching a skunk with me. We have been friends ever since.

## Chapter 9

# A Badeling of Birds

SOMEDAY *someone will write a usable book on how to look for birds, a book that will tell where and when to watch for each species. Until such a book appears, perhaps some of the hints in this chapter about habits and habitats will be of help.*

*According to an estimate* by Richard H. Pough, the conservationist, between twelve and fifteen billion birds regularly spend at least part of each year in the United States and Canada. This is almost 2,000 birds to the square mile, three birds to the acre. To a countryman this figure seems low. Mathematically, we would be entitled to only 300 birds on our hundred acres, and I am sure I hear twice that many within a hundred yards of my house any May morning.

The human population of this country averages only about fifty to the square mile, so there apparently are about forty times as many birds as people. Again this figure seems low, at least in the country. But here, of course, there are fewer people than the national average per square mile, and more birds than average. However you look at it, though, there are many birds and they are distributed over all parts of the country. This is a fortunate circumstance from any viewpoint, for besides being beautiful to look at and wonderful to listen to, birds are the best natural control of insects that we have. Even from a cold-blooded economic viewpoint, birds are a tremendously valuable asset.

Birds live almost everywhere on earth, certainly wherever there is food enough to sustain them. Penguins thrive in the Antarctic, waterfowl by the millions nest each year in the Arctic, ravens live in the furnace heat of Death Valley, horned larks and road runners thrive in the Southwestern deserts, condors live in the highest Andes. And the temperate regions of the United States have a great wealth of birds, some 1,200 species and subspecies.

The latest list of bird species state by state that I can find was published in 1936 and now may be quite out of date, but I doubt that the relative standings have much changed. On that list Texas stands first with 546 species and California second with 541. Both are big states with a wide variety of bird habitats. But number three is Nebraska, an inland state with no shore birds but still recording 418 species. New York, with 412 species, stands fourth. Then comes another surprise, Colorado, with 403. After that, in order, come Illinois, Missouri, Kansas, and Washington, with Arizona, the biggest surprise of all to me, tenth. Massachusetts stands eleventh. And my own state, Connecticut, is number sixteen on the list. Last of all is Idaho, with 210 species.

These figures are for the states as a whole. But even the major cities have a surprising quota of birds. John Kieran notes that more than 230 species have been recorded in New York City's Central Park, and he says that any observant person can see at least 200 species somewhere in the city in almost any year.

The bird watcher, no matter where he lives, certainly has no lack of birds to watch. All he needs is a good bird handbook, a pair of binoculars, and an interest in birds. If he has a friend who knows birds he is specially fortunate. That friend can give help and guidance. But even a person who doesn't know where to start can find help in any local or national conservation or ornithological group. For that matter, many able amateur ornithologists started with only the help of a handbook. Once started, the beginner will find bird watchers in almost every group he meets.

I live in a rural area and a good many of my friends are able amateurs and a few are professionals, but I didn't know how many bird watchers were around until a few Winters ago. I had gone to a crossroads garage to have my car serviced and half a dozen men were there, loafing and talking, a farmer, a storekeeper, a couple of retired teachers, a stone mason. I joined them and found that they were discussing birds. All were amateurs, but they knew their birds. They swapped news and opinions about redpolls, redbreasted nuthatches, grackles, mourning doves, kinglets, cardinals, juncos. Finally a gasoline tank truck drove up and the driver came in and announced that he had just seen a pair of snow geese down on the river road. He, too, knew his birds.

Spring is the ideal time to start learning to recognize

birds. The Winter species are relatively few in number and not too difficult to identify. And the early migrations bring only a few species at a time. Use a good handbook with illustrations that emphasize the identification points, size, markings, shape of beak, etc. Equip yourself with adequate binoculars. I prefer the size called "7 x 35," which gives ample magnification for general use, and I insist on coated lenses, which give far more light and clarity than uncoated ones. Such binoculars are moderately priced and will serve you for many years. Cheap binoculars strain the eyes, distort the vision, and aren't really worth whatever they cost. But it isn't necessary to buy the most expensive binoculars in the showcase, either. Ask the advice of an experienced bird watcher about which to buy, or go to a thoroughly reliable dealer. Preferably, do both.

The beginner shouldn't try to learn all the birds in the first season. Start with one related group, the sparrows for instance. Learn to recognize those common to your area. If the sparrows seem too difficult, start with the Winter woodpeckers, of which there are only a few. But take one group, learn to know its species, then go on to another group. Inevitably you will be lured to widen your knowledge with the more common members of other groups along the way. By late April you should have a fair foundation of knowledge of the cold-weather birds common in your area. From then on it will be a scramble, because the Summer birds will arrive in increasing numbers all through May. Among them will be warblers, which to me at least are the most challenging and most baffling of all. You won't learn them all the first season, but you will get a start.

By Midsummer the birds common to any area will all be there, and through June and July they can be watched daily. That is when the energetic bird watcher fattens his list. And, of course, is baffled time and again by young birds, which often lack the distinguishing marks of the adults.

By August some of the migrants will have begun to move south again. And some birds will begin to change to Fall plumage. This creates still another problem in identification, another challenge. By September the migration will really be in progress. And all through the latter part of August and well into September, in my area at least, the warblers will be passing through again, on their way south. The watcher will get the year's second chance to sort them out. But, again, many of the warblers change dress in the Fall, so the puzzles are compounded.

By October only the laggard migrants and the year-rounders will oe around. In my area the late migrants include the flickers, the red-wing blackbirds, and often the robins. And the ducks and geese, which sometimes stay in my area into December. Meanwhile, there has been a quiet return of a good many familiar Winter birds, some of which always move north a little way to nest. Among them are juncos, tree sparrows, red-breasted nuthatches, redpolls, and kinglets. By November we are reduced to our normal Winter bird population, which includes a few migrants that are going to spend the whole year here. There is always a small flock of robins, sometimes there are a few bluebirds, and often a few red-wing blackbirds stay. The farther south one goes, the more of these non-migrating groups of migrant species will be found. Even a hundred miles south of where I live there are twice or three times as many of these birds every Winter.

The bird watcher will find, in most communities, a variety of group activities, ranging all the way from local field trips to national conservation movements. Both national and local groups have general as well as specialized programs. Day lists, week-end lists, and year lists are encouraged. Library and museum exhibits are sponsored and arranged. Educational programs are undertaken in schools and among youth organizations. Or the bird watcher can go it alone and make his own discoveries.

The week-ender, the vacationer, and the occasional visitor to the country often are satisfied to learn to recognize the principal birds of an area by sight or song. But the person who lives in the country even a part of the time usually wants to know all the birds, and sometimes he becomes something of an amateur ornithologist. At the least, he learns that birds are good company the year around, and if he is a gardener he soon learns that birds are among his most valuable allies. Without birds, gardening and farming would be all but impossible. It is safe to say that if all the birds were to be destroyed, human life would be in constant peril from the insects. Those of us who were not stung and bitten into madness would starve within a few years because the insects would destroy the food crops.

Ever since the first primitive farmer scratched the earth

with a stick and planted a handful of seed, man has been fighting the war of the insects. Insect damage to farm crops in this country alone amounts to many millions of dollars a year despite all the use of insecticides. And since time began, the only real and continuing checks on the insects have been the birds and small animals.

This is not the place to fight the War of the Insecticides, but I must point out two facts. In the past ten years the insects, with their quick succession of generations, have developed immunity to the DDT-type of insecticides which were hailed as the killers of virtually every noxious insect we know. Stronger and stronger concentrations of the insecticides are used, and still the insects survive and do their damage. And, second, those poisons in the concentrations now used kill birds and animals, literally millions of them, and thus wipe out whole populations of natural enemies of insects in the very areas where they are most needed. Biologists warn that all bird life is being endangered by these DDT-type of poisons, which are potent enough to kill even so large an animal as a raccoon and possibly are a menace to human health.

We grow a large vegetable garden and, since we dislike poison in or on our food, we have never used any insecticide except non-poisonous rotenone. We also encourage the birds, which are busy in our garden all Spring and Summer. True, they take a little sprouting corn and a few beans, but they also eat countless grubs, cutworms, cornworms, squash beetles, potato beetles, cabbage and tomato worms, and many other pests including Japanese beetles. They also eat mosquitoes and add to our physical comfort. I am quite willing even to share the strawberries with the birds in payment for what they do. Year after year we have less insect damage than any gardener we know who uses DDT or any of its chemical cousins. To me, the significance of this is obvious.

Birds will come to any place where they can find food and nesting sites. Natural food is the best lure of all, but it can be supplemented with grain and suet in the Winter months. I am sure that dooryard feeders are welcomed by millions of birds, but I know that far more millions of them never visit a feeder. The vast majority of our birds are self-sustaining, as they always have been. The tons of grain and suet put out for the birds every year certainly are not wasted, but the more important result, it seems to me, is the constantly growing interest in birds and their protection.

The person who would have birds nearby all the year around will see to it that there is plenty of natural food. All berry bushes provide bird food, and scores of trees and bushes, both tame ornamentals and wildlings, are worth attention. Birds like the berries of dogwoods, both tree and bush, tame and wild. Junipers and mountain ash provide food many birds like. So do the hollies, including our northern winterberry. Wild grapes and Virginia creeper are high on the birds' dietary list. Most of the viburnums, both wild and tame, provide bird berries. Pyracantha (firethorn) is a special lure, and so are barberry and winged euonymus. Common pasture cedars and roadside sumac are favored Winter lunch counters for the birds.

Most of these trees and bushes also provide nesting places. Catbirds nest in our big lilac clumps. Song sparrows nest in the yews and barberries. Robins nest in the apple trees. Orioles hang their nests in the tall elms and maples. Goldfinches nest in the low juniper in the corner of the flower garden.

In the vegetable garden we grow giant sunflowers for the birds. I harvest most of the heads to shell out and put in the feeders in the Winter, but I always let a few heads ripen on the stalks. The chickadees, out of sight most of the Summer earning their own living in the woodland, know to the day when those heads are ripe. They come in flocks and have a wonderful time. Often a few cardinals get the word, too, and come to share in the treat. And I let the asparagus stand till first frost so its little red berries can ripen. Dozens of birds come all through September to eat those berries. And plant asparagus in their droppings all along the roadsides, where it grows vigorously every Summer and provides still more berries every September. I let the seed pods, the hips, form on the cabbage rose bushes in the sideyard simply because the birds like them, come Fall and Winter. I tolerate several huge plants of pokeweed along the garden fence because the birds feast on their berries, inkberries as some call them.

Weeds and wildflowers provide vast quantities of food for birds, especially those of the finch family. You will recognize any member of the finch family by its short, thick bill, typical in the grosbeaks and sparrows. Such bills are ideally adapted to cracking the hard hulls of many wild seeds. All the finch family are primarily seed-eaters, though they also eat a good many insects. The insect-eaters have longer, slimmer beaks, such as the beak of the kingbird, the oriole, and the meadowlark. Most of the insect-eaters also eat some seeds, especially in their Winter diet. In fact, most birds—except hawks, owls, herons, and a number of shore birds, which are flesh-eaters—have a mixed diet that includes both animal and vegetable matter. But the shape of the beak is usually an index to which type of food predominates. The beak shape is also important in identifying the bird's species. The strong, hooked beak belongs to a hawk, an eagle, or an owl, for instance. The extremely long, slim beak belongs to a heron, a crane, a snipe, a woodcock, or some other marsh or shore bird. The chisel beak belongs to one of the woodpeckers. The sharp, slender beak belongs to one of the insect-eating songbirds, and the short, cone-shaped beak belongs to a seed-eater, one of the finch tribe.

The various finches—and the finch tribe is one of the largest in birddom—eat vast quantities of ragweed seed, and should therefor have the thanks of all who suffer from hay fever and similar allergies. The seeds of the troublesome pigweed are a stock item on the sparrow diet, which makes them special allies of all gardeners. Goldfinches specially like the tiny seeds of the thistles and will be found wherever thistle heads are ripe. Goldenrod seed is another favorite for the smaller finches, such as field and tree sparrows. Every Winter I find a dark dust of hulls under the brown goldenrod stems, proving that my sparrow friends have been feasting there. Even the asters and Queen Anne's lace are acceptable fare for December birds, though the seeds are extremely small.

When Winter comes, and snow and ice, we put out the feeders here in the yard. Any kind of feeder will do. We have used all kinds but now prefer the top-loading cannister type. I have improvised such a feeder from a tall fruit-juice can and two aluminum pie plates, one for a cover, the other for a bottom tray. I hang the feeders on long wires suspended from tree limbs, a method that makes raiding by the squirrels more difficult. The feeders blow and sway in the wind, and they tilt when the blue jays crowd onto them, but the grain spilled onto the ground is salvaged by juncos and other ground feeders. In these feeders we use any mixture at hand or readily obtainable, sometimes the ready-mixed wild bird feed, sometimes cracked grain sold as chick feed, but always with sunflower seeds mixed in. Some people put out bread crumbs, peanut hearts, crumbled nutmeats, rolled oats. I have put out popped corn and seen it eagerly eaten. One year we had a quantity of stale mixed nuts, everything from pecans to Brazil nuts, and I put them through a food chopper, shells and all, and put them in the feeder. The birds liked them, and the shells probably helped supplement the sand they need for digestion. I put out sand in a covered box, but it has few patrons. I notice that our birds get the necessary sand during the Winter from the roads after the sander trucks have been out. Flocks of birds go to the sanded road every day.

Some people put out peanut butter, but now it has been shown that peanut butter can choke a bird to death. I understand that it is no longer recommended, not without something else mixed in, anyway. And some people grind dog biscuits and put them out. Other exotic foods include cottage cheese, doughnuts, even pancakes. Some birds apparently will eat anything.

Suet, or some kind of fat, is welcome especially in bitter cold weather. Chickadees, nuthatches, woodpeckers, and blue jays are our most persistent fat-eaters. We have used suet cages made of half-inch wire mesh. They are satisfactory and keep the gluttonous jays from making off with great chunks of suet at a time. Some advisers frown on using such wire cages, saying the metal can maim a bird in very cold weather if the bird touches it with an eye or other moist, unprotected part. Perhaps so, but I have never seen it happen. One year I bought a coconut, sawed it in half, and hung it out for the birds. They cleaned out the meat in a few days and I filled the empty shells with tallow fried out of beef suet and let it harden, then hung them out again. The birds loved it that way. Anyone who doesn't want to use a metal container for fat might try coconut shells. Incidentally, one year when there was a shortage of suet locally we filled the shells with Spry and Crisco, and it was eaten as eagerly as was the suet. Since then we have used any kind of fat or shortening, even bacon fat, and they eat it. You can buy or make suet packs with seed and nuts mixed in, but we never found the birds specially eager to get that combination. They never find it in nature; maybe that's the reason.

Some birds like salt. I first learned this when I saw a flock of pine siskins every day at a salt block that had been put out for the cows in a nearby pasture and left there over Winter. The siskins pecked at that salt, obviously wanted it. Other finches also like salt. Some bird folk accommodate them by pouring concentrated salt water on a log or stump in the dooryard and letting it crystallize there. I suspect that most rural birds get the salt they need in the sander-truck sand, always salted to hasten the melting of ice on the roads. The road salt is calcium chloride, but it probably substitutes well enough for sodium chloride, common table salt.

At one time or another I have heard dozens of taboos about feeding birds, and over the years I have seen nearly all of them disproven. I have been told that a feeder painted with a bright or shiny color will frighten the birds away, that brown or naturally weathered feeders are essential. One year I painted one feeder bright red and left another as it was, weathered brown. I hung them in the same tree and stocked them with the same food, and couldn't see any preference between them by the birds. The feeders I make out of juice cans are enameled in red, white, orange, and blue, and the birds pay no attention to the colors. The aluminum covers and trays seem to make no difference, bright as they are.

I have been told that a glass roof on a feeder will frighten off the customers. I made a tray feeder for a window sill and covered it with glass so we could see in, and every bird in the neighborhood used it.

I have been told that birds don't like salted fat. Our birds eat bacon fat as eagerly as they eat raw beef suet.

I have been told that robins like raisins and apples. The robins in my area won't touch them.

I have been told that squirrels will drive the birds away from a feeder. I have seen one truculent nuthatch drive a big red squirrel out of a feeder, and I have seen two squirrels and a dozen tree sparrows eating at the same feeder at the same time. That, incidentally, was at a window feeder. The squirrels haven't yet solved the problem of reaching the feeders I hang on wires in the trees. But they do eat grain spilled on the ground from those feeders. On the ground, they compete with the blue jays, but the juncos seem to have a truce with the squirrels—they feed together with few disputes.

One Winter a pair of ruffed grouse came down from the mountain and found the big window feeder. For several weeks they came and ate there, looking as big as Leghorn hens and practically filling the feeder. I've never heard of grouse in anybody else's feeder, and after that Winter they never came to ours again. But they often come down in late February to feed on the buds in the apple trees near the house.

I have heard it argued that food put out in feeders keeps normally migrant birds from going south and lures others here that shouldn't be here in the Winter. That I doubt. Those who credit—or blame—the feeders sometimes point to the sizable flocks of evening grosbeaks, normally Western birds, they say, which recently have made a habit of wintering in the East. They forget that the evening grosbeaks are habitual wanderers and that good-sized flocks of them Wintered in Massachusetts as early as 1889. They were regular Winter visitors there by 1910, long before Winter feeding became widespread. Others point to robins and bluebirds; but they, too, have Wintered in the North in occasional flocks for many years. Still others use the cardinal as an example. Actually, the cardinals were extending their range northward at least twenty-five years ago. Moreover, cardinals are seldom regular customers at the dooryard feeder. Some of them seem to like the easy life, but my guess is that hundreds of them fend for themselves for every individual that lives on charity.

It is almost impossible to set definite limits on the range of most birds. Nearly all of them are remarkably adaptable and they are likely to go anywhere they can find food. Even in the matter of food they are adaptable. Robins, for example, though they like a diet in which worms and insects constitute almost half, can and do live on a seed and berry diet for months. The flocks that Winter over in my area make many meals on the sumac berries and the cedar berries. About one fourth of the red-wing blackbird's Summer diet consists of insects, but in the Winter the red-wing turns vegetarian. I suspect that pretty much the same is true of all the birds who occasionally fail to migrate with the rest of their species. I have wondered if these habitual nonmigrants are not slowly evolving strains that are particularly hardy and more than normaly adaptable to northern Winters. I doubt that it is a matter of accident that certain flocks of robins spend the Winter here. Some of them must have spent previous Winters here. I know that as far back as I can remember it was possible to find flocks of robins in the swamp thickets every Winter. When the first relatively mild days of late Winter arrive, some of them appear in dooryards and someone announces happily that "the robins are back!" Actually, those robins were here all the time, and the migrants usually won't appear until late March.

Birds as a species are older than mammals and evidently evolved from the early reptiles. Their feathers are believed to be modified reptile scales, though if that is true the word "modified" is a most inadequate term. The scale is quite simple, and the feather is one of the most complex achievements of nature. I shall never cease to marvel at a feather, so ingeniously fashioned to its purpose, so nearly weightless, so incredibly strong, so efficiently insulating.

The capacity of birds for flight is one of the enduring wonders of nature. Albatrosses, vultures, and hawks can soar for hours without flapping a wing. The Arctic tern flies 22,000 miles a year in its incredible migrations. The ruby-throat hummingbird, which weighs only a little more than a bumblebee, makes its 500-mile migratory flight across the Gulf of Mexico without a stop, without food or drink. Such feats are all the more remarkable because of the physical limitations, especially of small birds. Their lives demand great quantities of energy, which is provided by a high rate of respiration, around 120 per minute when at rest, twice that when flying, and by high metabolism. Most birds feed almost constantly during the day and sometimes consume half their own weight daily. Nestlings of some species require their own weight or even more in food every day. These processes produce high body temperatures, as much as 108° Fahrenheit. But the temperature may drop to around 100° at night when they are at rest, thus conserving energy. The metabolism of the hummingbirds appears to have a wide range, day and night. Hummers, incidentally, contrary to legend, do not subsist entirely on nectar; they also eat large numbers of small, flying insects. The nestlings of some species, notably wrens, pass through an early stage of cold-bloodedness which anthropologists say proves their reptilian origin. But their warm-bloodedness is soon established and persists the remainder of their lives. During that early phase they must be hovered by a warm-blooded parent during the cool night or during a chill, rainy day or they perish.

The speed of birds in flight is often overestimated. Most small songbirds fly about twenty miles an hour, with a top speed of not much over thirty-five miles an hour. Crows can fly as fast as forty-five miles an hour, but seldom do; their usual pace is less than thirty miles an hour. Few ducks can fly more than sixty miles an hour except with a strong tail wind, and most plovers have a top speed of about fifty miles an hour. I have seen it stated that swifts can fly 200 miles an hour, but I am skeptical. Birds of prey can obtain high speeds in dives at their victims, but that isn't what should be considered flight. Flight is straightaway travel through the air.

All birds are hatched from eggs, of course, and with the exception of a few parasitic species such as American cowbirds and European cuckoos they all make some kind of nest in which to brood those eggs and care for the chicks. Some sea birds lay their eggs and brood them on bare rocks, but they evidently consider the spot where they lay the eggs as their nest and guard it carefully. Of our common land birds, the nighthawks and whippoorwills make the crudest nests I know of. I have seen a nighthawk's eggs in a "nest" on the bare roof of a city apartment building, nothing more than a spot where the roofing gravel was somewhat brushed away. And I have seen a whippoorwill's eggs on bare ground in the woods with a few small twigs around them, a token nest if I ever saw one. At the other end of the scale are the orioles, which I sometimes think must have taught man the art of weaving. And when I watch a pair of barn swallows building their mud nest on a beam in my garage I shake my head in wonder at their patience and industry, not to say the skill they have to build such a structure with nothing but their beaks for tools, since their feet are inadequate for anything but perching.

Some birds can be lured to the dooryard with nesting boxes or houses, especially house wrens, purple martins, and bluebirds. The Audubon Society and other nature and conservation groups publish plans for such birdhouses. The critical dimension is that of the entrance, which must be just large enough to admit the wanted tenant, small enough to keep out troublesome intruders. A house wren, for instance, will not use a house with an entrance larger than a silver half-dollar. A bigger entrance than that will admit an English sparrow, and English sparrows destroy wren nests and eggs.

Nesting boxes are often put up for wood ducks on posts in shallow ponds. If such boxes are not too close to an occupied house the colorful ducks will use them year after year. Wood ducks also nest, and by preference, in hollow trees. But always near the water.

Anyone who insists on trimming every dead branch from the trees on his place is robbing himself of the company of many birds, both at nesting time and through much of the year. Not only owls and woodpeckers nest in deep knot-holes in old trees and dead branches. Bluebirds nest in such places, and tree swallows, and other species from time to time. And, though this has nothing to do with birds, flying squirrels nest in such hideaways. Flying squirrels are good neighbors, though few people ever see them since they are nocturnal animals.

At one time it was considered quite proper for amateurs to make collections of birds' nests and eggs. Happily, that idea has now gone out of fashion. Only experts, collectors for museums and qualified researchers, do such collecting now. Birds' nests should never be disturbed when they are in use, and eggs should be left in the nest. Winter nest-collecting is quite in order, of course, for those who like that sort of thing. But most birds have lice, and even abandoned Winter nests often have lice or louse eggs; if they are taken into a warm house they may soon become thoroughly alive. If you collect Winter nests, however, don't be surprised if you find some of them occupied—by mice. Field mice often take over down-lined nests in low brush, roof them over with grass, and spend the Winter there, warm and snug.

Although most birds choose to sing and perch well up in the trees and bushes, a surprising number of the treetop songsters nest on or near the ground. Robins nest in tree crotches, often in dooryards, and bluebirds prefer to nest in holes in trees such as abandoned woodpecker holes; but hermit thrushes and veeries, though they are high singers, always nest on or near the ground, preferably in thick woods. Warblers' nests show great variety not only in materials, ranging all the way from bark and grass to moss and mud, but in chosen situation. The prothonotary warbler often nests in a woodpecker hole. The Cape May, Audubon's, black-throated green, Blackburnian, bay-breasted, blackpoll, pine, and several other warblers prefer to nest in conifers, some near the ground, some high up. All the sparrows are ground nesters or shrub nesters. One year I found a song sparrow nesting in a clump of phlox in my flower garden. Cardinals, which choose the highest branch from which to whistle, build a ragged nest of twigs and shreds of bark in a low bush. And brown thrashers, which also prefer to perch high when they sing, nest low, nearly always in bushes. If you have brown thrashers resident in your dooryard, look in your lilac bushes for their nest, especially bushes that are not trimmed too neatly at the base, so there is sufficient protection for a nest within two feet of the ground. Both thrashers and catbirds nest regularly in my yard. The catbirds build their nest five to eight feet above the ground in a big lilac clump twenty feet from the lesser lilac in which the thrashers nest.

If you have good eyes and are persistent you may find meadowlark nests in the nearest pasture or meadow. The nests will be on the ground in a tuft of tall grass—cups of deftly arranged dry grass, usually at least partially roofed over with a loose thatch that hides the nesting mother but gives her little real protection from the weather. Red-wing blackbirds' nests will be found in wetland, often in clumps of reeds. In damp meadows you may find the open-topped nests of bobolinks, well-hidden grass cups.

Crows' nests may be found in almost any kind of tall, deciduous trees, disorderly jumbles of twigs and grass assembled in a high crotch, sometimes as much as half a bushel or more of material. Gray squirrels from time to time appropriate a crow's nest for the Winter, stuff it with leaves and dry grass for warmth.

The eyesight of birds is phenomenal. In proportion to their body size, the eyes of most birds are larger than those of any other vertebrate creature. The muscles that focus a bird's eyes are so highly developed that a bird seems able to shift in a flash from examining something just beyond its beak to something else several hundred yards away. Hawks, eagles, vultures, and other high-flying birds of prey appear to have telescopic sight of unbelievable acuity. A hawk soaring a thousand feet in the air can distinguish a rabbit hiding in the grass, and I sometimes believe that a crow in full flight well above the highest trees can see a kernel of corn in the garden. Some birds have highly specialized vision. The kingfisher, for example, has egg-shaped eyes with bifocal vision, one phase of which it uses in the air, the other under water. Owls, nighthawks, whippoorwills, and other night birds have night vision at least as acute as night-hunting animals. Unlike most animals, including dogs and cats, which see the world in blacks and whites and cannot distinguish colors, birds have satisfactory and possibly acute color vision. Color vision, incidentally, appears to be a rare attribute except among birds and monkeys and men.

All birds have an acute sense of hearing, but apparently they have little sense of smell or taste. Nor do they have much sense of touch, having no sensitive antennae, like insects, or fingers, like human beings. But the expression "bird-brained" is quite unjustified as a jeering characterization. The brain of a bird, in relation to the size and weight of the body, is larger than that of any reptile or insect and proportionately larger than the brains of some mammals.

Two particular attributes, their colorful plumage and their voices, distinguish birds among all creatures. Only such insects as moths and butterflies can rival birds in physical beauty of color, and even they have no such seasonal color changes as many birds have. In most instances the male birds are more brilliantly colored, at least when in Summer plumage. But some, even such spectacularly beautiful ones as the goldfinches, change to quite drab Winter garb. The goldfinch, brilliant in black and dazzling yellow all Summer, is as sparrow-dull in color as his modest mate all Winter. But who can see a cardinal, an Indigo bunting, a Baltimore oriole, a scarlet tanager, or half a hundred other birds in full color and fail to marvel?

As for voices, the birds are the world's memorable songsters. No other living creatures except the occasional human being can create such sweet sounds. Only a few birds, such as the pelican and the cormorant, are voiceless. Some, such as the crow, have harsh voices with little or no music in them. But scores of birds not only have beautiful voices but a variety of melodies.

We think of most birds as having only a very few songs which they sing over and over. Actually, many of them have an extensive repertoire. Aretas A. Saunders, an outstanding authority on bird songs, has recorded fifty-three different songs from one male meadowlark in less than an hour. And the meadowlark is not generally known as a versatile songster. The thrushes have long been noted for the quality of their music, but not many people think of even them as being endowed with a great variety of song. Yet all thrushes have a considerable repertoire. Saunders says that the robin, probably the best known and most often heard of all American thrushes, has eight or ten different musical phrases that can be put together in a great variety of ways. And the hermit thrush, sometimes called the greatest of all American songsters, has at least ten different phrases, each composed to eight to twelve notes, which can be put together in almost countless combinations. The catbird, cousin of the versatile, sweet-voiced mockingbird, has been recorded by Saunders imitating more than twenty other birds as well as using seventy-four different song phrases of its own.

The warblers are also notable songsters, though not as vocally spectacular as the thrushes. Experiments have shown that warblers especially, but some other birds too, often sing notes and whole phrases above the range of the human ear. So it seems likely that most of us hear only a part of the bird songs that fill the air every Spring day.

There is even a variation in the songs sung by individuals within most species. Of the various Baltimore orioles that nest each year near my house I can usually distinguish four or five by their voices or the songs they sing most often. One of them, a few years ago, persistently sang a phrase identical with one from "I've Grown Accustomed to Her Face," a song in the musical comedy, *My Fair Lady*. We finally named that oriole 'Enry 'Iggins. And every year we learn to identify several robins by their characteristic songs.

I have a well-worn tape recorder, bought some years ago for quite another purpose, with which I have from time to time made tapes of bird songs for my own amusement and information. All the recordings have been made from here in the house or on the front porch, most of them through open doors and windows. The microphone I use is an ordinary voice microphone, not one of the extremely sensitive microphones used by those who make professional bird recordings. Mine are strictly amateur tapes, and they include early-morning choruses of all the birds nearby as well as individual songs such as the ecstatic outpouring of a house wren that one year nested in the big spruce just outside my study window. They also have crow calls, the jeering of blue jays, alarm calls of robins with nestlings learning to fly, night calls of the repetitious whippoorwill, the hooting of owls.

Such tapes can be made by anyone with a tape recorder. No special equipment is needed, though I do have a twenty-foot extension for the microphone line for use on the porch. I dub in the dates of the recordings and when I can I identify the birds, all for my own information. Thus I have a record, of sorts, of the birds that sing or call within earshot of my own house the year around.

Far better recordings, with accurate identifications, are available commercially, both on tapes and on records. These recordings are of great help to anyone trying to learn to identify birds by their voices. But homemade recordings can be of help, too, if only for comparison with the professionally made ones to make identity certain. I have found that the best time for recording is around sunup, when the birds are most vocal and in best voice. The best time of the year is the Spring, April and May, while the birds are nesting and the males are most articulate. I have never tried using the battery-powered portable tape recorders, which could be carried into the woods and open fields, but such an instrument should be completely satisfactory. Mine is a house-current recorder bought originally about fifteen years ago. Much better ones are available today.

# Chapter 10

# Sun, Moon, Stars, and Weather

POWERFUL *as he is, man cannot divert the hurricane or temper the blast of a lightning bolt, let alone alter the orbit of the least star in the heavens. All around him every day of his life play the eternal forces of the universe, to be watched in awe and wonder.*

*It sometimes seems* that the atmosphere around us and the natural phenomena in the skies, the sun, moon, and stars, are more taken for granted and are less generally known than any other aspect of nature. True, we are all aware of the weather, even though we live in air-conditioned houses or apartments, because we encounter it every time we step outdoors; and the weather is the atmosphere in action. But even the weather is, for most of us and most of the time, little more than a topic for forecasters to discuss and something for us to enjoy or regret, not something to understand and appreciate. Yet the atmosphere, which creates both weather and climate, is our lifelong environment, and the sun, moon, and stars are our neighbors and mysterious companions in this remarkable voyage we are making through the universe. It would seem only fitting that we be at least as aware of them, whether we understand them or not, as we are of the robin in the dooryard and the dandelion on the lawn.

There isn't room in this chapter, or this whole book for that matter, to discuss the atmosphere and the skies in any detail, but perhaps we can find a few guideposts and suggest a few paths into this fascinating and all-encompassing area. Let's start close at hand, with the atmosphere and the weather.

The atmosphere is the film of air that surrounds the earth. The specialists call it the earth's atmospheric envelope. Proportionately, it is even thinner than the skin on an apple, and it is invisible to the human eye. At least half of it, by weight, is concentrated in a three-and-a-half-mile layer next to the earth's surface. At sea level the atmosphere consists of approximately 78 per cent nitrogen, 21 per cent oxygen, and varying amounts of water vapor, carbon dioxide and other gases. Five miles up the oxygen becomes scarce, as climbers of high mountains have learned. Five hundred miles up the atmosphere consists almost entirely of hydrogen and helium, and from there on up it thins away until there is nothing but stray atoms of gas and dust in outer space.

Science divides the atmosphere into four layers. The one closest to the earth is the troposphere and is about five miles deep at the poles, eleven miles deep at the equator. Then comes the stratosphere, reaching up to about fifty miles. Then the ionosphere, extending out to about 650 miles. Beyond that is the exosphere, about which we know very little.

Man and all other animal life live in the troposphere, which is a kind of universal ocean of oxygen-rich air. We are as dependent on it as a fish is on water. We cannot swim in it, though birds can, but we are partially supported by it as we move about. Its oxygen feeds the fires of life, and its pressure holds our bodies together.

Weather is a result of what happens in the troposphere, though it is affected by changes and movements in the stratosphere. But what happens in this lower layer of air creates all our weather and dictates our climate. It is this layer of the atmosphere which makes the earth habitable for the kind of life we know. The heat radiated by our parent star, the sun, is essential to life, but without this atmospheric envelope the earth would be incredibly hot in daytime and abysmally cold at night. The moon, which has no atmosphere, has daytime temperatures as high as 212° Fahrenheit, the boiling point of water, and night cold reaching 238° below zero. Our atmosphere filters and moderates the daytime heat, allowing less than half the sun's radiation to reach the earth, and acts as a blanket at night, preventing the earth from radiating all its warmth back into outer space.

Being a gas, the air is easily compressed, expands when heated, and shrinks when chilled. When warm, it can hold a vast quantity of water vapor. When chilled, it precipitates that moisture as rain or snow. Air flows somewhat as water does, but it is very restless and flows much more swiftly. Heat it in one place and it expands and rises, leaving a pocket. Cold air from elsewhere rushes into that pocket, and that moving air is wind. If it begins to swirl it may become a tornado. If the swirl sets a great mass of air into motion it may become a hurricane.

The difference in air pressure creates what we call high- and low-pressure areas. These areas are what we call weather systems, and they are constantly in motion about the surface of the earth. Their broad direction of movement is from west to east, the same direction as the earth's rotation. But their paths are affected by many factors. Huge streams of air are constantly in motion high in the troposphere and in the stratosphere, and they affect the movements of weather systems. So does the land itself, mountain ranges, river valleys, deserts. And warm air is constantly rising in the tropics; heavier cold air is constantly flowing down from the polar regions. Warm air anywhere, but especially in the tropics and over oceans and lakes, absorbs water vapor, and cold air chills and precipitates this moisture. All these factors, and still more, affect the size, direction, character, and speed of weather systems.

Weather systems move across the earth on more or less regular schedules. In the Summer the tendency is for one such system to follow another at seven-day intervals. In Winter this speeds up to five-day intervals. The difference is caused by the fact that warm Summer air is lighter than cold Winter air and moves somewhat more slowly. The Winter wind, cold air, is literally heavier than the warm wind of Summer. Tests have shown that a twenty-mile Winter wind, for instance, exerts more pressure on a windmill than a twenty-mile Summer wind. When we have a Summer that seems to bring rain every week end, it is not mere coincidence. Summer weather tends to repeat itself in seven-day cycles. But don't count on it. One storm may be slowed up on the way and a new sequence will follow.

Storms are the most violent and dramatic of all weather phenomena. They vary from the local thunderstorm to the widespread devastation of a hurricane.

Thunderstorms are most frequent along the eastern part of the Gulf Coast and in the southern part of the Rockies and the nearby Plains area. Parts of Mississippi, Alabama, and Florida sometimes have ninety such storms a year. The upper Midwest averages about forty a year, and most of the Northeast has around thirty.

The thunderstorm is essentially local. It is caused by violent vertical movements of air, hot spots at the earth's surface often contrasted with nearby cool spots, as where plain and mountain meet or warm shoreline and cool ocean. Cumulus clouds build into thunderheads sometimes 75,000 feet high, whose interiors seethe with warring winds. Brief, heavy rain is typical of such storms, and so is violent lightning. You can estimate the distance of such a storm by timing the lag between the sight of a lightning flash and the sound of its thunder. The sight is almost instantaneous, but the sound travels only about 1,100 feet a second. There is a five-second lag if the storm is a mile away, ten seconds for two miles. Another warning is the wave of cool air ahead of the storm, usually about three miles. When you first feel the chill, the storm is probably still three miles away.

Lightning tends to strike the highest object. Never take shelter under a lone tree in an open field in a lightning storm. One is much safer lying flat in the open, even at the expense of a drenching. The mast on a sailboat is a prime target. If you are in a boat on the water when such a storm approaches, get to land as soon as possible. You are safe inside an automobile in the open, but not under a tree. You are safe in any steel-frame building or any building with lightning rods properly installed. A TV antenna is a prime target unless it is properly grounded. In the woods, stay away from the taller trees.

Tornadoes are the most violent of all storms, though their paths seldom are more than an eighth of a mile across. They are marked by twisting, funnel-shaped clouds inside which the wind force is incredible. They usually accompany heavy thunderstorms and heavy rain, sometimes severe hailstorms. They are most frequent in the lower Mississippi valley and the Midwest. The area west of Texas and Nebraska has almost none, West Virginia and Maine have very few, New England and the Northeast have only ten or fifteen a year. The extreme low pressure inside a tornado's vortex can cause even a large building literally to explode, and the winds can uproot huge trees, even knock a train and locomotive off the tracks. In recent years the Weather Bureau has been tracking tornadoes by radar and issuing warnings to all in their path.

In a sense, a hurricane is a tremendous tornado. Hurricanes originate near the equator and are created, at least in part, by the twisting forces of the earth's rotation. A mass of warm air, perhaps twenty or thirty miles in diameter, rises and starts swirling. It feeds on its own motion, condensing its moisture, generating more hot, turbulent air, drawing more and more surrounding air into its giant whirlpool. At first it is something like a big thunderstorm, but it becomes a tremendous wheel of growing winds and heavy rain. The winds may reach 200 miles an hour and the path of destruction may be a hundred miles or more wide. The storm may move only ten miles an hour at the start, but as it gains strength it may travel thirty miles an hour. Some hurricanes travel 4,000 miles before they die out.

Late August, September, and early October are the worst time for hurricanes in our area. The worst of their damage in the Northeast usually is within a hundred miles of the coast, and most of it often is caused by flooding. Now and then a hurricane, as the vicious one of 1938, moves inland in the Northeast and leaves a broad path of devastation caused by both wind and flood. The Weather Bureau now maintains a hurricane watch and warning system.

The northwestern part of the Pacific has more hurricanes, known there as typhoons, than any other part of the earth. But Australia and New Zealand have them, and so does Africa. The hurricane winds revolve counter-clockwise in our northern hemisphere, clockwise in the southern hemisphere.

All these violent storms are accompanied by clouds, but there can be clouds without storms. Often the clouds make the sky intensely beautiful and they always add interest to the sky. Clouds are responsible for colorful sunrises and sunsets, which are among the most beautiful of all natural phenomena.

Clouds are formed of water vapor in some state or another. The air always contains water vapor, even on a dazzling, cloudless Autumn day. Clouds form when the air cools below its saturation point and the water vapor condenses. The steam from a boiling kettle in a cool room is a miniature cloud. So is your breath on a cold morning. Fog is a cloud at the earth's surface.

Clouds are among the earth's greatest travelers, constantly in motion, constantly being renewed. I look out my window now and see cirrus clouds, mare's-tail streamers, riding the wind several miles high. Only six or eight hours ago those clouds probably were over Chicago, nearly a thousand miles away. If conditions are right tonight I may look up and see noctilucent clouds traveling in the stratosphere at the speed of a jet plane, yet so far away that they seem to be standing still among the stars.

These are high-flying clouds, which zip along at spectacular speeds up where eternal gales are blowing. But the everyday clouds of the lower atmosphere are also travelers of consequence. Scud, the ragged gray cloud which flies so low just before or after a rainstorm, is whipped along by winds of thirty, forty, and fifty miles an hour. The most spectacular of all, the big cotton-ball cumulus clouds, sometimes travel hundreds of miles, though at a stately pace of fifteen or twenty and rarely more than thirty-five miles an hour.

Cloud names come from the Latin. *Cumulus* means a heap, and cumulus clouds look like giant heaps of meringue. *Nimbus* means rain, and nimbo-stratus clouds are those gray masses that close in the earth, darken everything, and finally pour out a drenching rainstorm. *Stratus* means layer, and stratus clouds look like successive layers or bands. *Cirrus,* meaning a curl or strand of hair, aptly describes the high-flying cloud strands which sometimes resemble straight mare's-tails and often curl up at the ends in beautiful swirls. *Noctilucent* clouds are night-luminous, and *Nacreous* clouds are like mother-of-pearl. Both are visible only at night, since they occur at heights of sixteen to fifty miles, where they catch and reflect the sun's glow long after sunset. We aren't sure, but it seems likely that noctilucent clouds are composed of fine dust similar to that of comets and meteors rather than of water vapor. All other clouds are vapor clouds, though some contain smoke and other solid materials. Vast forest fires and volcanic eruptions create smoky clouds that sometimes completely circle the earth. The clouds created by the explosion of Krakatoa in the Dutch East Indies in 1883, the most violent of modern times, circled the globe within a week and remained in the atmosphere, creating brilliant sunsets, for nearly a year.

There are two broad classes of clouds—the puffy, piled-up cumulus clouds formed when warm, saturated air rises swiftly and the moisture is condensed into visible particles by the cool upper air, and the sheets of foglike layer clouds formed when a layer of warm, saturated air is cooled without much vertical movement.

Clouds are also classified by their altitude—low clouds, middle clouds, high clouds, and towering clouds.

There are three kinds of low clouds, which are seldom much more than a mile above the earth. *Stratus* clouds are a low, uniform cloud sheet, often dull gray. They make a heavy, dull sky but bring only drizzling rain. *Nimbo-stratus* are the rain clouds, darker than ordinary stratus and having a "wet" look. Streaks of rain often can be seen in them, reaching to the ground. Nimbo-stratus clouds often are accompanied by fracto-stratus, or low, scudding clouds whipped along by a strong wind. *Strato-cumulus* clouds are puffy masses of cloud that form a moving, sometimes rolling layer, usually gray with deep, dark shadows. Strato-cumulus do not produce rain, but if they roll into great masses and form nimbo-stratus they can and usually do become the source of rainstorms, sometimes mild thunderstorms.

Middle clouds are nearly always either stratus or cumulus and they ride about two miles above the earth. *Alto-stratus* are veils or sheets of cloud, either blue or gray in color. They often give a striped appearance. The sun or moon seen through them looks as though it were behind frosted glass but does not form a halo. *Alto-cumulus* are patches or layers of fluffy clouds. They may be dazzling white or pearly gray. They seem to have no special form, are clots of cloud that never seem to come together. The sun may appear as a disc with a corona of blue or yellow with a reddish rim when seen through alto-cumulus clouds. Neither alto-stratus nor alto-cumulus clouds produce storms.

High clouds are composed almost entirely of minute crystals of ice and they fly about four miles above the earth.

*Cirrus* clouds are feathery, wispy. They form the mare's-tails I mentioned earlier. *Cirro-cumulus* are rare. They are streaky clouds that form waves and ripples and create the true "mackerel sky." *Cirro-stratus* clouds look like ragged patches of veiling, very high and gauzy. They are the clouds that create large halos, big luminous circles, around the sun or moon.

The towering clouds are the thunderheads, the *cumulo-nimbus*, which may have their bases close to the ground and their tops, often flattened and anvil-shaped, as much as fifteen miles above the earth. They are frothy and turbulent, white with deep, dark shadows. Ordinary *cumulus* clouds are quite harmless and sail like ships with towering sheets of canvas across the Summer sky. They form at almost any altitude, sometimes as much as three miles up but more often half that high or less. They are the great clouds of the West, the picturesque ones that make the clear sky look twice as blue, and they often accompany a brilliant, sunny Summer day. When in the western sky at sunset they can be dazzlingly beautiful, shot with silver and gold and even with red and orange, but more often with pink and yellow.

The droplets of moisture in a cloud average only 1/2,500 inch in diameter, so small that they float in air that has any motion at all. The average raindrop contains about one million times as much water as one of those cloud drop-lets. *Hail* is formed when raindrops are frozen into ice par-ticles in high, turbulent clouds, then carried up and down by the turbulence through warm, moist zones and cold, dry ones, building bigger and bigger all the time, until they finally are hailstones and come pelting down. Hailstones as big as a hen's egg have been found. *Sleet* occurs when rain falls from high clouds through a layer of freezing air. Sleet actually consists of ice pellets, usually very small as con-trasted to hail. *Snow* remains something of a mystery. As far as is known, droplets of water vapor in saturated air at-tach themselves to very small particles of dust or other mat-ter, then are frozen into crystals. Those crystals are six-sided and amazingly delicate and beautiful. But it has also been found that at high altitudes snowflakes will form without those dust particles if the air is supersaturated and the temperature is at least 38° below zero. *Snow pellets* are like soft sleet and are differentiated from sleet, usually, only by meteorologists. *Ice prisms* are tiny ice crystals, often needles and columns, so small that they fall very slowly. They are seen as a dazzling shimmer in the air on very cold Winter mornings and often accompany a Winter morning fog. They sometimes create beautiful colored halos around the sun.

*Dew* and *frost* form from moisture in the air at the earth's surface. They form on clear nights. The "sweat" that collects on a glass containing a cold drink on a hot day is a form of dew. Frost out of doors, especially near a river, a pond, or other source of water vapor, sometimes makes a spectacular display. This is sometimes called hoarfrost. It often takes one of two typical forms, tabular or spicular. *Tabular frost* forms in tiny plates, usually on edge like the leaves of a partially opened book. *Spicular frost* consists of spikes or needles, smaller than a pin in diameter and bristling on a grass blade or weed stem. Either frost or dew can make spider webs into fantastically beautiful, delicate designs of crystal. Another form of frost forms on windowpanes in a room with moist air on a very cold night. These *frost patterns* often are feathery, intricate beyond belief, and remarkably beautiful. They are found in our centrally heated houses usually in bedrooms, where our own breath has created enough moisture for them to form. Elsewhere in the house the air is too dry, though sometimes they will appear on a kitchen window, where cooking has moistened the air with its steam.

Man's own works have somewhat altered the weather and climate. Cities, with their concentration of heat-absorbing structures and of heating machinery, are warmer both Summer and Winter than the country. The haze over cities and factory areas also holds the heat. City air has more carbon dioxide than the air of the open country, relatively less oxygen.

Both climate and weather will vary somewhat within a region because of local differences of geography and plant life. Valleys are generally cooler than hilltops, especially at night and in the Winter, because cold air flows downhill. Lakesides and riversides are more humid than inland areas, have more dew, often have later Autumn frosts. Woodlands are cooler in Summer, warmer in Winter, than open land.

The question of whether our climate is growing warmer or not has often been argued, to no conclusion. Some say we are still emerging from the last Ice Age and the trend is toward a warmer climate. Others say we are moving into a new Ice Age and the long-time trend is colder. The evidence seems inconclusive. Despite the grandfather tales of bitter winters in the past, we have only about one century of weather records made with comparable instruments, by no means enough to make a judgment either way. It does appear that the West Coast of the United States is getting somewhat cooler and the East Coast somewhat warmer, but the evidence is slight and short-term. We who are living today probably never will know the answer, but perhaps our great-great-grandchildren will.

When we come to matters outside the earth's atmosphere, there is the whole universe to consider, and that is a subject for more awe and speculation than precise information. Perhaps we can touch a few of the highlights. Let's start with the moon, the earth's own satellite, our companion in the annual trip around the sun.

The moon is about one quarter the diameter of the earth. It has an elliptical orbit but averages about 238,000 miles from the earth. The moon is a "dead" planet with little or no atmosphere, no light of its own, and probably with no form of life we would recognize as life. The moonlight we see is reflected from the sun. Because the moon rotates only once in each circuit of the earth we always see the same side of it.

The moon's phases are created by the fact that the moon revolves around the earth just a little slower than the earth revolves on its own axis. The difference averages about fifty minutes a day. That is another way of saying that the moon rises an average of fifty minutes later each day. When we have a new moon, the moon rises in the east soon after sunrise, is invisible all day in the sun's overpowering brilliance, and can be seen at dusk as a thin crescent low in the west, its horns pointing to the east. The cresent is the reflection of the sun on the moon's lower side.

Each day the moon rises a little later, and about seven days after new moon it appears overhead as a half moon soon after sunset. Now the whole lower half reflects the sun there below the horizon. Another seven or eight days and the moon rises in the east at about the time the sun sets in the west. Now it is entirely illuminated by the sun and we see it as a full, round disc. This is the full moon and it remains in the sky all night long. Still rising later each night, in another seven days it doesn't appear until midnight and is a half moon again, waning. And, after still another week, it rises just before sunrise, a crescent once more but this time with the horns pointing west. After that it is out of sight about seven days because it rises so near sunrise that it is invisible. This is what we call the dark of the moon. Finally its daily lag sets it in the western sky just after sunset and we have the crescent new moon again. Each phase of the moon is repeated about every four weeks.

The daily lag of the moon varies from season to season. It is at its minimum, only about twenty-three minutes a day, in the Northeast at about the time of the Autumnal Equinox. So the full moon nearest the Autumnal Equinox gives us four or five days in a row with the moon practically full and in the sky almost all night. This is the Harvest Moon, and it occurs only then.

The gravitational pull of the moon and the sun causes the tides in the earth's oceans. Because the sun is so far away and the moon so close, the moon's effect is about three times that of the sun. When the sun and moon are in line, at the times of new moon and full moon, their combined effect causes the highest tides, the spring tides; and when they are opposed to each other, in the first and last quarter of the moon, the tides are lowest, or neap tides.

Because it once was believed that the moon also caused tides in the human brain, we have the word "lunacy," meaning madness, from the Latin word for moon. Some people still believe that the moon's phases have an effect on crops, and they plant by the moon's phases. The moon on the increase is supposed to favor crops that grow above the ground; the moon on the decrease, past full moon, to favor those below the ground, root crops.

The sun is the star around which the earth and other planets of our particular system revolve. It is only a medium-sized star, as stars go, but is twice as big as the orbit of the moon, more than a hundred times the diameter of the earth. The earth's orbit around the sun is elliptical, but the average distance between the two is about 93,000,000 miles. Paradoxically, the earth is about 3,000,000 miles closer to the sun in January than in July.

Celestial distances are almost inconceivable. The next nearest star to us is about 300,000 times as far away as the sun, some twenty-six million million miles. Since miles lose their meaning, out there in space, astronomers measure distances in light-years—the distance light will travel in a year. Since light travels 186,000 miles per second, a light-year is nearly six million million miles. Sirius, the brightest star beyond the sun, is 8.7 light-years from us. Some other stars are millions of light-years away.

On a brilliantly clear night a person with good eyesight can see about 2,000 stars in the sky at one time. Different stars are visible at different seasons, but the total number visible to the naked eye over the entire year is only about 6,000. An astronomical telescope reveals literally millions more, and the total number in the universe is estimated in the billions. And each star is a sun somewhat like our own, the center of its own system of planets and other satellites.

The solar system to which we belong consists of the sun, nine planets, thirty-one known moons or other satellites, thousands of minor planets and asteroids, dozens of comets, and millions of meteors. In the order of their distance from the sun, the planets are Mercury, Venus, Earth, Mars, Jupiter, Saturn, Uranus, Neptune, and Pluto. Earth and Venus are about the same size, Mars a little over half the diameter of the Earth, Saturn nine times as big, and Jupiter eleven times as big. Mercury, which is only 36,000,000 miles from the Sun, is the smallest of the family, less than half the Earth's diameter. We have so far discovered that Jupiter has twelve moons, Saturn nine, Uranus five, Mars and Neptune two each.

Mercury, Venus, Mars, Jupiter, and Saturn are what we know as our Morning and Evening Stars. Their positions vary in the sky and they are visible only when they are in a position, like our own moon, to reflect the sun's light. All of them are, by turn, visible in early morning or early evening, their positions varying from season to season and year to year. Their schedules can be found in a good almanac. Mars always appears to have a reddish glow. Saturn has a ring, a flattened belt, which can be seen through a small telescope; this ring apparently consists of fragments of meteoric material or disintegrated satellites. Jupiter's moons can also be seen through a small telescope. Some details of all the visible planets and many details of the moon's surface can be seen through a good pair of binoculars, the ones you may use for watching birds.

The stars appear to move from hour to hour and even from night to night. The apparent movement is a consequence of the earth's rotation and seasonal shifting of position, but the visual effect is that the heavens wheel from east to west as though pivoted on the North Star, which moves so little and so slowly that we can rely on it for a directional guide. Among the stars there are fixed patterns which ancient man recognized and named as constellations. The old names persist, and the fables about the constellations have endowed many of them with fancied resemblances —The Big Dipper, as an example, and Draco the Dragon and Cygnus the Swan. Some of these names and identifications of form are difficult to believe, but they do help the amateur to find his way about in the starry heavens. And their relative positions are sufficiently constant to be guides as long as any of us are going to look at them. The stars even in the fixed constellations are changing position, but so slowly that those the early Greeks named are still the same shape and in the same relative position that they were thousands of years ago.

Someone who knows a little about the stars can help the beginner a great deal, but anyone can start to learn the constellations with a star chart or handbook. I would start with the North Star, which is not really a brilliant star but can be found any time after it has been identified. From it, one can easily find Ursa Minor, the Little Bear (or the Little Dipper) whose tail-tip is the North Star itself. On a Summer evening the Little Bear will be standing on his tail above the North Star. And off to the left of him will be the Big Dipper, with the two stars at the end of the bowl pointing toward the North Star. The Big Dipper will be standing on its head, handle up toward the zenith. Near the horizon, almost on a line from the tip of the Big Dipper's handle through the North Star, will be the irregular "W" of Cassiopeia.

With those constellations to begin with, it is easy to go on with a star chart, for you have a starting point and known groups to guide by. Draco the Dragon winds its tail between the Big and Little Dippers. Lyra is just to the east of Draco, and Cygnus the Swan is just below Lyra.

Summer is the most comfortable time to watch the stars, but the Summer skies are less interesting to me than those of late Fall and Winter. By November the Big Dipper is down on the horizon in the northeast in mid-evening, Cassiopeia is high in the sky, the Pleiades are almost overhead, and Orion, with its three unmistakable "belt" stars, is well up in the southeastern sky. To see the Seven Sisters of the Pleiades, which are quite faint, I look somewhat away from them and catch them in the corner of my eye, as it were. Then they are clearly visible. The Pleiades are not visible on a Summer evening; they are still hidden below the eastern horizon and do not appear until late at night.

There are five or ten comets that appear in the skies every year, but most of them are so faint that they can be seen only with a telescope. Halley's Comet is the most famous of all we know. It was reported as early as 240 B.C. and has made periodic appearances every seventy-six years since. Few people will see a large, spectacular comet more than once in their lifetime. Comets are now believed to be members of the solar system, closely related to meteors but traveling in regular, predictable orbits. They have long, glowing tails, probably of gas and meteoric dust. Those tails appear to be harmless. The earth has passed through the tail of Halley's Comet without being scorched or in any way affected. Halley's Comet's next visit to the earth's vicinity will be in 1986.

There are countless meteors or shooting stars. They streak across the night skies, often visible, and occasionally fragments of one strike the earth. There are large craters in Arizona, near Hudson Bay, in Siberia, and in Estonia where large meteors once struck the earth. The one which made the Arizona crater is estimated to have weighed 50,000 tons. Most meteors burn up in the atmosphere before they reach the earth. There are predictable meteor "showers" of considerable intensity. These periodic showers are named from the constellations from which they appear to come. Among them are the Lyrids in April, the Perseids, most spectacular of all, about August 10, the Leonids in mid-November, the Andromedes in late November, and the Germinids about December 10–13.

And now, a few final notes:

There are two Equinoxes each year, the Autumnal and the Vernal. The Autumnal Equinox occurs on or about September 21, the Vernal about March 21, at which time day and night are supposed to be equal (but aren't exactly) and the sun stands directly overhead at midday and rises due east, sets due west.

There are two Solstices each year, the Summer and the Winter. The Summer Solstice occurs on or about June 21, the Winter Solstice on or about December 21, traditionally the year's longest and shortest days, though not actually so by a matter of a few minutes. The Summer Solstice marks the point of the sun's apparent movement to its farthest point north and the Winter Solstice the sun's farthest apparent movement south. The span of daylight decreases after the Summer Solstice and increases after the Winter Solstice.

The Solstices and Equinoxes mark the changes from Spring to Summer, Summer to Autumn, Autumn to Winter, and Winter to Spring—by the almanac and calendar, but not by the weather and the birds and plants, which only approximate those seasonal dates.

The solar day is exactly twenty-four hours, though the actual spans of daylight and darkness vary with the season and the latitude. The lunar day is twenty-four hours and fifty minutes, which is responsible for the moon's phases described earlier.

Twilight and dusk in the Northeast vary in length from about an hour and a half in Winter to more than two and a quarter hours in Summer.

Rainbows are always seen in that part of the sky opposite the sun and are rarely seen when the sun is near midday. They are caused by a combination of refraction and reflection of sunlight on raindrops. On rare occasions moonbows are seen, the parallel phenomena caused by moonlight on raindrops.

Sundogs are streaks of rainbow color, one on each side of the sun, usually seen at or soon after sunrise in the Winter. Apparently they are created by ice crystals in the air which refract the sunlight like prisms. Occasionally they occur at midday, when they are a part of a halo type of phenomena; sometimes the halo is complete, a circle of rainbow color. Both sundogs and the halo can on occasion occur with the moon, also in Winter. Then, of course, they are moondogs.

The Aurora Borealis, or Northern Lights, can be spectacular and are so varied in form and color that no general description suffices. They may be white, yellow, green, red, or yellow, or all colors. They may be rays that seem to radiate from the northern horizon or writhing streamers or nothing more than a suffused glow. I have seen Northern Lights that looked like the sky glow of a tremendous fire beyond the horizon, I have seen them look like a giant fan of green and yellow and white, and I have seen them like rippling ribbons in the northern sky. Often they have the appearance of faint neon light. Scientists say they seem to be caused by electrically charged particles in empty space as much as 600 miles above the earth. The earth's magnetic poles seem to emphasize the phenomenon, which is why Northern Lights are typical of the polar latitudes. A friend of mine who spent some time in both the Arctic and the Antarctic tells me that the Aurora is even more spectacular in the South Polar area than in the Far North. We frequently have brilliant Northern Lights in the Autumn, especially, where I live.

# Chapter 11

# Biotopes
# and the Lay of the Land

*Soil, climate, and the prevailing winds determine which forms of life will thrive and which will perish in any area. He who would know the botany and biology of his homeland must first know where he lives in those fundamental terms. He must know his own biotope.*

*In the terms of science,* the word "biota" means the organic life, the plants and animals, of a particular region; and a "biotope" is an area of uniform environment for life. So we all are part of the "biota" of our own regions, and each of us lives in a "biotope." Man, being an adaptable creature with the means of warming or cooling his own habitation and the ability to import food from a distance, can live in many different kinds of environment. Few other animals can. And plants have to live where they sprout and take root and find hospitable growing conditions. So the biota, the plant and native animal life, of any particular region is more or less predictable.

Broadly speaking, the northern and eastern parts of the United States consist of only a few major biotopic regions —the seashore, the inland valleys, the hill country and mountains, and the lake areas. But within each of these regions there are lesser "biotopes" or relatively uniform environments. For instance, although I live in the hill country of western New England, a biotope in itself, I have within short walking distance of my house four smaller biotopes, each rather specialized in the wild life it supports. In my dooryard is the river, with flowing water and damp banks. Behind the house is the pastureland, the meadow, an area of brooks and grassland. Beyond the pastures is the mountainside, rocks and woodland. And down the road a mile or so is a small bogland, stagnant water and marginal muck.

Each of these four areas has its own assortment of life,

172

some of it specially adapted to or characteristic of the river, the meadow, the hillside woodland, or the bog. There is a good deal of overlapping, since the climate is the same for all four areas, but there are no rabbits in the river, no catfish in the meadows, no woodchucks in the bog, and no snapping turtles in the woods. So to find a particular plant or animal, I must go to the right place; and when I am in a certain place I can rightly expect to find certain plants or types of animal life.

Man sometimes thinks he has changed the face of the earth tremendously, and in limited areas he has. His ax and his plow and more recently his bulldozer have removed forests, stripped the grass from the plains, and cut sizable gashes across the countryside. His dams have created lakes and his channels have diverted rivers and drained swamps. But the major changes have come in the wake of man's doing, and most of them have been the results of erosion. Topsoil has been washed or blown away, rivers have become silted, lowlands have been flooded, marshes have dried up, shorelines have been altered, underground water levels have been lowered disastrously. Natural environments have been irrevocably changed, and not always to man's benefit.

But even these effects, unhappy in too many instances, are minor in comparison to fundamental changes that have been going on since time began. Nature not only made the continents and lifted the mountain highlands; it created hill and valley, plain and tableland. And the essential elements of geography as we know them were created long before man invented the first stone ax. Change is still going on, but so slowly that we are scarcely aware of it.

This part of New England where I live, for example, was shaped substantially as it is today long before the first white man, or the first Indian, for that matter, saw it. As a land, this area is probably among the older places on earth and its geologic history is somewhat typical, certainly of the eastern part of the United States.

Parts of this area were thrust up from the primeval seas about half a billion years ago, back in the Cambrian era, in the form of very high mountains. The core of those mountains was limestone and marble, formed of sediments which had settled in the oceans over the eons. That is where Vermont marble comes from, and the fine-grained limestone that crops out in many parts of New England. Those mountains are now worn down into the Berkshire Hills and the Green Mountains, relatively low upthrusts, but in the beginning they probably were as high as the Andes, possibly the Himalayas.

Over the eons those high ridges were eroded away. There were more upheavals. Deep valleys were formed, new hills thrust up, valleys filled again. But apparently some part of the New England mountains remained above the oceans through all that time. Finally most of New England was worn down to a vast high plain that sloped gradually into the still-warm sea, at the margin of which was a broad tidal marsh. Lush vegetation grew there. We know this because in succeeding ages some of it turned to low-grade coal which is still found in the vicinity of Boston and Narragansett Bay.

Then, in another of the earth's vast convulsions, the Rocky Mountains were thrust up, and in the continental upheaval the whole New England area was lifted several hundred feet above the ocean. With this new tilt of the land, the rivers that had wound sluggishly across the plain became hurrying streams again and gouged deep canyons in their rush to the sea. The land became scarred and rugged. And finally, about a million years ago, the first of the great Ice Ages began. Tremendous ice sheets formed in the North and flowed down across the land. The ice was more than a mile deep in places, a tearing, gouging, rending plow of ice that slowly sliced southward.

There appear to have been four waves of ice across New England and most of northern United States. At one time or another, ice covered all of New England, reached southern New Jersey, flowed down both sides of the Alleghenies, covered much of New York State, reached down the Ohio River almost to its mouth, covered all the upper Mississippi valley, and reached as far west as the Dakotas. All these areas still show the marks of the glaciers.

Each wave of ice melted back before the next one came, always with great flooding and deep erosion. The last Ice Age ended, perhaps 12,000 years ago, with what might be called The Big Melt. We speak of the ice "retreating," but it didn't actually retreat in the sense of moving back north. It melted where it was, the southern edge first, of course. And in the melting, the hilltops and mountains were the first to be ice-free. Once the ice was gone from them, they were wide open to all the forces of erosion, wind, rain, frost, water. As they eroded, the debris was carried into the valleys. The ice was laden with all kinds of geologic trash, picked up on its way south—rocks, sand, silt, all kinds of scrapings from the land. This debris was dumped as the ice melted, and it formed hills and ridges, dammed valleys, created new features on the land. The tremendous volume of water from the retreating ice created surging rivers and huge lakes. Some of these lakes were soon filled with silt and created what man, when he arrived, called plains—the patches of flat, plainlike land here in the East, not the high plains of the West. Elsewhere the debris from the ice settled on the bedrock where the ice dumped it, a miscellaneous collection of sand, silt, clay, gravel, and boulders, the "glacial till" of today, which is characteristic soil in many parts of New England.

As the ice melted, the oceans rose. The rise of the oceans drowned the mouths of the rivers all along the northeast coast and created the fantastically irregular coastline and the wealth of harbors characteristic of Massachusetts and Maine today. And the new rivers redistributed the surface soil and the glacial debris all over the landscape. Long Island was built of such debris.

During the advance and retreat of each of these vast waves of ice, the plant and animal life retreated and advanced, driven southward by the cold along the ice front, then creeping back as the climate warmed up again. Actually, the retreats were not as far as used to be believed. The constant melting of the ice at the southern edge, even when the ice was advancing, created heavy fogs which somewhat confined the cold. Not far in advance of the ice there seems to have been a relatively mild, very damp climate. The animals, birds, and plants that had been displaced by the ice moved southward, but not far ahead of the ice itself; and each time the ice melted back, all forms of life crept northward again. Even plant life spread northward in those intervals, the seeds sometimes carried by the wind, sometimes in mud on the feet of birds and animals, sometimes in bird and animal droppings. Plant life's return was somewhat more leisurely than the return of bird and animal life, but it came back each time.

At one time or another, all New England was swept clean by the ice. All the plant life that was here before the ice came was killed or swept away. The plant life we know today has crept back in the last 10,000 or 15,000 years. Tundra plants came first, of course, the Alpine and Arctic types of hardy dwarfs, shrubs, bushes, and low-growing plants that can endure severe cold. Then came the pines, the spruces, and the hemlocks. Last to return were the hardwoods. And of the hardwoods, the birch, the beech, and the maple were the first to get a foothold. After them came the oaks, the chestnuts, and the hickories.

With such a history, the Northeast provides a great variety of geographic and geological material for study, as well as a variety of biotopes or plant and animal environments.

The surface of the land is made up of soil and rocks. Soil consists of finely divided rock materials and decayed or decaying plant and animal material. The soil is a result of eons of the whole erosion process, together with the continual cycle of life, growth, maturity, death, and decay. But underlying the soil, and thrusting up through it in many places, is the basic rock of the earth's solid crust.

The geologist classifies rocks according to their origin, igneous, sedimentary, or metamorphic.

*Igneous* rocks were formed by the cooling of molten material from within the earth's crust. There are two basic kinds of igneous rocks, those that cooled inside the crust and formed such rocks as granite, and those that cooled outside in the form of lava, which produced such rocks as obsidian, basalt, and pumice.

Rocks erode and some of the minerals in them are dissolved in water. When surface rocks erode they become pebbles and sand and finely divided particles such as clay. These eroded materials are carried off by wind and water and deposited, usually in layers, and they become the materials for *sedimentary* rocks. Sandstone and shale and conglomerate, which is like sandstone with pebbles scattered through it, are typical sedimentary rocks. Natural cements such as lime, silica, and iron are filtered out of solution into such layers of sediment and bind the materials together. In the ocean, limestone is formed when the remains of shellfish and other animal life accumulate on the ocean floor; they have a high calcite or lime content, another natural cement.

When rocks already in existence are crushed together by the tremendous pressures of a convulsive earth and acted on by the earth's internal heat and the heat resulting from those pressures, *metamorphic* rocks are formed. Such action changes sandstone into quartzite, limestone into marble, granite into gneiss (pronounced "nice"), shale into slate. The degree of change depends on the pressure and the amount of heat present.

Theoretically, there is a sequence in these processes. The magma, or internal igneous rocks, become lava. The lava is eroded into sand and pebbles and carried off and deposited as sandstone, sedimentary rock. Sedimentary rock is squeezed and heated by the earth's convulsive pressures and metamorphosed. If the heat and pressures are sufficiently high, the metamorphic rock may be melted and changed to magma once more, which could spew out as lava and start the whole cycle over again. Actually, what we have is an overlap rather than a clear-cut differentiation, not only the three basic kinds of rocks but gradations of all three. And, of course, in almost every area there is a variety of rock forms, for the earth has jumbled them about and all the forces of erosion, from wind to glaciation, have scattered them. And because some rocks are more durable, more resistant to erosion than others, we have the geographic features of the land, the hills and valleys, the plains and mountains. These factors, as well as the variety of soils from one area to another, combine with weather and climate to create the various biotopes or particular areas of somewhat specialized forms of life.

There is the temptation to continue with geological speculation, which must be resisted. Anyone living in the Northeast is specially favored with a vast museum of geological material for study, with the whole story of rocks and the land lying there waiting to be read. I could spend years puzzling over the mysteries of the stones in the tumbled walls on my own land, for example, many of which were brought here from distant places by the glaciers and most of which still show the indelible marks of that long-gone age. On my desk right now is a small bowl of garnets I plucked from a weathered ledge of mica schist on the mountainside. In what ancient time and what warm seas were those magnesium silicates deposited in that rock, and what incredible forces metamorphosed the rock and created these dull red crystals that can be polished into semiprecious gems or crushed into abrasive covering for sandpaper or garnet-cloth? What convulsions and what vast erosions brought them into the open here on my ancient mountainside?

But the purpose of this chapter is to examine and speculate on the various kinds of environment for life. Let those whose deep interest is in the rocks follow out such questions.

In broad terms, that part of the continent which was covered by the glaciers of the Ice Age still shows traces of that time not only in its terrain but in its plant life. Perhaps we are still recovering from the effects of the ice. For example, there is an irregular line across New York, Pennsylvania, and the Midwest where certain kinds of plants seem to stop short—south of it you find such plants as sweet buckeye, Hercules'-club, and mistletoe, and north of it you do not find them. The soil, the climate, and even the terrain seem to be almost identical on both sides of that invisible line, and there is a wealth of plant life that pays no attention to the line. But there are certain trees and lesser plants that obey some invisible barrier. Actually, that line is the southern boundary of the ice sheet, and geological evidence proves it. The ice killed those plants, and they have never returned, for some reason. So we have two major biotopic areas still separated by a line that vanished perhaps 15,000 years ago.

There is another biotopic division of major proportions in the mid-South, and again it is a result, at least in good part, of the Ice Age. In the Cumberland Mountain area of Tennessee, Virginia, and western North Carolina is a region of remarkable variety of plant life. The hardwood forests there are both venerable and widely diversified. They include birch, black cherry, cucumber tree, ash, red maple, sour gum, several kinds of basswood, tulip tree, sugar maple, red and white oak, hemlock, beech, hickory, black walnut, and a score of other species. And the lesser plants are equally varied, the underbrush and the wildflowers, a vast wealth of them. The plant life of this area was in process of development long before the glacial ages. It is, in a sense, the mother greenhouse or nursery for most of the Northeast. Before the Ice Age, this wealth of plant life undoubtedly extended out from that area in all directions. It certainly reached well over the whole Appalachian area and probably into New England.

Then came the ice. This northern land of ours was denuded. That parent nursery was not only untouched by the ice but apparently not affected greatly by the climatic changes. Its wealth of plant life continued to flourish. Then the ice finally melted. Here lay the land, vastly changed, its soil reconstituted where any soil was left, its climate relatively mild once more. And as the land began to emerge from the boggy, chill, foggy state in which the melting ice left it, hardy plants from the Cumberland began to move in. Oaks, chestnuts, and other nut trees that thrive in a mild climate were among the first, perhaps because returning animals such as squirrels helped plant their seeds. It seems now that the oak forests of the Northeast established themselves about 5,000 years ago, when climates all over the earth were warmer than they are today. Since that time the climate has turned cooler again, but the oak forests adapted themselves to the change.

Logically, in terms of the climate the white man has always known here, all of New England should have the North-woods type of forest cover, completely lacking in oaks and related hardwoods, with spruce, hemlock, white pine, birch, and maple predominating. Actually, this natural tendency creates botanical pockets here and there, special biotopes as the scientists would call them. In shady ravines, on north-facing slopes, on damp slopes above swamps even in southern Connecticut, typical North-woods trees are often found, hemlocks, black birch, beech, and sugar maples. And oaks and hickories are scarce. Such areas are always marked by damp soil, shelter from drying winds, and some natural protection from the intense heat of the Summer sun. Often you can go just over the ridge from such pockets and find a totally different environment, drier soil, more direct sun, and oak-hickory woods, an entirely different biotope though less than a mile from the little North-woods area.

The kind of trees has a profound effect on the soil and on the lesser plants. Maple, walnut, birch, basswood, and ash enrich the soil. Their leaves are relatively soft and sweet; earthworms eat them, bacteria work on them, and they soon become a layer of leafmold, a rich topsoil. Oak leaves, tough and full of tannin, decay slowly and sometimes form thick, fibrous mats where few bushes or lesser plants can find roothold and sustenance. If other trees take root there, they are the lesser ones—dogwood, hornbeam, sassafras—and few shrubs except blueberries, laurel, and hazel thrive. On the forest floor itself you will find Canada Mayflower, partridgeberry, wintergreen, sometimes trailing arbutus, but few others of the flowering tribe.

On the other hand, the type of terrain and the quality of the soil largely determine the kind of woodland that grows there. For example, rocky ledges and places with thin, poor soil are likely to have a growth of red cedar. Upland ground, dry and relatively poor in fertility, is typical oak and hickory country. Fertile but moderately dry soil invites sugar maple, walnut, white ash, white birch, and white pine. Damp, cool soil is preferred by spruce and hemlock. Riverbanks and swamp margins, especially those with full sunlight, invite swamp maple, black ash, willow, tamarack, cottonwood, and basswood. Almost invariably there is some overlapping of such areas. Red cedars, for instance, are constantly creeping down from the dry, sterile ledges on the mountainside and gaining a foothold in the margins of my moist, fertile pastures. There are a few oaks in the rich, damp soil along the riverbank. And there is an occasional swamp maple on the mountainside where I am sure it lacks the damp rootbed it usually prefers. But this merely proves that the boundaries of any biotic area are approximate, never clear-cut.

These overlaps make life interesting for the person who explores the outdoors, for there is always a surprise possible. Purple vervain, for instance, is a riverbank, damp-soil plant which I find only in the bogland or along the river. Usually. But one afternoon I was high on the mountainside when I saw a flash of color that certainly was the blue flower of that misnamed vervain. I made my way through the woodland toward it and came out in a tiny opening where a trickle of a seep spring oozed up among the rocks and made a little patch of bog, a wet spot not five feet across. A thread of spring water flowed from it perhaps twenty feet, then disappeared among the rocks. But that little damp spot had a patch of lush green grass, a couple of marsh violet plants, and one thriving stalk of vervain in full bloom. It had no business growing there, theoretically at least. Probably the seed from which it grew was carried to that unlikely spot by some bird with muddy feet. However it got there, it sprouted, grew, and was now in bloom.

In a sense, that tiny spot of boggy soil, so small I could jump across it, was a special biotope, a particular environment for such plants as purple vervain and marsh violets. Possibly there were a couple of green frogs there, too, though I didn't see them.

Almost any area, even one of only a few square miles, will have its lesser specialized environments, just as my own place has. Even without a river or a bog, there may be meadow and woodland, or a low hill and a shallow valley. Even two or three trees can create a small environment of their own, with their shade and the effect of their decaying leaves on the soil beneath them. And any hill will have a slightly different type of life from that in the valley at its foot.

I can illustrate this even in our vegetable garden, a patch only about a hundred feet square, or in the lawn beside the house.

The soil here is typical valley soil, deposited first by the river, long ago, then added to by the wash from the mountainside, and finally topped by a layer of natural topsoil. Logically the soil in the garden should be uniform. But one half of the garden is dark, fairly heavy soil, and the other half is lighter, somewhat sandy soil. The division line runs right down the middle of the garden. The dark soil is ideal for leaf crops, the lighter soil is perfect for root crops. And even our ten years of cultivation, on top of perhaps forty or fifty years of cultivation before we came here, have not greatly altered the character of the soil in either side. There in that garden we have two different natural environments, side by side. If it were left to go back to natural growth there would be a slight difference in the wild plants that established themselves there.

Here on the side lawn the soil seems to be fairly uniform, but the presence of a big Norway spruce makes a noticeable difference. Under the spruce the grass needs constant care and pampering, but only a few feet away the grass grows lush and luxuriant. The tree makes all the difference, as any suburban householder learns. The tree casts shade, and its slow fall of needles alters the chemistry of the soil. Ground ivy, dandelions, and plantain, which thrive in shade and more acid soil, are constantly trying to crowd out the grass under the tree. Again, I have two minor biotopes, two separate plant environments, side by side.

Multiply such slight differences by a hundred or a thousand times and you have the difference in natural conditions between, say, a meadow and a woodland, or even between two areas in the same meadow.

But even these are essentially minor differences in the big picture, details to be noted after one has taken account of the major differences between the larger natural regions. Climate is the first of the governing factors. Then comes geography, the lay of the land. And after those first two come the matters of soil and moisture.

Climate is a matter of average temperatures, prevailing winds, and normal rain and snowfall. The United States has a variety of climates because of its size and varying terrain. Average annual temperatures, for instance, range from below 40° to above 70°. Average Summer temperatures range from below 60° to above 90°, and average Winter lows vary from minus 40° to plus 20°. Maine, upper Wisconsin, and North Dakota and the Rocky Mountains are the coldest areas; lower New Mexico and California, the hottest. Most of New England, upper New York State, and the upper Midwest are cool, and a broad area from the mid-Atlantic coast west to the Rocky Mountains is, on the averages, moderate in climate, averaging from zero to 20° below in Winter, 70° to 80° in the Summer. There are hotter and colder spots in all these areas, of course, caused by the lay of the land. But each of them is essentially one major biotope or environment.

Average annual precipitation, both rain and snow, is between 30 and 50 inches throughout New England, the Northeast, and the Midwest, with little patches of heavier precipitation here and there. The Deep South, except most of Georgia, has a wetter climate, between 50 and 70 inches of rainfall a year. But when it comes to the amount of sunshine and the number of clear days each year, the picture changes again. Lower New England and most of the Midwest have 140 to 180 clear days a year. This number drops to 100–140 in the Great Lakes area. And the pattern of snowfall is still different, snow-covered days averaging around 60 a year in the lower Midwest and lower New England, and 100 or more in the upper Midwest and upper New England.

And, finally, the growing season, the period of frost-free weather, follows still another pattern on the map. All New England and most of the Midwest as far as the Rockies averages from 80 to 120 frost-free days a year. But when you try to plot the dates of last Spring frost and first Fall frost you create a pattern even more complicated than the daily weather map. Frost follows the pattern of the land. My place here close beside the river, for instance, has almost two weeks more of frost-free weather than the hilltop farm of a friend only two miles away. Frost normally follows the valleys, so my place should be colder than his; but the river tempers my climate and reverses the normal difference from hilltop to valley. This one factor somewhat affects the character of all the natural growth on my land and that of my friend.

All these factors—soil, terrain, average temperature, frost dates, amount of sunshine, annual rain and snowfall—determine the natural life in any area. Even trees respond to slight changes in natural environment. To pick one example, the black walnut, though common in the Midwest and much of the Northeast, is rare in Connecticut and Massachusetts. But here in my own area, in a pocket of only a few square miles, the black walnut was thriving when the white man first arrived. Go fifteen miles in any direction and you won't find a black walnut tree, but here it still grows vigorously. There must be something in the soil and climate of this small, particular area that satisfies the needs of the black walnut.

Or take another example. Just up the road from my place, in the lower edge of Massachusetts, is a state park called Bartholomew's Cobble. It is only a few acres in extent and consists primarily of a rocky upthrust bordered by the Housatonic River. The rocks there are quartzite and dolomitic marble, and the soil is ideal for ferns. In that little plot of rocks and thin topsoil is one of the finest natural collections of native wild ferns in the country. Species that can't be found elsewhere in the East grow there. How they came there in the first place is a mystery, since there isn't a transplant among them. But there they are, simply because that particular combination of soil and climate is ideal for ferns. It is a special biotope, a botanical island in this rocky region of weathered hills and valleys.

Broadly speaking, then, there are big areas or biotopes, such as New England, the Middle Atlantic States, the Upper Midwest, the Lower Midwest, the Lakes area, and the Southern Appalachians. Each of these big areas has its broad range of plants—and animals and birds and even insects—typical of that area. You can be reasonably sure of finding spruce and hemlock in upper New England, for instance, and white pine over most of New England and the Northeast. In New England and the upper Northeast you will find maples and birch and beech, as well as many other hardwoods. In lower New England and much of the Midwest you will find oaks, both red and white. And with these trees you will find typical undergrowth, both low trees and bushes as well as flowering plants. Blueberries are typical of oak woodland. Christmas fern and partridgeberry often grow in pine woods, and sometimes ladyslipper grows there. Birch, poplar, and wild cherry often grow in maple groves or mixed forests of hardwoods.

Within each of these big areas there are always the lesser biotopes, the distinctive environments created by local geography. There is the meadow, there is the riverbank and lake or pond shore, there is the swamp or bogland, and there is the hillside woodland. Again, there will be certain plants typical of each of these environments, as well as many plants that are common to the larger area. When I want to find black alder, our smooth-leafed northern holly, I go to the wet places, along the shore of a pond or in the margin of the bog. When I am looking for wild columbine I go up the mountainside to the sun-warmed ledges; columbine often grows elsewhere, but I know I will find it up there among the rocks. If I am looking for pussy willows, I go to the swamp. If I want to find black birch and chew its wintergreen-flavored twigs, I go to the thin woods on the mountainside.

Nature has her own patterns, her own way of organizing and establishing communities of living things. Sometimes they may seem to be untidy patterns, but I am convinced they always have logical reasons for being as they are. Any confusion is, I am sure, in me. Nature recognizes neither state lines nor regional distinctions that man may make. She is the original pragmatist, dealing with conditions as they are, abandoning experiments that do not work. When I find a plant or animal in a place that seems wrong to me, the chances are a thousand to one that I, not nature, made the wrong appraisal.

So when anyone ventures to say that such and such are the boundaries of a particular biotope, or uniform environment, that person is simply making a guess, a generalization. He is stating the probabilities. Nature herself states the facts. I doubt that I shall ever find a grove of date palms growing in my New England valley, but if I ever do I will know that I, not nature, guessed wrong.

# Chapter 12

# No Need
# To Go Hungry

**THE FIELDS** *and forests are full of food that
will sustain the starving man if he knows
where to look. But most of us have our
preferences in what we eat. This chapter
discusses food that is there for the taking,
as well as how and how not to cook it.*

*In the first chapter* of Genesis, God is quoted as saying to Adam: "Behold, I have given you every herb bearing seed, which is upon the face of the earth, and every tree, in the which is the fruit of a tree yielding seed; to you it shall be for meat." This is a fine, large statement on which a vegetarian can rest content. But I note that only a few pages further on the diet begins to broaden and there is a good deal of meat-eating from there on. And the anthropologists tell me that man's dental equipment has always been that of an omnivorous creature. Apparently he ate what was at hand—plants, meat, fish, and, on occasion, insects.

Theoretically at least, a man should still be able to live on what grows around him. But both man and nature have changed, over the centuries, and the civilized appetite has rather well-defined preferences in food. With swift transportation and refrigeration, we are no longer limited to what grows in our immediate area, and canning and freezing have made Summer fruits and vegetables available the year around. Anyone with a garden, seal-top jars, and a freezer, or even with daily access to a moderately well-stocked food store, can live better today and eat more variously than any Roman emperor. But in spite of this plenty there is an urge in many country folk, especially newcomers, to partake of nature's own bounty, the food that grows without the helping hand of man.

We live on the land, not off it, for the most part. But there are a good many edibles, some of them tasty fare indeed, to be had for the taking if one knows where and when to look for them. And, I must add, if one knows how to prepare them. The cooking, to me at least, is the critical point in the use of all wild fare.

For instance, there are wild greens. My grandmother gathered wild greens every Spring and she cooked them the way she cooked tame greens, boiling them for hours and usually with a ham bone or a chunk of salt pork "for flavor." I never liked cooked greens, wild or tame, until my own wife began cooking them for me. She cooks them quickly and in a minimum of water. That way she makes wild mustard palatable fare, and I can even enjoy a few servings of early dandelions or young nettles. But I still revolt at some of the other traditional wildlings. Purslane, for instance, which comes out a tasteless, gelatinous mess; and dock, which is too bitter for my taste; and pokeweed, which isn't worth the bother. Others may like them. I don't. They are edible, though.

We always pick a few messes of dandelion greens as soon as they appear in the Spring. After they are sorted, which is a tedious job, we pour boiling water over them in a colander, to leach out the worst of the inherent bitterness. Then we cook them quickly and eat them with a dash of butter, a bit of salt and pepper, and I add a dash of vinegar. But we choose only the young leaves, and we tire of them in a week or two.

The wild cresses and mustards, and especially yellow rocket, make excellent greens if picked before they are fully budded. We choose only the tips, which makes for tedious picking but also makes better flavor. They don't need the boiling-water treatment; we just put them in a pot with a little water, boil briefly, and season and eat. Our favorite Spring green is marsh marigold, also called cowslip. As with the cresses, we pick only the tips and take them before the buds show color. Again, a quick cooking in a minimum of water is best. And all these greens are good in a raw green salad, especially when mixed with store-bought lettuce, the only lettuce available when the wild greens are ready. They give character and taste to the practically tasteless lettuce.

I mentioned pokeweed. Those who care for it pick it very young and pour off the first water in which it is boiled. Then they cook it in a second water and eat it like spinach. The plant as it grows develops a mildly poisonous element, so it shouldn't be eaten after it is more than six or eight inches high. But there are relatively few poisonous plants that even suggest themselves as greens, and most of them give warning in a bitter or sharply acrid taste. If they don't taste good, don't eat them. That is a fairly safe rule.

Very young nettles make an acceptable dish of greens, but one or two tastes satisfy me for the year. Some people say that skunk cabbage can be eaten if it is cooked in several waters and fully drained each time. It doesn't sound worth the bother, to me, and I doubt that I could appreciate skunk cabbage no matter how it was cooked.

Then there are fern fiddleheads, which some people think are better than asparagus. The tradition is that bracken is the best of all, but I think bracken is tough and stringy. My choice, if I must eat ferns, is the big ostrich fern, which sends up fiddleheads with stalks as big as a lead pencil. They should be cut before the fiddlehead begins to uncurl. The fuzz can be wiped off between the fingers. Then the stalks, including the curled tips, are boiled till tender in slightly salted water and treated like asparagus. They are palatable, but I prefer milkweed stalks. We even freeze milkweed, most years, to have a few packets for Winter eating. The milkweed must be gathered while very young, before the leaves have opened, while the stalks are only six or eight inches tall. Then we cook it exactly like asparagus. It becomes rank and bitter if picked too old, but when prime it is, for my money, just as good as the asparagus which doesn't appear until the milkweed is too old to eat.

In the wild green salad of which I spoke we also use sour grass, sparingly, peppergrass, wild chickory when we can find it young, now and then a touch of clover, and often a few very young leaves of horseradish. Horseradish is not technically a wildling, but it escapes and thrives near most rural gardens. Sour dock can be added, in moderation, and lamb's-quarters can be added. Lamb's-quarters makes a good cooked green, by the way. I didn't mention it earlier because it doesn't grow in profusion in my area. Actually, the wild-greens salad is more of a stunt than a stand-by. We make one almost every Spring, just to prove that we can do it, but it takes half the morning to gather the greens we want, and that at a season when we should spend the time planting the vegetable garden.

Of wild roots, there aren't many that are really palatable or worth the work. Jerusalem artichokes are treasured by

some people. These plants are really sunflowers, with no relation either to Jerusalem or the artichoke, but they produce
knotty roots that are edible, Spring and Fall. We find them
a satisfactory substitute for water chestnuts in Chinese food.
We also eat them with Hollandaise sauce. They are hard to
peel raw, but the skins slip off easily after they are boiled.
They are sometimes called Indian potatoes, and I assume
that the Indians roasted and ate them. I understand that the
Indians also roasted and ate the fat root of the Jack-in-the-
pulpit, which is sometimes called Indian turnip. Raw or
even partially cooked, that root is fiery hot to the taste. The
Indians can have it, as far as I go. Groundnuts, which belong to the same family as clover and peanuts, also have
edible roots which, when boiled, taste something like turnips. But for the turnip flavor I prefer turnips, which are
more easily dug and much more easily peeled.

Real nuts are in another category. Hickory nuts, walnuts,
butternuts, pecans, hazelnuts—they are all good fare. And
if one lives in or visits the Southwest, I would definitely add
piñon nuts, tedious though they are to gather and to shell.
Squirrels also know the virtue of wild nuts, however, and
there is always the question of who will harvest first, you
or the squirrels. If the squirrels get first chance, those that
are left for you will be the culls. Although there is a good
deal of hazel brush on my place, I have yet to pick a quart
of ripe hazelnuts for myself. The only way I can beat the
squirrels to them is to gather the nuts still green and hope
they ripen on the stem in my woodshed. Even then, the
squirrels get half of them, since the squirrels get into the
woodshed.

Some acorns are edible, chiefly those of the white oaks.
The Indians are said to have eaten quantities of them, even
to have made a kind of bread out of acorn meal. I've never
gone that far. But a white-oak acorn sometimes tastes to me
like a chestnut tinged with tannic acid, just enough to
pucker my mouth a little. I have roasted them and found
them moderately tasty, after the first one or two had accustomed my mouth to the flavor. But the acorns from the
red oaks all are bitter, heavily tinged with tannic acid. The
Indians gathered both kinds, white and red, leached them
with water after the nuts had been ground into meal. I have
heard of white folk using acorn meal, leached under running water, to make muffins, using a corn-muffin recipe, but

I have never tasted them. If you like the unusual, you might try it.

When it comes to fruit and berries, you will find a wealth of them in nearly any woodland, brush patch, or old meadow. Wild strawberries are classic gourmet fare. Once or twice we have made wild-strawberry jam, which is very special; but we prefer to eat them as they come from the vine, sun-warm, or to have a handful in cream at breakfast time. Occasionally we mix them with tame berries in the breakfast bowl. And always wish we hadn't because the wild ones make the tame ones taste flat and flavorless.

Wild raspberries are also special with us. If you have the red ones in your area, appreciate them. Ours are mostly the small black-caps, but we pick all we can find and eat them raw or freeze them for a special treat in Midwinter. We have made jam from them and jelly; but the jam is rather seedy. The red ones make better jam but not as good jelly as the black-caps. A mixture of the two makes excellent jam.

Wild blackberries are perfect in any form, raw in milk or cream, in jam or jelly, or frozen. Raspberries and blackberries grow on country roadsides, in the edge of the woods, and in fence rows.

Blueberries and huckleberries are traditional New England fare but I have never acquired a taste for them. I eat my blueberries as I pick them, in the open, and a few handfuls satisfy me. But that is a personal matter. Look for blueberries in oak woods or on high hillsides where there once were groves of oaks. They like acid soil and seldom grow in broad-leaf woodlands except where oaks predominate.

Chokecherries make excellent jelly with a special tang, but the birds love them and usually force us to pick ours before they are fully ripe. I always find the best chokecherries near a bog or other wetland. Elderberries present the same problem as chokecherries—the birds beat us to them. But we usually get our share, enough for jelly. Some people make elderberry pie, which is quite a chore. And the result reminds me of blueberry pie. Elderberries also prefer damp soil near bogs or along stream banks. Look for them there.

Among the lesser berries are those of the pimbina or "high-bush cranberry." We have made jelly from them as well as sauce, both of which have much the same flavor as true cranberries. Real cranberries also grow wild throughout the Northeast. You will find them in lowland bogs, and you will have to wear boots to gather them. And among the thornless bush berries are a number of viburnum fruits that are edible. You might try nannyberry, or wild raisin, whose fresh fruit is rather insipid but tastes much like commercial raisins when it shrivels in late Fall. Shadblow or serviceberry has a mild, sweet-flavored fruit with a texture like a mellow, juicy apple. But the birds and squirrels usually beat me to them, in my woods. They also grow in moist soil, near streams, usually.

All roses, since they belong to the same family as the apple, have edible seed pods or hips. They have a rather sharp tang, and I am told that they are full of vitamin C. I pluck them occasionally in September, when they are apple-red, and suck their juice; and once we gathered a quart of ripe hips from the wild roses along the pasture line, crushed them, stewed them, strained out the juice, and made a couple of glasses of jelly. It looked like apple jelly, and it had a fine, sharp, wild tang. But the job of making the jelly is tedious, and there aren't enough wild roses around to provide many hips.

The wild grapes are really our stand-by for wild jelly. They grow in the woods and at the roadside all over my area. There is even a tangle of them on one section of the garden fence which about one year in three bears heavily. They happen to be the tiny river grapes, only about a quarter of an inch in diameter, but they make superior jelly. We pick them by the bunch, wash them, sort out the twigs and leaves and stems, simmer them, crush them, set them to drain in a jelly bag, and make wild grape jelly every year. One year when the wild crop was short I mixed them, about half and half, with domestic Concords, but the result was a compromise, good enough but not the real wild grape. We've never adulterated them since.

On my mountainside there is a small grove of wild plum trees. I don't know where they come from, but they are beautiful in May, when in full bloom, and they bear plums about the size of my thumb-end. When those plums ripen to a ruddy red, early in September, I pick a few pecks of them and we make jam. It is one of the best of all jams, we think, especially with roasts and particularly with venison. The jam process takes time, since we slit each plum, take out the seed, and save both the seeds and the pitted plums. We cook seeds and plums separately, then add the juice from the seeds to the simmering pulp and throw the seeds away. This way we save the flavor of the pulp that has clung to the seeds. Then we add about one cup of sugar to each two cups of pulp and simmer pulp, skins, and juice until the skins are tender and the color has deepened. It takes hours, but when the mixture has reached the right point for jam we pour it into jelly glasses, seal it, and stow it away. This is one tedious job well worth the bother.

There are also edible wild mushrooms, quite a number of them. But unless one knows which are which among the mushrooms, it is downright stupid to eat them. Some are mildly poisonous, some are deadly poisonous. We pick and eat morels and puffballs, which are quite easy to recognize; but I wouldn't even attempt to describe them because there are poisonous mushrooms that somewhat resemble both of them. If you want to eat wild mushrooms, study micology, learn which are which. There are about two dozen poisonous forms, many of which are quite common and several of which resemble edible species.

Some of the bracket fungi which grow on dead or dying trees are also edible, but again the same warning holds—unless you know which are which, don't eat them. It is my experience that even the edible bracket fungi are rather tasteless and usually tough. All the fungi, whether edible or poisonous, are interesting to study as forms of plant life. But only the expert, or at least the well informed, should eat those which grow wild.

When it comes to fish and wild game someone always raises the question of the propriety of killing birds and animals—few people seem to have strong feelings about killing fish. I have no prejudice about taking birds, animals, or fish for food if the laws allow it, if the species is plentiful, and if the hunter or fisherman doesn't kill and catch just to be killing and catching. When a species is scarce, only a fool kills. And the hunter or fisherman who doesn't use the meat he takes is nothing more than a slaughterer. I hunt and fish, in season, and make no apology for it. We eat the game I take. When a species is scarce, I stop hunting it and forbid all shooting on my land until that species has re-established itself. To me, that only makes sense. I think that bag limits, both for hunting and fishing, should be set according to the supply, not the demand, and they might well be changed from year to year and certainly from area to area.

With a river in our dooryard, we do a good deal of fishing, as I said in an earlier chapter. Most years we freeze fifteen or twenty pounds of fillets from the fish we catch for Winter use. In the Summer we eat a good deal of fresh fish. Our river has, in numbers that vary from year to year, brown and brook trout, yellow perch, rock bass, various of the sunfishes, both small- and large-mouth bass, and an occasional pickerel, as well as catfish, suckers, silver carp, and other fish that we do not eat. Even these are edible. They are best in Spring and Fall, when their flesh is firm and relatively sweet in taste. In hot weather they are soft and sometimes taste of mud.

When we get big bass or trout, we usually bake them whole. Smaller trout we usually fry whole. All other fish I skin and fillet, and we fry or broil the fillets. We freeze only the fillets, and in Winter we fry or broil them or make fish chowder from them. I skin all except trout and big bass because I think it is easier than scaling them.

I have tried all kinds of tools and gadgets for skinning, scaling, and filleting fish and have come down to an ordinary fish knife and a pair of common pliers as most satisfactory of all. To skin and fillet a fish, I slit the skin all the way around the neck just back of the gills. Then I make a deep cut the length of the back, with an added slit on both sides of the dorsal fin. Then a shallow slit all down the belly, just through the skin, and again a deep cut on both sides of the anal fin. Next I pull out the dorsal and anal fins with the pliers; they come out quite easily, and this removes the small fin bones. Then, holding the fish by the head, I get a firm hold with the pliers on the skin at the top of the neck and peel off one side, all the way to the tail, turn the fish over, and peel off the skin from the other side. There is the fish, skinned and with the big fins removed. To fillet it, I go in along the backbone with the knife, working as close to the ribs as possible, and slice off the fillet toward the tail. The same on the other side and the job is done. Head, bones, and entrails are left intact, to be discarded or buried in the garden. When the fillets are washed, they are ready for the pan or the freezer pack. With this method I can fillet a dozen fish in ten minutes.

I know fishermen who take their fillets by gutting the fish, slicing through the ribs close to the backbone, then slicing neatly downward with the knife and removing the bones in what seems to be one deft gesture. That, too, is a good way, but I prefer mine.

The only rule I would suggest about cooking freshwater fish is to have them cooked through but not overdone. Our test is to have the cooked fish flaky. When we bake fish we strip them with bacon and often put bacon inside as well. The only seasoning we use is salt and pepper; I have a prejudice against sauces on fish. Sometimes we dot fillets generously with butter, salt and pepper them, then wrap them, several in a pack, in aluminum foil, and bake or broil them. This is a good method for cooking fish over an open fire, too. Any good chowder recipe works for making fish chowder, but my preference is for a minimum of herbs in it. Fresh fish, like fresh game of any kind, has its own flavor which should not be smothered with herbs. But I insist on having my fresh fish fresh. While we are fishing, we keep those we have caught on a stringer and in the water. If any are dead before I am ready to clean them, I discard the dead ones. I kill the live fish just before I dress them at the fish-sink, an old kitchen sink I have rigged with running water out beside the garage.

Game birds, on the other hand, benefit by being hung or even frozen for a few days. But I prefer to have them gutted soon after they are killed, even though I do not pluck them until the day we eat them. The flavor of any bird depends in large part on its diet, and game birds eat different food at different seasons of the year. Fish-eating ducks have a fishy flavor. Winter grouse often have a cedar or hemlock flavor because they have been eating cedar berries or hemlock needles. In the West, sage grouse have the flavor of the sage leaves they eat. And any bird badly shot up will have a strong taste from the fluids in the intestinal track unless gutted as soon as it is killed. It is my experience that game birds with an unpleasantly rank flavor have been taken at the wrong season, have been improperly dressed, or have been hung too long. If I find any bird has an unpleasant odor when I dress it, I don't try to eat it.

In cooking all game birds, we treat them much the same as tame fowl. We stuff ruffed grouse with bread stuffing made from the same recipe we use for roasting chickens, and we roast them the same way. With all game birds, however, it is necessary to baste with oil or fat, since they have drier meat than pen-fed domestic birds. We sometimes strip those we roast with bacon. This holds true for grouse, pheasant, ducks, even geese, though wild geese are fatter than any of the others.

Nearly all birds are edible, but I wouldn't shoot a song bird for anything. In Europe they even eat larks, which seems to me barbaric. Besides, there isn't a mouthful of meat on any lark I ever saw. I have eaten doves, but haven't shot one since I was a boy; to me, it is almost like eating robins, which I would deplore utterly. There are places in this country where people eat blackbirds, and I have heard of people eating crows. They seem to me like starvation fare, both of them. But ducks, geese, grouse, partridges, pheasants, woodcocks, and quail where they are plentiful—all are legitimate fare and all have their merits at the table. But, as with fish, I frown on sauces and elaborate flavoring for birds. Their own flavor should not be masked. If one doesn't like that flavor, one should eat domestic birds, chicken or turkey.

Much the same rules hold for game animals, and again it is essential that the meat be fresh and properly handled. When I shoot rabbits I like to gut them in the field, and when I take a deer I bleed it at once and hog-dress it as soon as I can get it hung up. Game animals, just as domestic meat, should be bled thoroughly and cooled at once if the flavor of the meat is to be right. When I see hunters carting a deer carcass for miles on the fender of a car, usually in the hot sun and always with the car's engine keeping it warm, I know why so many people find venison a "strong" meat. If they did the same thing to beef or lamb it would be just as rank.

The quality of venison—all wild meat, for that matter—depends on whether it is fat or lean and what it has been feeding on. Winter deer that have lots of evergreen browse in their diet are, to my taste, inferior venison. I'll take my deer in the late Fall, when they are well larded with fat and before they have started eating cedar or hemlock. There is a firm difference of opinion about whether does or bucks make the best venison and whether a buck with a trophy head—a big, old buck—is worth eating. I prefer my venison young, and if I have a choice between a big, old buck and a three-year-old doe, I'll take the doe. But some hunters whose opinion I respect say the biggest buck in the herd, if he is fat, makes the best meat. Such a buck will be satisfactorily fat only before the rutting season. It is generally agreed that late Winter or Spring venison is inferior, lacking fat, tasting of evergreen browse, and generally tough. And only a fool or a starving man would kill a doe in the Spring, when she is carrying fawns.

After a deer carcass is hog-dressed—the intestines and other organs removed—it should be left hanging to cool. I prefer to skin my deer before it cools; some wait till they are ready to cut it up. I have heard deer hunters say that a venison should be hung for two weeks before it is cut up. I think this is nonsense. Venison is ready to cut up, to cook, to eat, to stow in the freezer, as soon as the carcass is thoroughly cooled. Some of the best venison we ever had was cut up the second day after it was taken. Some of the most unpalatable venison I ever tasted was given to me by a man who left it hanging for ten days. No wonder such meat has to be soaked in wine and vinegar, marinated is the term, before it can be eaten.

Once we have fresh, properly butchered venison, we treat it like any domestic meat. We broil the chops and steaks, dotting them liberally with butter unless the meat has plenty of fat of its own. Sometimes we fry chops and steaks. Venison shouldn't be broiled or fried too long. Medium rare is about right. And the only seasoning it needs it salt and pepper.

We treat venison roasts like lamb roasts, and again don't cook them too long. And we make venison stew exactly as we make lamb stew. Never do we marinate venison. We tried it, egged on by cookbooks written by people who apparently never had prime, fresh venison; we soaked venison chops and steaks and roasts for hours and days in spiced wine and vinegar, according to the recipes. And after we had cooked them we tasted them and threw them out. The marinades and elaborate sauces and gravies just didn't go with our kind of venison. They spoiled good meat.

The same is true of rabbit. Young rabbit is as sweet a meat as chicken, and we cook it much the same way, frying it or roasting it with none of the tricks the cookbook writers think up for disguising the flavor of old meat or rancid meat. Old, tough rabbit isn't worth eating, no matter how it is disguised.

Gray squirrel is considered good eating in some places and in certain areas is hunted as a game animal. I have eaten squirrel stew and don't care for it, certainly not enough to shoot squirrels and cook them. Squirrel meat is somewhat more gamy in flavor than rabbit, but quite palatable.

Raccoon is thoroughly good to eat and makes a tasty roast with a flavor something like rabbit. Opossum is regarded as a delicacy in the South, with a flavor something like pork; it is a fat meat and the fat, I understand, is rather strong in flavor. Roast 'possum and sweet potatoes make good fare, if you like 'possum.

Woodchuck is not only edible but, I understand, quite palatable. It should be. The woodchuck is a rather fastidious vegetarian, clean in habits and diet. Call it a ground hog and there should be no particular distaste about eating it.

Bear meat, if from a young, fat bear, is excellent, particularly when roasted. Beaver meat is good, and beaver tail is a food of long and honorable tradition, even regarded as a delicacy by beaver trappers of the past. The meat is dark but not especially strong in flavor.

In fact, most animal meat can be eaten, as hungry men have proved time and again. A friend of mine tells me that he ate wolf meat once, a roasted ham of fat wolf, and found it tough but palatable. Since the Indians ate dog meat, I can accept his appraisal and stand on that. Men lost in the woods have killed and eaten porcupine and survived, though none that I know would recommend porcupine as a gourmet item. I once heard of a man who had cooked and sampled skunk meat. He didn't recommend it, though he insisted that it didn't taste really bad; he just kept remembering how the animal smelled when it was alive.

Muskrat makes quite acceptable table meat, something like rabbit. In fact, a good deal of muskrat meat is sold and eaten in Louisiana under the name "marsh hare." I have never known of anyone eating fox or bobcat, but either one would certainly be edible if a man were hungry enough. Long ago I ate fried prairie dog and found it much like jack rabbit. The prairie dog is a minor cousin of the woodchuck, a vegetarian like the rabbit, and if it weren't for the name it might have become a common item in the country diet of the West. But prairie dogs were starvation fare and weren't eaten even by hungry men as long as they could get prong-horn antelope or rabbits. The prong-horns' meat, which I have eaten, tastes like lamb; like strong mutton, if the prong-horn is an old buck.

Even snakes and insects are edible, though most of us want none of them. Years ago I was tricked into eating rattlesnake meat, which tasted something like fishy chicken. But when somebody began canning rattlesnake meat for sale to experimental eaters a few years ago I didn't see any rush to buy it. Probably most people feel as I do about eating snakes. And although roasted grasshoppers and chocolate-covered ants have been offered to devotees of exotic foods, they don't seem to have stampeded the market.

Turtles, of course, are not only edible but provide gourmet items such as turtle steaks and turtle soup. The big snapping turtles are the best flavored of our common turtles. They have to be butchered with an ax, however, and one must know how to choose and extract the meat. The amateur will be wise to leave turtles alone unelss he is an insistent experimenter or lost and starving.

To sum up, the person who knows what to look for and where to find it would have no reason to starve in the woods, even today. A natural abundance is available, though it takes a bit of knowledge to find it and make the best use of it. Few of us, however, are equipped by either knowledge or inclination to live entirely on this abundance. Most country folk, when they use wild plants at all, eat them only a few times a year. Fish and game are more common than wild plants on the rural table.

All wild fare, plant, animal, bird, or fish, demands care in the taking, the preparation, and the cooking. Unless one knows how to handle it one is better off with bread and butter, meat and potatoes, fruit and vegetables, all from the nearest market. But those who take game or fish should remember two things. First, treat all wild meat, from butchering to refrigeration, with the same care you give expensive beefsteak or swordfish. Second, cook it simply. Most cookbook recipes for wild meat either mask its flavor or ruin it for any sensitive palate.

## Chapter 13

# Out of This
# Nettle, Danger

THERE are some things, but not too many,
toward which the countryman knows he
must be properly respectful if he would
avoid pain, sickness, and injury. Nature
is neither punitive nor solicitous, but she
has thorns and fangs as well as bowers
and grassy banks.

*What*," the newcomer to the country sometimes asks, "are the hazards? There must be vicious animals, poisonous snakes and insects, and poisonous plants. Which are the dangerous ones, and how dangerous are they?"

Of course there are hazards. There are hazards everywhere. But, on the whole, city life is more hazardous than life in the country. The principal difference is that those accustomed to urban life are aware of the hazards in the city and avoid them almost by instinct; they are less aware of rural hazards, and the unknown is always disturbing. But this must be said: There are practically no vicious animals left in the United States, very few in the East, and even they will run from a human being unless they are wounded or cornered. Poisonous snakes are rare and seldom bite unless cornered or stepped on. Insects can be a painful nuisance but almost never worse than that except to unusually allergic persons. There are poisonous roots, berries, and mushrooms, but only a fool eats those he cannot positively identify.

Actually, the most dangerous living thing I know of in this country, plant, animal, snake, or insect, is poison ivy. And it grows in cities and suburbs as well as in the country. I believe that more people suffer from ivy poisoning every year than from any other natural hazard except possibly sunburn. For every person bitten by a snake or a spider, clawed by a bear or made ill by eating poisonous plants, ten thousand others probably require medical help or hospitalization for ivy poisoning.

I shall take up the other hazards one by one, but let's start with poison ivy.

Botanically, poison ivy is a cousin of the harmless common sumac. It grows both as a climbing vine and as a sprawling shrub, and it grows in almost any kind of soil, in sun or shade. It is most common in good soil, in damp places, and in partial shade. Every part of the plant—root, stem, leaf, and berry—contains an oil called cardol that is an extreme irritant to the skin. Some people are immune to it—I seem to be; but that immunity sometimes disappears overnight. One friend of mine was acutely susceptible until he was in his twenties, was then immune for ten years or so, and without warning became susceptible again, even more so than in his youth.

Contact with the plant usually has no immediate effect, but within hours, nearly always within a day, a rash appears. The rash soon becomes a mass of small blisters. If much of an area is affected it can be not merely painful but serious. Susceptible persons can be infected by handling clothes someone else has worn in ivy-grown places. They can get it by touching dogs or cats that have been in an ivy patch. They can even get it by standing in the smoke from a fire in which any part of the plant is being burned.

Any number of "cures" and "preventives" have been tried, including pills and injections. I know of none that is universally effective, probably because of the individual differences in susceptibility and skin sensitivity. Among everyday remedies, washing with strong soap soon after exposure usually is of great help because it removes and neutralizes the poisonous oil, which is chemically acid. The application of any alkaline substance seems to help. Some people wash exposed areas with white gasoline and get relief. Among natural remedies, the juice of the common jewelweed appears to be effective for some cases. A handful of the plant's juicy stems and leaves is crushed and rubbed on the affected skin. Unless one uses a strong alkaline soap and uses it generously, a bath after exposure can spread the infection and make it worse.

The best means of protection I know is to recognize the plant and avoid contact with it. Poison ivy is easily identified, once one knows it by sight, but the uninitiated sometimes confuse it with Virginia creeper, another common but harmless vine.

Virginia creeper, sometimes called woodbine, grows as poison ivy does, in old stone walls and on trees. But Virginia creeper leaves, lance-shaped, saw-toothed, and deep green, grow in groups of five, occasionally seven. Poison ivy leaves grow in groups of three, never five. Poison ivy leaves are smooth-edged lighter green, and broader in shape than Virginia creeper leaves, and have a shiny, oily look. Virginia creeper leaves tend to droop on their stems. Poison ivy leaves stand up straight. Virginia creeper's stems are smooth, like grapevines. Poison ivy stems often have grayish-white, whiskery-looking rootlets by which they cling to stones and tree trunks.

The blossoms of both plants are small, dull greenish-white, but those of poison ivy are in compact clusters, those of Virginia creeper in loose clusters. In late Summer and early Fall poison ivy berries, about one-eighth inch in diameter, ripen to lead gray or lusterless white. Ripe Virginia creeper berries are purple; they look like tiny Concord grapes. Poison ivy berries are borne on green stems. Virginia creeper berries are on red stems. When the leaves turn, poison ivy usually is lemon yellow or rich orange, sometimes red. Virginia creeper leaves turn deep crimson, sometimes scarlet, seldom yellow or orange.

If there is any doubt about whether a plant is poison ivy or Virginia creeper, avoid it until you are sure which it is. But once it has been identified, poison ivy is recognizable anywhere. You seem to know it, almost by instinct, at a glance.

Two other plants, both cousins of poison ivy, can be equally painful and in much the same way. One is poison sumac which, although it grows from Maine to Florida and west to Minnesota, is usually found in low, wet ground and boggy places. In the Northeast it is said to be seldom found far from the seacoast. However, I recently identified a specimen only a few miles from my house and more than a hundred miles from the seacoast. It is growing in relatively dry soil on a side road frequently used by bird watchers. I wonder how many persons have carelessly brushed against it and mistaken the consequent skin eruptions for an unusually virulent attack of ivy poisoning. It is the only poison sumac I have seen for miles around, but the birds will eat its berries and plant its seeds elsewhere. We may yet have poison sumac as a common menace in this unlikely area.

Poison sumac looks much like the common, harmless sumac, though it grows as a round-topped bush or low tree while the harmless sumac usually is flat-topped. Poison sumac's blossoms and fruit are borne in loose, slender clusters at the junction of leaf-stem and branch. Harmless sumac blossoms and fruit come in tight clumps at the branch tips. Poison sumac berries ripen to dull greenish-white, something like poison-ivy berries. Harmless sumac fruit ripens in stiff, upright clusters, usually conical in shape and velvety maroon in color.

The other poisonous relative of the ivy is poison oak. It is said to grow only from Virginia southward and in the Deep South, always in thin woods and waste places. Having found poison sumac in my own unlikely area, I hesitate to agree with the guidebooks that poison oak is always confined to those areas. I know it also grows in California, for instance. Poison oak's leaves look something like the familiar oak leaves but, like those of poison ivy, they grow in groups of three. Its berries are much like those of poison ivy in shape, size, and color. If you should find an "oak" shrub bearing greenish-white berries instead of acorns, even if you find it in Maine or New Jersey or Iowa, leave it strictly alone. It is not a true oak and it is not harmless. It is *poison* oak and as treacherous as poison ivy.

I know of no other plants as poisonous on contact or as potentially dangerous as these three allied cousins of the common sumac, poison ivy, poison sumac, and poison oak. Nettles are troublesome, but they cause only a stinging itch that is gone in a few hours. Thistles are prickly. Various briers and thorny bushes can be a nuisance but they are not dangerous, certainly no more of a peril than the rosebushes in any flower garden. Cat brier, a well-armed cousin of the common smilax, creates impenetrable tangles now and then. Wild raspberries and wild blackberries can be punishing to clothing and skin. Barberry, which often grows wild, can be a thorny proposition. There are thorn trees, such as the hawthorns and locusts, which any sensible person will avoid. But the person who is afraid of all thorns and briers had better stay at home and indoors.

As for poisonous berries, there are a few which will

make the person who eats them distressingly uncomfortable. Children especially should be warned not to eat strange berries, no matter how pretty and inviting they may look. The red baneberry looks good enough to eat but it can cause stomach cramps or, if taken in quantity, illness that may call for a doctor. Some of the nightshade family have poisonous berries that are invitingly red and juicy-looking.

The best advice about wild berries is that one should not eat any that cannot be definitely identified. Almost everyone knows wild strawberries, raspberries, and blackberries, and the novice who confines his wild-fruit diet to those will have no trouble. He may miss a good many other edible berries, but he will also avoid possible nausea, cramps, and even the attention of a doctor.

When it comes to wild mushrooms, the word for the novice is: "No!" Unless one knows, for sure, which ones to pick, it is foolhardy to eat them. Many people know puffballs and morels, but there is a poisonous false-morel, and several non-edible mushrooms in their early stages look like young puffballs. Many wild mushrooms are edible, some of them delicious, and only a few such as the *Amanitas* are critically poisonous, though at least a dozen of them can cause acute distress. Anyone who wants to learn which are which can, with proper study and guidance, soon identify and classify as edible or inedible the common ones in his area. But until you know your wild mushrooms, don't eat them.

As for ferocious animals, virtually none are left in the East and few in the West, if one excludes the temperamental bears that often beg for food in the National Parks. Here or there in the East there is an occasional report of a panther or cougar—one was reported on the mountain just back of my house this past Winter. There certainly could be a few panthers in the more rugged areas, but unless they were cornered or wounded they probably would run at the sight of a man. The one reported on my mountain fled from the man who saw it and apparently kept on going, because several of us looked for it and never got sight of it.

The panther is America's biggest cat except the jaguar, weighing as much as 250 pounds and sometimes more than seven feet long, tail and body. In the West it is called a mountain lion and sometimes kills sheep and young cattle; but I never knew of one making an un-provoked attack on a man. In colonial days panthers were well known in the Northeast, at least by reputation. The panther's scream was a byword for terror in the night, and hair-raising tales were told about the beast, most of them by people who never had seen a panther. I have heard of panthers trailing a man and of wounded panthers attacking and even killing foolhardy hunters; but I have yet to see an authenticated instance of unprovoked attack by one. It is safe to say that not one person in a million of those who tramp the woods will ever see a panther, and even then it will be a panther in full flight away from him.

Our other two wild cats are the lynx and the bobcat. The lynx is now gone from nearly all parts of the United States except certain wilderness mountain areas of Idaho, Washington, and Oregon. The lynx fights back only when cornered or wounded, and in any case will not be found in the Northeast. We do have bobcats in wooded and mountainous areas. There are a few on my own mountain and one once mauled my dog. The bobcat is smaller than the lynx, less than three feet long, is in no sense dangerous, and will run from a human being. Or from a dog, if it has a chance.

In the United States, outside Alaska, there are only two kinds of bear, the black bear, sometimes in a cin-namon phase, and the grizzly. In 1950 there were only 750 known grizzlies in this country, most of them in a wilderness area of Montana but a few in similar areas of Wyoming, Idaho, and Washington. Few Americans except hunters and professional guides will ever see a grizzly outside a zoo. Black bears, on the other hand, persist in the mountain areas of the East as well as in the western mountains. Now and then a black bear wanders down out of the hills and prowls through the countryside, raids garbage cans and public dumps, hides in the woods, scares suburban housewives, and gets shot by a policeman. A few years ago one wandered through my area, frightened a few motorists out for Sunday drives, dug up a few compost heaps, and vanished over the hills unscathed. Black bears don't care for human company and will run at the sight of a man. But a mother bear with cubs can be dangerous and probably will be truculent. If you ever see such a bear, leave her alone, and particularly leave the cubs alone, and she will go on about her business, glad to get away from you. If you visit parks such as Yellowstone, where bears seem quite tame and often beg for food, be wary of them. A bear isn't a dog. Its moods are unpredictable. Otherwise, there is no danger from bears, even in the thickest eastern woodland.

Porcupines can be both painful and even dangerous if one tries to bother them. Left alone, they will amble off without bothering anyone. If camping in porcupine territory, however, make sure that boots and all other leather gear, even canoe paddles and axes, are safely out of their reach. They will wander into camp in the night and rip boots to pieces or gnaw canoe paddles and ax handles, apparently liking the salty sweat on them. And keep dogs away from porcupines. Most dogs are tempted to attack the lumbering creatures, and if they get a mouthful of quills they probably will need the help of a veterinarian.

Skunks are too well known to need much additional warning. They, too, will amble off if given a chance. But they refuse to be crowded or hurried, by anyone or anything, including an automobile. Their nauseous spray is contained in twin glands situated on each side of the tail, and each gland has enough for four of five shots. The spray can be squirted twelve or fifteen feet. Besides being nauseating, this spray can burn the skin and blind the eyes. A dog which has been skunked can be made moderately acceptable socially by rubbing him thoroughly with tomato juice, catsup, almost any tomato preparation, then washing him with a strong soap or detergent. That is the method I use with my own dog. I have heard that a vinegar bath is also effective, but I have never tried it. The tomato-scrub is also effective on a person who has been skunked; but the best thing to do with the clothes such a person was wearing at the time is to burn them or throw them away. I have never heard of an effective way to clean an automobile that has hit a skunk and been sprayed. The odor persists for weeks. Avoid skunks, afoot or in a car. They are willing to avoid you if you give them a chance.

Probably the most vicious animal in America, if not in the world, when considered ounce for ounce, is the shrew. Fortunately, shrews are very small animals, even smaller than a field mouse. In appearance, the shrew is something like a small mouse with a long, tapering nose and inconspicuous eyes and ears. It is usually mole-gray in color, often almost silvery. As mentioned before, shrews live in open fields and thin woodlands, eat almost anything they can find, mostly insects and grubs, and have such a high metabolism that they must consume about twice their own weight every twenty-four hours. A friend of mine has caught several of them in humane traps, but all were caught at night and were dead by the next morning, apparently starved to death.

The shrews I have seen were all very hungry, scurrying about in search of food. They can be truculent and surprisingly aggressive for such small creatures. Few people ever see shrews, so they are not really a hazard. But if you try to catch a field mouse in your bare hands, be sure it is a mouse, not a shrew. If it has visible ears, it isn't a shrew.

Most wild animals will bite or scratch if they are cornered or caught. Even a rabbit can scratch like a cat, on occasion, and both red and gray squirrels can give one a painful bite with needle-sharp teeth. Young raccoons may be cute as kittens, but their teeth can be painful and their tempers can be short. All wild animals resent loss of freedom, and usually they will fight anyone who captures them with whatever means they have. It is a good rule to leave them alone, even young animals. The mother is probably somewhere around and will return to take care of them as soon as you go away.

As for snakes, there are only a few poisonous ones—the Eastern coral snake, the cottonmouth or moccasin, the copperhead, and the various rattlesnakes.

Despite its name, the Eastern coral snake is found only in the South, no farther north than central North Carolina. It is the only American snake with a black snout and body rings of black-yellow-red-yellow-black, in that order. There are other snakes with alternate color rings on the body, but none with the black snout and the same sequence of color rings. But, to repeat, the coral snake is never seen north of the Carolinas.

The cottonmouth is also a southern snake, sometimes found as far north as coastal Virginia. It tends to be a big snake, as much as six feet long, and is brown with wide, indistinct black bands. It is almost invariably found in or near bogs, marshes or other wetlands, including riverbanks. Again, to repeat, the cottonmouth is never found north of Virginia, and there only near the coast.

The copperhead is found from central Texas to the East Coast and from the Gulf to southern Illinois, Indiana, and Ohio, in most of Pennsylvania, lower New York, all of Connecticut and Massachusetts. It is usually found in dry upland woods, on rocky hillsides and ledges, and especially in rocky hills or mountainous country. In Summer it may move into more lowland areas. It grows to about four and a half feet in length. The northern copperhead is marked with dark, hourglass-shaped bands that enclose patches of light tan or a pinkish shade. Its head is coppery brown or even almost pink. The dark bands are somewhat less regular in pattern in the southern copperhead, and the color is somewhat lighter. The copperhead bites only if stepped on or touched. If exploring rocky hillsides or ledges known to have copperheads, be cautious. Wear stout leather boots in snake country, and don't reach blindly onto a ledge or down among the rocks.

Rattlesnakes can be distinguished by the loose, horny links at the end of the tail that form the rattle the snake vibrates as a warning. It has been said that the rattler is a gentleman because he always gives warning before striking. But don't rely on this. If stepped on, a rattler will strike first, then rattle—maybe. But the rattle, actually a high-pitched buzz, is fair warning if one is too close.

There are a number of types of rattlers, from the little sidewinder of the deserts to the seven-foot Western diamondback, from the small massasauga of the upper Midwest to the timber rattler of the East which sometimes grows to six feet in length. This timber rattler is the only one common to the Northeast, but the massasauga is found as far east as western Pennsylvania and New York. The timber rattler may be almost all black, or yellowish with brown or black crossbands. The massasauga is brown with squarish dark markings on its back, sometimes so dark as to look almost all black. Both species carry rattles on the tail and will give warning, if they have a chance, before they strike. The massasauga is a wetland snake, usually found in swamps. It is the only American snake that still carries the original Indian name. The timber rattler likes the same kind of terrain where one finds copperheads, but sometimes is found on the edge of swamps.

The number of people who die of snakebite is still so small that an instance is headline news. If one is bitten, open the wound, let it bleed, apply a tourniquet above the wound, and get to a doctor as soon as possible. Antivenin is usually effective. But best of all, avoid being bitten in the first place. Learn to recognize the poisonous snakes in your area, know where they are likely to be, and use ordinary caution. I live in copperhead and timber-rattler country, but I have never seen a snake of either species on my place though both species have been killed every Summer within a few miles of here. In the past ten years I have not heard of anyone in this whole area being bitten by a poisonous snake.

As I said earlier, most insect bites and stings are a painful nuisance and nothing more, for most people. The black-widow spider got a good deal of publicity a few years ago, but I have not heard of anyone seriously hurt by one. Black widows can be found here and there, but if they have half a chance they will run away and hide. They do not attack. Other spiders may bite if provoked, but usually with little more effect than a bee sting. There is little need to be wary of spiders.

Bees and wasps can cause more pain than any other insects I know, and some people are acutely sensitive to their sting. My wife is, and she has been painfully ill from the sting of a wasp. But the prompt administration of cortisone is an effective treatment, and we keep that drug on hand; and she works among the wasps in the garden just as I do and has been stung only three times in ten years. If a wasp or bee sting makes you sick, call a doctor at once.

Wasps are far more resentful of human intrusion than are bees. A few years ago I was watching a work party of paper wasps (hornets) at an old stump in the dooryard. They were suspicious of me but made no hostile move until I got out a magnifying glass. They took offense at that and four of them attacked me. One hit me on the forehead with a stinger like a red-hot needle. I got away from there in a hurry, but my forehead swelled up until my eyes were hooded. The pain was gone in a few hours but the swelling remained for three days. Leave the wasps alone if you don't want to get stung. Particularly avoid hornets. If you insist on watching them at work, sit or stand quietly and not too close to them.

Bumblebee stings can be almost as painful as a wasp sting. But bumblebees are less easily annoyed than wasps. They sometimes buzz noisily around me when I approach the delphiniums in the flower garden, which they regard as their own, but they have never stung me there. I have never been stung by a bumblebee except when I trapped one in my bare hand, for some stupid reason I now forget.

In early Spring there are gnats and midges to contend with—we speak of them as sap flies because they appear when sap is in full flow and leaf buds are opening, and as midges or no-see-ums. They are all midges, the smallest of all insect bloodsuckers, and can be a painful nuisance because they often arrive in swarms. An insect repellent, of which there are a number available in drugstores, helps to fend them off. A little later there are mosquitoes, especially in damp places. There are deer flies, bigger than house flies and with dark markings on their wings. Deer flies are persistent and inflict painful but not serious bites. I find insect repellents more effective with mosquitoes than with deer flies. In the North woods, and sometimes well south of that area, especially in boglands and along streams, the Summer is sometimes made almost insufferable by black flies. They have close cousins known in other areas as buffalo gnats and turkey gnats. They are all humpbacked insects as big as mosquitoes, and they are vicious biters. At the height of black-fly season in the North it is often necessary to wear head nets, and those hardy souls who disdain the nets use "fly dope," a repellent that is moderately effective. It also is quite effective against the swarms of mosquitoes that often accompany the black-fly hordes.

In case of insect bites, almost any mild alkaline substance helps to relieve the pain, since the toxic agent is acid. We use household ammonia applied to the bite. A paste of sodium bicarbonate, common cooking soda, often helps. As a boy I used a dab of mud on a bee or wasp sting and sometimes still do. For years, oil of citronella was believed to be the best repellent, but now there are others that seem to be more effective. For a time we used several of them that came in stick form, like camphor ice, but now prefer the spray-on type. But even among those we find some to be of little use, even though they work for other people. I suspect that the individual chemistry has something to do with this. I know that when I am sweaty I seem to be the special target of deer flies and mosquitoes, and at such times none of the repellents does much good.

There still remains the matter of fish and turtles. Any fish of the bass family can inflict minor wounds with the spines on the dorsal fins if you handle them carelessly. I have never known these punctures to be more than momentarily painful. All the catfishes have viciously sharp spines on the pectoral and dorsal fins. They can cause painful punctures in the careless hand, and sometimes these wounds become inflamed and fester. I doubt that there is any poison on the spines, but they can and probably do carry mud and muck into the wound. Ordinary care in handling catfish will avoid such sometimes painful but really minor injuries.

The only dangerous turtle is the snapper, and only an idiot would give a snapping turtle a chance to grab a finger. A big snapper could sever a man's finger in one bite. I have known a ten-pound snapper to bite a fishhook in two. On the few occasions when I have caught a snapper on my line while fishing I have cut the line above the hook and let it go, a procedure I recommend to anyone who isn't interested in eating turtle—or being wounded by one. If you want the turtle to eat, shoot it in the head or kill it somehow and certainly before you get your hand close enough for the snapper to reach with those steel-trap jaws.

One final entry and we have finished with the hazards. Under certain conditions, be wary of birds. Birds with young in their nests, particularly. Catbirds, robins, blue jays, even barn swallows sometimes become boldly truculent in their zeal as parents. Usually they do nothing more than scream repeated warnings when a person approaches the nest where the fledglings are almost ready to fly, but now and then they will attack. Such attacks can be frightening. A bird swooping at a person's face with angry beak and claws is nothing to be laughed at, and if both parents attack at once it is wise to retreat with an arm up protecting one's eyes.

Last Summer a pair of barn swallows nesting in my garage took offense at my wife and me even when we went to our rural mailbox fifty yards from the garage. They dive-bombed us angrily and one day attacked my wife so vigorously that, blinded by their swooping at her face, she fell and was painfully hurt. When I went to her rescue they attacked me the same way. I later went out with an umbrella, and when they returned to the attack I zoomed it open in their faces. The defense eventually was effective. The next afternoon the fledglings were out and flying and the parents' truculence ended. I recommend the umbrella treatment for any such unfriendly birds.

Adventurous ornithologists who have tried to examine or photograph the nests of hawks and eagles, especially when they have eggs or young, tell of vigorous attacks by the sharp-taloned parents. Such attacks, however, were invited by the intruders themselves. Most of us never get into such a position, and I have never known of hawks or eagles attacking anyone who left their nests alone.

Screech owls and great horned owls have been known to attack a person in the woods at dusk. They do it only on rare occasions. The screech owl is no bigger than the blue jay and can do little damage, but the great horned owl is a big bird and can inflict painful scratches. I suspect that owl attacks are mistakes, that the owls mistake the person for an animal that they can frighten off. But as I said, such attacks are rare; and they usually result in nothing worse than a few scratches.

So there are the hazards, all that I can think of. None of them is critical except snakebite and ivy poisoning. And for every person who even sees a poisonous snake, I will guess that 10,000 get ivy poisoning. Learn to recognize and avoid poison ivy and you will be as safe in the country as in any city apartment.

# Chapter 14

# Month by Month: What To Look For and When

EVERTHING has its season, but no season is without color and life, wonder and surprise. He who would know the world of which he is a part must know the way the January wind shapes a snowdrift as well as the ecstasy with which an oriole greets the June dawn.

*The march of the seasons* is fairly constant, not day by day but almost week by week. Winter may be what we call late or Spring may be early, but it is my experience that the seasons themselves tend to even out. I have kept a daily journal for twenty years, and when I go back and compare dates I usually find that two years out of three the first anemones, say, are in bloom the first week in April. Occasionally they appear a week or ten days earlier than that or a week later, but those years are exceptions. And the height of color in the trees comes, in my part of New England, four years out of five, some time during the week of October 12—though I admit it is hard to pick one particular day when the color is more magnificent than it was two days earlier or two days later; it depends on the sky as well as the trees. And, regardless of the actual date, there are certain seasonal matters that can be timed by each other. For instance, when the first migrant red-wing blackbirds appear I can begin to look for pussy willows, and when the pussy willows are in sight I watch for the returning robins. When the robins are here I listen for the call of the Spring peepers.

Such relationships, and the whole sequence of events outdoors, hold true almost everywhere. Therefore, a timetable for my own valley should be valid, within reasonable limits, for most of the Northeast if one makes a simple correction for latitude and elevation.

Spring moves northward at approximately sixteen miles a day or, roughly a hundred miles a week. This applies, however, only on level ground. When one begins to climb, the northward pace slackens, since Spring moves uphill only about one hundred feet a day. To take an example, I live approximately a hundred miles north of New York City. If forsythia begins to bloom along Riverside Drive in New York City on April 1, it would bloom here on April 7 or 8—if there were no difference in altitude. But New York is at sea level, and my valley has an altitude of almost 800 feet. That adds another eight days to the lag, so if forsythia blooms in New York City on April 1, it probably won't bloom here until around April 15.

A friend of mine in the Philadelphia area reports that his records of Spring events outdoors show about three weeks' head start over my records here. That is about right, by the formula—200 miles, north to south, and about 800 feet difference in altitude. Washington, D.C., would be another week ahead of Philadelphia. Northward, another friend in central Vermont, just about a hundred miles from here, reports that Spring is normally a week behind its schedule here. Again, that conforms to the formula, since his area is about the same altitude as mine. There are variations because of local conditions, of course. Places near the seashore are somewhat warmer than those inland, hence somewhat earlier; and places on major lakes are also somewhat warmer than their latitude might imply. But that hundred miles a week, hundred feet of altitude a day, can be taken as a reasonably accurate guide.

In the Fall, of course, the whole process is reversed, since Autumn moves southward. However, Autumn moves south at just about the same rate that Spring moves north.

The timetable in this chapter, then, is set down in terms of my own valley's natural happenings. If a reader lives 300 miles south of here—calculate from the northern boundary of Connecticut, which is only a mile or so from my house—then what is happening here in the Spring probably will be happening in the reader's area at least three weeks earlier. If the reader lives at or near sea level, another week must be added to account for the 800 feet difference in altitude making almost a month's difference. If I find anemones in bloom here the first week in April, that reader probably will find them the first week in March. And the reverse will be true in the Autumn; what happens here in September will happen there in October. Mid-summer and Midwinter dates, however, will be approximately the same.

The events mentioned in the timetable are only a sampling of what one may expect, month by month. They are highlights, drawn from my own journals, and those I have included are here because they seem to be typical and I have experienced them year after year. There are many exceptions even to these typical incidents. It is the exceptions that make the outdoors everlastingly interesting. My friend in Pennsylvania, for example, once found trailing arbutus in bloom on February 22, though the usual date is more than a month later. And one year I saw migrant bluebirds here in the valley on February 24, though March 25 is early for them normally.

I have begun the timetable with March, which long ago was considered the year's first month because it marked the turn from Winter toward Spring. To me it is the beginning of the natural year.

## March

MAPLE SYRUP TIME. Some years the sap begins to rise in February, but more often it waits for March. It flows best when days are mild, in the 40's and 50's, and nights are still frosty. It may start in a warm spell, stop if the days turn cold, then start again. Old-time sugarmen think snow on the ground helps. I know when the sap flow starts by watching the squirrels. They seem to know instinctively, go into the maples, nip off a few twigs, and lap the sap as it oozes. Chickadees also watch the squirrels and drink at the "taps" when the squirrels are away.

Geese sometimes fly north now. They fly high and their gabble is like the distant barking of small dogs. If they fly in fairly regular V's they usually are Canada geese; if in loose, wavery V's or long, wavy lines they more likely are snow geese. Snow geese gather by the thousands and are a famous sight, Spring and Fall, at Fortescue, New Jersey, and Cap Tourments, Quebec.

Mergansers appear on my river, both the American

and the hooded mergansers. The males, with lots of snowy white on them, are eye-catching; their heads are green, their beaks orange-red. The females are drab in grays and browns with only a little white on their sides. Soon after the mergansers come the ducks, black ducks first, then wood ducks, occasionally mallards.

Skunk cabbage blooms in the bogs; the flower has a carrion odor. Now and then someone finds hepatica in bloom, but I never find them till April. In a very early Spring, anemones may bloom in March; I look for them in damp, leafmoldy places at the edge of the woods.

Birch catkins fatten around the time of the Equinox. And pussy willows, the male catkins on the willow, appear. Catkins on the aspens and poplars burst bud and begin to grow. The tiny catkins on alders perk up, show new life.

Red-osier dogwood stems glow blood-red. Willow stems and withes turn lively amber. Grass shows new, fresh green on south slopes and beside the brooks. In sun and shelter near my house the dandelions send up tentative new leaves.

The lively green of celandine leaves appears at the road-side, sometimes at the edge of melting snow. Giant mullein shows new life. I have seen new green in these mulleins during a mild spell in February. But new growth waits for April.

In the vegetable garden our chives begin to show new shoots. We dig parsnips now, as soon as the ground thaws enough. In the flower garden we watch for crocuses, daffo-dils, squills, hyacinths. In favored years the crocuses bloom in March. Lilac buds often look as though they would pop into leaf next week, but they won't for another month.

Woodchucks emerge from hibernation. Gray squirrels bear their young. Sometimes the first migrant robins and red-wing blackbirds arrive.

## April

SPRING PEEPERS emerge and begin to make late afternoon and evening ring with their calls. I expect to hear them when daytime temperature reaches 50° and stays there for a few days. Before the month is out the bog water will be full of frog eggs and toad eggs.

By April's second week I watch for the first flickers. And for kingfishers over the river. Barn swallows usually arrive the week of April 20 and start repairing their nest in my garage. Towhees are very busy, very eye-catching, in the dead leaves in the flower garden. Woodpeckers signal each other in the woods, tapping out messages on dead limbs. The big pileated woodpeckers yawk and hammer at dead trees and telephone poles. They are big as crows.

Warblers begin to arrive by the third week. They are busy in the trees, twittering rather than singing. The big warbler migration here comes at the end of the month and laps over into May. Mornings now are loud with the songs of robins, Baltimore orioles, scarlet tanagers, rose-breasted grosbeaks. Song sparrows and whitethroats are specially vocal now.

Maples bloom, swamp maples first with their crimson flowers, sugar maples soon after with their yellow-green. By the end of the month the birches show tiny leaves, make the woods look green-misty. For a few weeks the woods and woodlands will be rich with pastel shades of young leaves, many shades of green, yellow, and pink.

First violets bloom. Jack-in-the-pulpit shoots up, opens its spathe and leaves. Bloodroot opens big, white, waxen petals beside old walls and in the edge of the woodland. Trilliums and dogtooth violets bloom nearby. Wild ginger sends up its leaves, will bloom next month.

We go to the damp places for marsh marigolds and have to hurry before they are in bloom. We also pick wild cresses, spring cress, bitter cress, yellow rocket, for cooked Spring greens.

Early saxifrage is in bloom. Sometimes I find wild strawberries in bloom in the pasture now, but more often in May. Trailing arbutus often blooms in April. I look for first leaves of wild columbine in rocky places. First fern fiddleheads pop up. Sometimes, but not often, I find baneberry in bloom now. A few bluets come to flower in April, millions of them in May. Both rue and wood anemone come to blossom now. I always find hepatica in bloom in April, on rocky ledges. In the woods I sometimes find partridgeberry's small twin white blossoms. I have found partridgeberry in bloom as late as the last week in June.

Bees are out and hungrily busy.

Baby chipmunks are born now, in the dens, but won't be out for another month. By then they will be almost as big as their parents. That's why I never see what looks like a baby chipmunk. Young muskrats are born in April but won't be weaned and out till late May. Gray squirrels are born now, stay in the nest till June. Red squirrels mate now. Deer drop fawns. Young does have only one fawn, older does two, rarely three. Young skunks are born now but stay in the den till late May. Raccoon kits are born now or in early May but don't forage with their mothers till late June.

Lilies of the valley open leaf, show buds. Peonies send up crimson shoots. Shirley poppies, self-sown, are up. Lupines and delphinium send up leaves. Daffodils bloom, and early tulips.

First cattail shoots appear in the bog, looking like iris. Wild iris shoots appear, looking like dark cattail leaves. Water snakes are out but still sluggish. First turtles appear, also sluggish. Toads sing the shrill, high-pitched mating trill, and pickerel frogs trill in the twilight. Peepers have finished their nightly choruses by the end of April, except a few loners who always are late waking up from the Winter sleep.

Fishing is good on lake and river, and worms are plentiful in the garden soil. It's still too early to plant anything in the garden except peas, onions maybe, some early lettuce if one is impatient, and radishes.

# May

A GREEN WORLD. Pasture grass is tall enough for grazing. First buttercups are in bloom. Maples are in leaf and there is shade again. Poplars and aspens and birches begin to whisper, their leaves full size. Catkins on the big cottonwood are like long, reddish-brown caterpillars, millions of them. Willows shed catkins, turn green with leaf. All in May's first week.

Lilacs open bud, leaves purple-tipped as though stained by the color of the tight cluster of pinhead-size flower buds. Tulips in full flower. Grape hyacinths out and host to swarming bees. Daffodils in the flower garden are through by mid-May but keep blooming where naturalized on the riverbank, probably because they were planted deeper there.

In the woods, Canada Mayflower blooms with elusive sweetness. Moccasin flowers are out in damp, woodsy places, and a few yellow lady-slippers in a secret place. Showy lady-slipper won't be out till early June. May apples, at the edge of the woods, hide their white blossoms under their big leaves. Foamflowers are proud in fluffs of white. Cranesbill (wild geranium) is in full flower beside the brook. Wild columbines in bloom on sunny ledges. Mountain laurel and pinkster flower, New England's wild azalea, will be in bloom before May's end.

Solomon's-seal and false spikenard are in bloom. So are Dutchman's-breeches and their modest cousins, squirrel corn. Wood sorrels (oxalis) opens its tiny yellow flowers, looking something like yellow strawberry flowers. Wild strawberries, real ones, begin to drop first white petals and set fruit to ripen the first week in June. Robin's plantain, looking something like low, pinkish-white asters, blooms at the roadside. So does red clover and white. Blue-eyed grass opens tiny yellow-eyed blue stars in the tall grass. Milkweed shoots up, particularly clean-looking yellow-green.

So many wildflowers now one can't keep count. This is the time of burgeoning and swift, insistent growth. Wild raspberries, the little black-caps, come to white blossom. Wild grapes, sprawling on the riverbank and climbing the trees, seem to grow a foot a day. All the bush dogwoods are in flower, tufted with white. Shadblow, foamy, filmy white when May began, fades after ten days or so.

The fruit trees are huge bouquets. All are loud with hungry bees. Pear trees are pure white, cherries pink, apples pink as the buds open, then white. When apple blossoms open I go to find showy orchis in damp, leafmoldy places, and always find it in bloom too. Wild ginger blooms with its three-lipped brown cups close to the root. Late bloodroot and anemones are nearby. They all like the same kind of soil.

Of all the birds, the busiest seem to be the fox sparrows, the towhees, and the redstarts. The fox sparrow, to my mind the jauntiest of all sparrows and one of the biggest, is conspicuous for his rich cinnamon-brown crown and tail; I see him scratching like a Leghorn hen among the old leaves in the flower garden. The towhee, only a little bigger than the fox sparrow, is also an energetic leaf-scratcher, but he carries his warm cinnamon-brown on his sides, has a black head and back and a white belly, really eye-catching. Some call him chewink, for the most common of his calls, and some know him as the ground-robin. The redstart is a flutterer who dives after insects the way a flycatcher does. He is one of the larger warblers and one of the few warblers with much black plumage—predominately black except for red wing and tail patches and a light-colored belly. In May the redstarts are busy on my lawn and surprisingly tame. I seldom see a redstart or a towhee as late as mid-June, though I know they nest in my area.

By late May the June bugs, big, bumbling scarab beetles, thump the screens at night and bang at outdoor lights. They look and fly like awkward tin insects, and if one gets indoors, it lies on its back on the floor, legs waving, like a mechanical toy running down. There are dozens of different kinds, but all are big and bumbly and, like moths, can't resist the light.

## June

THE BIG SURGE of green is past. Now there will be several weeks of urgent growth before the Midsummer lull when that growth will be completed and the energies will go into seed maturing. Trees are a more uniform green. Meadows are lush. Farmers begin to cut hay, always early, I think, but always on time. The undergrowth in the woods is full-leafed, a green carpet waist-deep.

Pasture roses are in bloom along the fence rows. Wild strawberries ripen in the grass. Yarrow is in bloom, gray-white. Daisies frost the roadside. The first black-eyed Susans appear, orange-yellow and eye-catching. We pick our first garden peas and luxuriate in garden asparagus and new lettuce, scallions and radishes.

Young woodchucks appear outside the dens. Up in the woods I see a mother partridge, who squawks, drags a wing, feigning injury, tries to lure me away from her brood of chicks. The chicks are no bigger than a dandelion bloom and scatter at her signal, vanish. I stand still and look, finally see one chick wink an eye, the only motion it makes, and thus can distinguish it from a dot of shadow in the dead leaves. Perfectly color-protected, the chicks hide by squatting motionless among the woodland litter. Baby raccoons begin to travel with their mother, chiefly at night.

Garden iris is in bloom, and ruby-throat humming-birds are feeding at it until the bee balm, still in bud, opens. Another few weeks and they will be at the jewelweed, another favorite. Nettles are thick along the garden fence. A few drops of 2–4D solution, applied with an oilcan to each of them, stops them in their tracks.

Baby barn swallows are so big they crowd the nest. The parents force them out, make them learn to fly. Two evenings of practice and they are flying circles over the river, catching mosquitoes.

Kingbirds are still nesting. Kingbirds are tough fighters, but a ruby-throat hummingbird can rout a kingbird. I've seen it happen.

Red squirrels are birthing. Cottontails have a second litter. I found a litter, only a few days old, in a nest under a rosebush in the flower garden. Young gray squirrels, half grown, are out and climbing, but stiff-tailed with fear at leaping in the treetops.

A big snapping turtle digs a hole for eggs in the pasture 200 yards from the river. She is there several hours, covers the eggs with dirt, then goes back to the river. The sun will hatch the eggs and the young will make their way to water they never saw.

Spring peepers are now through the tadpole stage, have lost their tails, are frogs the size of a honey bee. Cattails are in bloom. And wild iris, beautiful deep purple that catches the eye in the bogland.

The Summer Solstice occurs about June 21. The year's longest span of daylight comes, and from here on, till December's Winter Solstice, nights will slowly lengthen, days diminish. Summer has begun by the almanac, but the light already leans toward Fall.

## *July*

WASPS ARE NESTING. Mud wasps try to build their adobe structures on my front porch, have to be discouraged. I let them build in the garage. They build the nest cells, paralyze spiders with their sting, stuff the nests with spiders and caterpillars, lay the eggs. Eggs will hatch and wasp larvae will have food at hand. In the garden I see dozens of holes in the path where ground wasps are laying eggs. I resent them there, for their tempers are short. Then I see them stocking those nests with bugs from my potato vines. Two days and they have cleaned the vines. I change my tune. Welcome, wasps!

Few bird songs except in early morning and at dusk. Robins never sing at midday now. Sometimes I hear the brown thrasher in mid-afternoon, more musical than a catbird but just as versatile, almost as talented as the South's mockingbird. The thrasher repeats his phrases, each one twice over. As dusk comes on I hear the mourning doves and the wood thrush, that magnificent contralto. And at dusk the whippoorwills begin to call. Just now they start at 8:15—I can almost set my watch by them. But I deplore the habits of a few who also sing at 3:30 a.m. Sing? Well, call. One night I lay awake and counted 456 calls in a row from one bird. John Burrows once counted three times that many in one series.

Queen Anne's lace is in full bloom. Chickory flowers at the roadside. And the first goldenrod, late in the month, which somehow makes it seem later than it is. Bouncing Bet makes a pleasant pink-white accent—it will be blooming till hard frost. And wild bergamot now is in full bloom, mostly the lavender here, but a few patches of bee balm, the deep crimson variety. Bumblebees compete with the hummingbirds for bergamot nectar.

Wild raspberries, black-caps, begin to ripen. Up in the woods I find the first bloom of the lavender-flowered raspberry, big as a wild rose, beautiful; but the berries that follow are insipid. At the roadside a creeping raspberry with small white bloom is in flower; its berries will be sweet but few next month.

Moles are busy, heaving runs across the lawn. It's a toss-up what to do. They eat grubs that feed on grass roots, but the moles kill the grass over their runs. I give in, invite a neighbor to come and gas them with his cyanide gun. Let them kill the grubs in the pasture.

I see raccoon tracks in the mud at the river's edge. And a fresh corncob. They have been helping themselves to my sweet corn before I got a taste. I look, and they are right; it's ready.

A doe and two fawns are in the edge of the pasture at dawn, the fawns well spotted.

Frogs clunk the night. And an old drake, probably one of the black ducks that nested in the reeds just upstream, has the bad habit of squawking loudly two hours before dawn. I see a mother swimming near the far bank with eight ducklings in her wake. They keep to the shadows, wary of hawks, muskrats, turtles.

Bush dogwood has green berries in clusters. The birds have cleaned the shadbushes of their fruit—I didn't get a taste. Milkweed is in bloom, sweet as tuberose. I look for the tiny golden beetle in the dogbane blossoms. And for the pink and yellow moth, only an inch long, in the evening primroses at the roadside.

The big moths are out now, the spectacular ones. At night the lovely light green Lunas, with the long, trailing "tails" on their wings, come to the screened windows and fray those fragile wings trying to reach the light inside. Occasionally I find a Polyphemus on the screen. This big brown moth, sometimes six inches across, has one big blue "eye" and one yellow one on each hind wing.

In the flower garden at dusk I see Sphinx moths, dusky brown, hovering at the petunias and nicotiana. As a boy I thought I had found a hummingbird at the giant evening primroses on the High Plains of Colorado. I caught it and held in my hand the first Sphinx moth I had ever seen. And I marveled, as I still do, at the coiled tongue case which it can straighten out, like a beak, to reach deep into a flower to tap a hidden nectar sac. I didn't know then that this lovely moth was once a big, ugly green tomato worm in the vegetable garden. It still seems incredible.

I always think of the roadside asters as Fall flowers, but most years I find the panicled white asters competing with the daisies at the roadsides, often in veritable clouds of blossom, by mid-July. The branching stem, with a host of tiny white flowers, sometimes grows six feet or more tall. And by mid-July I often find Joe Pye weed, another "Fall" flower, coming to magneta-crimson bloom in a damp spot beside my pasture brook. It catches my eye because the lance-shaped leaves at the tip, just below the buds, are flushed with the same color that marks the blossom. It reminds me that daylight shrinks, Fall approaches.

## August

DOG DAYS. Algae thick on the stagnant water at the bog, and a steamy smell of ferment and rotting vegetation. And mosquitoes. I am content to watch the bog from a little distance, preferably in the evening and with a breeze, which keeps the mosquitoes in the bog and off of me. The swallows are busy there at that time of day, caracoling, feeding in the air. What would we do without swallows?

Dragonflies and damsel flies follow the boat when I go out on the river, curious. Some are still laying eggs, dipping into the water with the tips of their abdomens to lay them. Water striders swarm in the warm shallows, dart about like skaters. None of the fish bites well, probably sated with natural food ready at hand. Little spotted turtles sun themselves on old logs, slip into the water when I come near. I hear a bittern thumping in a backwater slew, but can't catch sight of him. A great blue heron stares moodily at me, awks testily, and flaps into the air, trailing its long legs as it flies down the river.

Flocks of cowbirds follow the cows in the pasture, but they are getting restless. Orioles begin to sing more often, but the robins sing little, scold much. Bobolinks, a great flock of them, are restless in a damp meadow not far from here; I see many of this year's young ones in the flock. The yellow-breasted chat that was so noisy just up the river a few weeks ago is silent. The barn swallows begin to leave, and so do the chimney swifts; I see fewer of them than even two weeks ago.

Goldenrod in bloom everywhere. And asters. Even the big purple New England asters now are in bloom, some of them five feet tall. But relatively few other wildflowers. Daisies hold on, and so does Queen Anne's lace. The sunflowers are at their prime. Milkweeds have formed their pods, still green and tightly closed. Wild clematis (virgin's-bower) sheds its small white petals and what were blossoms become twisted tangles of wiry green stamens; they will gray with age and justify the name Old Man's Beard in a few more weeks. Wild cucumber vines bear their soft-prickled, thumb-sized pods. Wild blackberries ripen.

Green acorns hang on the oaks, green cones on the pines. The nightshade's purple star flowers turn to green berries. Pimbina, the high bush cranberry, begins to show orange on its fruit, to ripen to cranberry red in a few more weeks. We freeze sweet corn and lima beans. Pickles can wait a bit. Chokecherries ripen, and if we would make jelly of them we must compete with the birds. The same is true of the elderberries, which weight the brittle branches so heavily that when the birds swoop to the harvest they break the stems.

By August's end the warblers are moving through here again, on their way south. But more quietly than they came north in May. I see them, but I have to listen to hear them. Now and then I hear a burst of special song, a house wren that just can't contain himself another hour. But nothing like the flood of song he made in May and June. I hear a fox bark in the night.

The Summer wanes, well before the Equinox.

## September

THE SUNFLOWERS we grow ripen, and the chickadees know it before I do. They flock and feed, and I cut the heavy sunflower heads to dry and shell and dole out during the Winter. But good to see the chicks again. They have been up in the woods all Summer.

One year, the first week in September, I saw a huge flock of nighthawks starting their migration. There were thousands, circling slowly in a stream that must have been two miles long. I watched them almost an hour before they passed my house. Such sights are rare.

Whippoorwills sometimes continue to call here till well into September. One year I heard one the first week in October, but that was most unusual.

Flickers gather in flocks, ready to migrate, and move restlessly up and down the valley. They will act this way for several weeks, then be on their way. Robins chatter and also flock, but still call this home. But my Winter birds begin to appear by mid-September. I see a brown creeper or two, a few nuthatches, quite a few whitethroat sparrows, now and then a couple of juncos. Blue jays are more noisy. They were either quiet or outvoiced most of the Summer. And the crows talk loudly. They were very noisy a month ago, bringing their young off the nests, screaming at them and at each other; then they were quiet for a bit. Now they are shrill again, talking of days ahead when they will own the valley. Catbirds are quiet, strangely subdued. I see no more kingbirds; they have gone south.

Sumac always shows traces of red in August, here and there. Now it begins to color in earnest. And some maples show color, on only a few branches. Tiny seedling maples turn early, like children being sent to bed before the grownups. The elm trees look tired and rusty and begin to shed old leaves, crisp and sere and tattered.

Our Fall rains begin. Brooks that were mere trickles all through August chatter again. I hear them in the stillness of the night. There is a yellow tinge to the birches, which turns to gold as the month advances. The aspens and cottonwoods shake down their leaves, thick and leathery, in the wind; they have turned a green-gold, not really yellow. White-ash leaves begin to turn. At a certain stage they look almost blue to me, from a distance; close up they are still green tinged with shades of yellow. As box elder trees, ash-leafed maples really, begin to shed their leaves I see their big tufts of seed, twin keys like the other maples. Those seeds cling to the branches far into Winter, quite unlike the other maples.

First frost often comes in late September. If light, it does no harm to the color in the trees. Hard frost kills the color before it really comes. The old myth of Jack Frost painting the leaves is all wrong, contrary to fact. We have our best color in a mild, dry Autumn.

Wild grapes ripen. We pick, simmer, and make jelly. Birds love the grapes. So do foxes, and 'possums.

Milkweed pods are silvery green and ripen daily, pop open, strew seeds to the wind. Sweet gum and sassafras become vivid with reds and oranges. Squirrels are busy harvesting nuts and acorns. I mark the crop on the hazelnut bushes each year, hoping to get some, but the squirrels always get there first. Bittersweet ripens, tan husks opening to reveal the orange berries.

The Autumn Equinox passes scarcely noticed. The season is well ahead of the almanac, always. All September belongs to Autumn.

## October

TRADITIONALLY, Columbus Day, October 12, is the height of the color in my part of New England. It seldom varies a week either way. By then, in most Autumns, the soft maples are ruby-red, the sugar maples are dazzling gold, and the oaks have begun to show their leathery browns and purples as well as an occasional splash of burgundy. I am always so overwhelmed by the color that I can't really see the trees. Now and then we have a day with mist at this time of year, sometimes fog enough to mask the hills; and then I always go out to look because the backdrop is at least half hidden and the individual trees in the foreground stand out.

The goldenrod has begun to fade. The Fall asters are uneven, but the big purples ones, the New England asters, are still making a vivid show. Bouncing Bet still stands, pinkish white, along most of the roadsides. Queen Anne's lace has largely matured and begun to form those heads often called "birds' nests," actually the bare stems of the flower head now curled into a fist-size ball. The gentians, both the closed bottle kind and the lovely fringed ones, bloomed in late September and are still spectacular among the birches. The last chickory flowers make vivid blue accents at the roadside.

Goldfinches are busy at the ripe thistle heads; they have begun to show their inconspicuous Fall and Winter plumage and may be mistaken for sparrows now. Flickers flock in my pasture early in the month and are gone south by the twentieth. The hawks begin to migrate and are sometimes seen in sizable flocks. Some of the Winter birds appear in greater numbers—juncos, chickadees, tree sparrows, nuthatches, particularly. Some of these species migrate somewhat, going a hundred miles or so north to nest, then coming back for the Winter. They mingle with those that nested here, all of them more evident now that the leaves are falling and the other birds have gone south. Even some blue jays make a short annual migration. But they come back to my corn crib for the Winter. Some years we have a minor Winter population of the red-breasted nuthatches, a more northern species than the white-breasted ones we always have. But the red-breasts come later, in December.

Woodchucks are almost ready to hibernate, though I have seen one out as late as mid-November. Chipmunks are very busy building Winter nests and stocking granaries for their long retirement. Gray squirrels are busy in the woods. I find a litter of acorn cups under every white oak, a litter of green hulls and opened shells under the hickories. Now I can see squirrel nests high in the trees, big as crows' nests and only one degree tidier.

When I walk now I bring home a harvest of burs and stick-tights on my trouser legs and socks. Even a brief walk at the roadside or in the pasture gathers half a dozen different kinds. Plucking them off, I marvel at the variety of ingenious ways a seed can hitch a ride.

Frost crisps the leaves, begins to break them down. Fall rain compacts them. Leafmold is in the making. The leaves provide a blanket for lesser woodland plants and the slow heat of decay warms them somewhat.

Muskrats are stocking Winter pantries with cattail roots. Frogs and turtles have already hibernated in the mud.

## November

HARD FROST BY NOW, and virtually all the leaves have been brought down by rain and wind. Except on the oaks and the beeches, which sometimes hold their sere leaves until Spring is near.

Several of the handbooks indicate that the Catocala moths are not seen later than September. I find them in my woods in November, especially the birch moth, which at rest so closely resembles the color and marking of birch bark that I have stood and looked for five minutes and not seen one two feet in front of me. These moths are about the size of the common "miller" moths of Midsummer nights. Some members of the family have brightly colored hind wings, but they are covered by the grayish or brownish forewings when at rest. One night in late November, with the temperature near 20°, I was driving through a birch woods and a cloud of these moths appeared in my headlights. There were hundreds of them. When I go to the woods now at dusk I nearly always see a few of them on the wing.

Geese move south. When I hear them in the night, if there is strong moonlight I often get up to look; something about a flight of honkers against the moon touches me deep inside. One raw November day when I would have bet ten to one it would snow before dark I saw a flock of thirty Canadas on a pond not far from here. I thought they were daring fate, not migrating. But they knew the weather better than I did. It cleared in early afternoon and stayed clear almost a week. Then I heard them go over in the night, a brilliant moonlit night, and within thirty-six hours it really did storm.

Frosty nights now bring frosty dawns—dawns when every bush and twig and weed stem along the river is covered with hoarfrost. Until the sun is well up and the day has begun to warm, it is a fantastic world of filigree. The river mist was deposited in billions of frost particles in the night. I can enter this astonishing world a little way with my ten-power glass, whch reveals the shape and arrangement of these frost particles. One heavily frosted morning many of the needles on the big Norway spruce had star-flakes at their tips, perfect six-pointed stars of frost, like snowflakes, none of them more than an eighth of an inch across.

Deer are rutting. Last Spring's fawns have lost their spots and are almost as big as their mothers. They come down to eat windfall apples on quiet nights with a late moon. They usually are specially wary now, but one November morning just after 8:00 a big doe and her twin fawns came across my home pasture to an old apple tree and ate windfalls for twenty minutes, in broad daylight, until a farm truck came along the road and sent them bounding back to the woods.

Now I hear the owls almost every evening, sometimes just before dawn. I have heard barred owls in August and the great horned owl in April, but they as well as the little screech owl seem to be most vocal in frosty November.

The screech owls call at late dusk. The call isn't really a screech. It is a quavery, lonely wail that starts high and slurs off and down, higher pitched than any other owl call. And with nothing in it that even resembles a hoot. The hooters in my area are the great horned owl and the barred owl.

The great horned owl's call is a gruff, wooflike series of hoots, deep-pitched. Some call this owl the "three-hooter." It often hoots four notes, however, and the call I most often hear consists of a three-hoot series, a slight pause, then a four-hoot series, seven in all: "Hoo, Hooo-hoo. Hoo, Hoo, Hooo-hooo."

The barred owl is an "eight-hooter." Its characteristic call might be interpreted as: "Who cooks for you? Who cooks for you-all?" with the final note, the "all," slurred sharply downward. Sometimes several barred owls will call to each other and there will be an assortment of voices, bass, baritone, and very low tenor. The voice seems to vary with the individual.

## December

IT IS EASY ENOUGH to identify the trees when they are in full leaf, but it takes a bit of knowledge to sort them out in December. All trees carry their own fingerprints in their bark pattern, however. Learn that language and you can readily tell them apart. Shapes are important too, but not all elms are shaped like wineglasses, not all maples egg-shaped, not all oaks globe-shaped. The shapes are clues, however, and worth noting. Bark color is important, the brown of oaks, the dark gray of maples, the dull red-brown of black birches. And red oaks hold their acorns over the Winter, white oaks don't. The conifers are easier to sort out than the deciduous trees, but the cedars can be confusing unless one remembers that red cedars look browner than white cedars in Winter. And red cedars have purple berries; white cedars have small cones, tiny ones, even smaller than hemlock cones.

If I find a green fern in the woods now I know it is a Christmas fern, the only evergreen fern in my area. But even those ferns whose fronds are frosted and fallen still show their spore heads, wood-brown and stiffly erect. Most interesting to me are those of the ostrich fern which look like brown leaf fronds. But each brown "leaflet" on them is a spore case. Pluck such a spore head and shake it and a mist of spores, finer than dust, drifts out, so light it hangs in the air like a dark mist.

Shrews have to eat, even in December, even when the ground is covered with snow. One December morning, with several inches of snow on the ground, I saw a short-tailed shrew, the most common species here, darting here and there in a bare patch under the big spruce. It was so hungry it dashed from one tuft of grass to another, diving into each, pawing at it, apparently finding some mite-size insect or larva to eat. I went out for a close look and it paid me little attention. Its fur was pewter-colored, looked soft as moleskin, and its eyes were like tiny black beads. It stayed there ten minutes, burning up energy in its frantic search, active as a frightened red squirrel. Then it hurried to a snowbank, plunged in, and was gone, probably to tunnel along at ground level and continue its driving search for food.

The river is frozen over now, the first freeze-up. The ice is crystal clear, for it was a quiet night when it froze. The ice is so clear it doesn't look like ice, but I know it is ice from the way the sun glints on it and the absence of ripples in the morning breeze. A few more cold nights and the ice will turn gray, then white. As it deepens it will trap air bubbles from the water beneath, tiny bubbles that make it look gray and opaque. If I am sufficiently curious, as I am once in a while, I can stretch out on the clear ice and watch big air bubbles float past, like toy balloons. Sometimes fish come up and poke their heads into those bubbles. But most of the fish are down near the bottom. Once in a while "frost flowers" appear on the ice, clusters of white frost crystals sometimes in tufts two inches high, sometimes like complex stars flat on the ice.

The year's shortest days come now, latest sunrise, earliest sunset—but not on the day of the Winter Solstice. These are perfect nights to study the stars, for the air is clean and clear. And cold.

## January

THE SOLSTICE PAST, the year tends toward Spring. But you would never know it. The old saying, "Days lengthen, cold strengthens," is proved in January. But it's a good time to study snowflakes. I go out wearing a dark coat or carrying a piece of black cloth and catch a few flakes and examine them, first with the naked eye, then under the glass. Perhaps there are two alike, but those who have studied them most say they never have seen duplicates. The late W. A. Bentley, of Jericho, Vermont, who made thousands of snowflake photographs, said he never found two exactly alike. His snowflake pictures, incidentally, are classic.

It is a good time, too, to study window frost. Those intricate patterns that form on panes in a cold room where there is moisture in the air are often unbelievably complex. They come in swirls and feathers and fronds and trees, fantastic in their elaboration and beauty. I have never seen two of these frost patterns alike, either.

Splitting fireplace wood one cold January day I was surprised at how easily tough oak billets popped open. I figured out why and now I leave the tough oak stacked green in the open, let the sap freeze and create inner tensions. Then when I swing the ax it starts a crack and the frost tensions pop it open.

Frost is the silent, powerful lever of erosion. A drop of moisture in a hairline crack in a rock becomes a tremendous force when deep cold turns the moisture to ice. Water expands when it freezes, and the expansion opens the crack. The ledges on my mountain are cracked and splintered every Winter by the frost, and when I go there in the Spring I am always wary of my footing because slabs have been loosened that way.

If I would see the wind, I go out after a windy snowstorm. There is the track of the wind in the drifted snow, the way it went over a hummock or a rock. Snowdrifts are frozen motion of that most fluid of the elements, the wind. Even the curl at the lip of a snowdrift is the curl of the wind as it was sucked back by the drift. Last Winter the big drift left by one storm in my sideyard was marked by big scallops that baffled me until I looked at the contours of the lilac bushes and rosebushes just beyond. The wind had been shaped and guided by those bushes, and the scallops were in the same pattern as the height of the bushes.

January is a good time to look for animal tracks in the snow, but not if it is too cold. I went out in zero weather after one storm last Winter and found not one track, not even of a rabbit. It was two days before rabbits, foxes, and squirrels were hungry enough to come out in that bitter cold. Only the birds were out. They flocked to the feeders. Small birds can starve to death in thirty-six hours in such weather.

Some years the snowy owls appear about now, often as far south as New York City, sometimes as far down as Washington, D.C. These big birds are usually seen in daylight, perching on posts, poles, and other high places. They have good daylight vision. They are basically white but often look gray because of a scalloping of small, dark feathers. The notion that their appearance means an especially hard Winter has no basis. Arctic lemmings are a principal item in their diet, and lemmings follow a mysterious four-year propulation cycle. When they are scarce in the snowy owl's Far Northern homeland, the owls come south to feed on rabbits, voles, and other small animals. We see them, because of that lemming cycle, about every four years. The snowy owl's call is a deep, defiant, four-note sequence, *khoog-go-go-gook*.

## *February*

PERHAPS there are places where the woodchuck, or groundhog, comes out of hibernation on February 2, but not in my part of the country. Here the woodchucks sleep till late March or early April, then come out driven by two urgencies, hunger and the desire to mate. They are then short-tempered and truculent, often fight bloody battles among themselves. But on February 2 they are still deep in the sleep of hibernation, no matter what the day's weather.

February brings snow-melt. Actually, snow will melt in zero weather, especially in February. It really evaporates, never going through the water stage, and is absorbed by dry air passing over it. I have seen a snowdrift shrink six inches in four days without the temperature getting above 20° Fahrenheit. But February almost invariably brings its own thaw, often a more authoritative one than the traditional one of January. The sun is warmer, daylight is longer, nights are shorter.

After a February thaw last Winter I walked in the pasture and saw how dry grass stems can pick up enough heat from the sun to melt holes in the snow. That day there was still two inches of snow on the ground, but every blade of grass, every weed stem, every twig, had melted its own hole. The snow looked like what the embroiderers of my mother's day used to call "punch work"; it was an elaborate lacework. Even in hollows where there was two-inch ice the pattern was the same—a melt-hole around every stem.

On a sunny February day I can expect to hear the blue jays calling, a cheerful, almost musical two-note call quite unlike the raucous jeer characteristic of the jay most of the

Winter. Tree sparrows begin to sing. Their songs are not in a class with those of the song sparrows, but they are sweet, high-pitched, and quite surprising after hearing nothing from them but a kind of pleasant tweet-twitter for so long. Even the nuthatches change their inflection if not their notes; they still *yark*, but more happily. Such sounds convince me that change is in the air and in the earth.

Gray squirrels began mating in January. They are still at it, chasing and scurrying in the trees, now so interested in each other that they sometimes forget me until I am almost upon them.

Some years I find the first tips of skunk cabbage up by now in the bog, brownish-green horns that at first glance seem to have no relation to plant life. Even if the bog is still iced over, they may be up. They generate enough warmth to melt a hole several inches in diameter.

We usually cut forsythia twigs during the February thaw and bring them indoors to force in a vase in a sunny window. Sometimes I cut twigs from the pussy willows and add them to the bouquet. A couple of weeks and we have forstyhia gold and pussy-willow silver, which makes Spring and wildflowers seem closer than they really are. February is still Winter, often is full of snow, but its changing light marks the season unmistakably. By February's end it is still daylight, though somewhat dim, at 6:00 in the evening. By then we know that March and April and Spring are just ahead.

# Chapter 15

# The Names
# and the Naming

THERE IS *folk poetry in the common names;
but science, devoted to order and systematic knowledge, insists on classifying and
defining. The poet's buttercup is the botanist's Ranunculus. If you would walk with
scientist as well as poet, learn both languages.*

*I like the old names* for things, especially the common names for plants, even though they can be confusing and are frowned on by the specialist. With good reason, I know, since science must have specific, unmistakable terms. But the old names have a lot of folk poetry in them, and I am sure that is what appeals to so many of us.

In this book I have used the common names in the text for two reasons. First, because they *are* common, known to so many people even when they may be regional names. And, second, because the use of scientific names in such an informal book as this might confuse some readers and certainly would distract others. But because exactitude is desirable, and because the common names sometimes apply to several different plants, I am including in this chapter a list of the plants and animals mentioned in previous chapters and identifying them with their scientific terminology. Where there are several common names, I have given those most often used. I wish it were possible to include literal translations of the scientific names, which sometimes are baffling, sometimes amusing, and often picturesque. But there isn't space or any urgent need for that.

Before we get to the list, however, I should like to discuss this whole matter of naming things.

In the Book of Genesis we are told that Adam named "every living creature." Nothing is said about the plants and their names, but for a long time both plants and animals had the kind of names that Adam might have given

240

them. Those names varied from place to place and from time to time, and they were what we today call the "common" names, that is the names the people generally used. They varied from country to country, which is to say from language to language; but there were also various names in the same language for the same plant or animal. For instance, we who speak English still speak of a cow, a bull, steer, a heifer, a calf, all the same animal, differing only in age and sex.

In the early days this variety of names caused little confusion, because everyone used the common names and there was little travel from one country to another. But as the known world expanded and men tried to tell each other about the plants and animals they saw elsewhere, misunderstanding was inevitable. Probably the first attempt to bring order out of this chaos was made by the Greeks. Aristotle, who is sometimes called the father of zoology, made a list of names for animals, all the animals in the world he knew. The names he used were those given to the various animals by hunters, fishermen, and occult priests who foretold events by examining freshly killed birds and animals. Aristotle's list was classified by the uses made of the birds and animals, with no attempt to group them physiologically.

And Aristotle's student, Theophrastus, "the father of botany," compiled a similar list of plants. The Theophrastus list was based on the names used by herb gatherers who supplied roots and plants to those who practiced herbal medicines. And he, too, grouped the plants by their use, not by physical similarity.

After Aristotle and Theophrastus, as men traveled more and more and more, the bestiaries or animal lists and the herbals or plant lists were expanded. The Romans superseded the Greeks and, even as they took over other good things from Greece, they adopted and expanded the bestiaries and herbals. In Latin, of course. And as the Latin scholars tried to be more and more precise, the names themselves grew until in some instances a name, explicitly descriptive, became a whole paragraph. This led to a point of absurdity where nobody but the specialized scholars could understand them and the whole matter of naming things became academic. Meanwhile, ordinary people went right on using the common, everyday names and clung to essential simplicity. The common names of plants especially were those given them by down-to-earth herb users, most of whom couldn't read Latin in any case.

To take one example, there was the word "wort," which still persists in everyday plant names—Webster's unabridged dictionary lists more than 150 "wort" names for plants in use today. The word "wort" came from the Old English "wyrt," meaning a plant or a root. The herb folk simply tacked onto it a descriptive term—feverwort, for instance, which we now know as horse gentian and which the botanists list as *Triosteum perfoliatum*, was a plant from which the herb doctors brewed an infusion to reduce fevers. Sneezewort was supposed to stop sneezing, cankerwort was good to cure cankers, and fleawort probably helped to make life miserable for those hopping insect pests.

At any rate, the learned men had their long-winded Latin names for plants and animals and the country folk had their descriptive and often colorful names for them, and nobody had yet thought of a really logical system of classifying either plants or animals. The learned compilers of herbals and bestiaries merely expanded their formless lists, and the common folk went right on using the descriptive names in their mother tongue. Common names were of some use in rural herb medicine, and occasionally they showed flashes of folk poetry, but otherwise they were just names.

In 1552 an Englishman named Wotton tried to organize animal names on the old Aristotelian system, but even his modifications got nowhere in particular. Then late in the seventeenth century another Englishman, John Ray, made a systematic list of animals, chiefly vertebrates, grouping them by structural characteristics and using the term "species" much as we use it today. But Ray didn't have the genius to do the job.

Finally, early in the eighteenth century, a young Swede with a Latin name, Carl Linnaeus, came along. Linnaeus was the son of a preacher and avid gardener and grew up with plants. He wanted to be a botanist, so he studied medicine—the doctors of his day used herbs and had to have at least a working knowledge of plants. He became a teacher and the father of modern botany. Taking some of Ray's ideas and adding his own genius, his passion for order and organization, he published a pamphlet called *Systema Naturae* in 1735, which for the first time pointed the way toward what is now known as taxonomy, the orderly, scientific classification of plants and animals. Before he died he published many books, two of which are enduring landmarks, *Species Plantarium*, the foundation of modern botany, and a greatly expanded *Systema Naturae*, which brought order to the world of animal life for the first time.

Basic to Linnaeus's system were two tremendous achievements. First, he grouped and classified both plants and animals according to structural similarities. Second, he inaugurated a simplified system of names, what we now know as the binomial system. Each plant or animal was given a two-word name; the first indicated the genus or family to which the plant or animal belonged, and the second specified the species within that family. Since Latin and Greek were the languages of science in his day, the names he used were of classic extraction, hence understandable to men everywhere who were familiar with the language of scholarship. So Linnaeus not only systematized and simplified botany and zoology, but he gave them a universal language.

That was the beginning, the first great breakthrough toward scientific understanding of the natural world. Many changes have been made since, particularly in classification, but the basic system that Linnaeus evolved is still used. Scientists have expanded it for their own purposes, sometimes to the bewilderment of the layman and the beginner, but they have never utterly confused it. Order is still there. For instance, fully to describe any particular plant and animal they now use a whole string of terms—first, the kingdom, plant or animal, then the phylum or line of descent, then the class, the order, the family, and finally the genus and species. But for everyday use only the last two terms are ordinarily stated, genus and species. Sometimes a third term is used, to indicate a subspecies, and sometimes a fourth is used to give credit to the person who first described and classified this particular example. But the two terms, genus and species, usually suffice.

Looking back, Linnaeus's method of naming things, just

to take one phase of his system, seems so simple and so obvious that one wonders why nobody thought of it earlier. For instance, he decided that the dog, the wolf, and the fox belonged to the same genus, which he designated as *Canis*, the Latin word for dog. So he designated the dog as *Canis familiaris*, literally "the dog of the family," or "domestic dog." The wolf became *Canis lupus*, from the Latin word for "wolf." The fox he called *Canis vulpes*, simply appropriating the Latin word for fox. The old, pre-Linnaean system would have called the fox something like "the small, doglike animal with a long, bushy tail and big, erect ears." It might even have gone on to describe the color of the coat and the fact that foxes eat grapes as well as birds and rabbits. Linnaeus compressed the essential information into the two words which said it was the species of dog known as a fox.

Not all scientific names are that simple and direct, I grant you, but they all have a logical meaning. And some of them are as graphic as the common names; some even more so. The American skunk, for example, gets its common name from the Algonquian Indian word for the beast, "seganku." But its scientific name is *Mephitis*, Latin for "noxious vapor," as appropriate a name as could be imagined.

In the field of botany a good many of the common names have been appropriated in the scientific names. Some are quite obvious, as the anemone or windflower. Anemone is simply the Greek word for "wind," and we use it in anemometer, an instrument for measuring the wind. Botanically the windflower or anemone is still *Anemone*— *Anemone quinquefolia* in the case of the wood anemone because its leaves have five divisions, *Anemone trifolia* for the mountain anemone which has three-part leaves. The genus name is from the Greek and the species name is Latin, but that doesn't seem to matter. Scholars object loudly when coiners of words tack a Greek ending onto a word with a Latin root, but I have never heard such criticism of the mixed origins of many scientific names. I am not one to venture a judgment, having forgotten most of the Latin I once had and never having had any Greek, I am sorry to say.

In any case, the scientific names have their own fascination and the person with a curious turn of thought can play all kinds of games with them. They are the precise language of botany and zoology, and they have order and reason and system in them. Most of them are descriptive, though I must admit that some of the descriptions baffle me. For instance, the common clothes moth is *Tineola bisel-liella*, literally the "double-seated little moth." The bluebot-tle fly is *Calliphora erythrocephala*, literally a "red-headed beauty bearer." The house martin is *Delichon urbica*, the "city swallow"; but that *Delichon* is an anagram for *Cheli-don*, which is Greek for "swallow." Somebody was playing word games, and I wonder who and why.

But to come back to the common names, before we go on to the list.

I mentioned that the common names, particularly of plants, sometimes had flashes of poetry as well as homely descriptive turns of language. It is the poetry of country folk, the imagery of people who live close to the earth, and sometimes it is quite graphic. Take "buttercup" and forget that it is a flower. Pure descriptive poetry. Or "Dutchman's-breeches," poetry with a grin. Or "bitter-sweet" or "checkerberry" or "moneywort," the common myrtle of the beautiful golden-yellow flowers. I wonder if he who gave it that name was calling it, in his own way, a money-plant because of its golden blossoms or if the plant had some commercial value at one time. There is also a pennywort.

Take bee balm, the scarlet bergamot beloved by bum-blebees and hummingbirds. Take mad-dog skullcap, a mixed figure if there ever was one, but certainly picturesque. Or St. John's-wort, named for its petals, which supposedly imitate the cross of St. John. Or one of the same family, St. Andrew's cross, whose four yellow petals form a cross like that of St. Andrew.

Take tear-thumb, that thorny-stemmed member of the buckwheat family which must have wounded many a care-less thumb. Or take buckwheat itself. The "buck" comes from the German "boek" for the beech tree. The seed of the buckwheat looks somewhat like a miniature beechnut. Hence, buckwheat, the wheat or grain that looks like a beechnut. Take meadowsweet, that fragrant wildflower with tufts of pink blossoms full of the sweet fragrance characteristic of most members of the rose family, to which it belongs.

Take liverwort, presumably once used by the herb doctors to treat a liver complaint. Another common name is Hepatica, and *Hepatica* is its botanical name. And Hepatica? It comes from the Greek *hepaticos*, the liver, made familiar in recent years by the disease hepatitis. Liverwort, hepatica, and back to liver, through the Greek.

Every time I leaf through a botany text or a wildflower handbook I am fascinated by the names. There is history and poetry and geography and even biography in them.

One more example.

Out in the edge of my pasture is a small patch of horse balm or rich weed, botanically *Collinsonia canadensis*. Curious, I began to search for the origin of that botanical name, and I came at last to Peter Collinson, who was an amateur botanist and naturalist in England in the early eighteenth century. He was one of that group of inquiring minds, both in England and in America, which poked into all kinds of natural phenomena and, by the very act of inquiry, helped lay the groundwork for natural science.

Collinson had a number of American correspondents and exchanged both plants and ideas with them. He introduced a number of American plants into England, and he had a part in introducing the culture of hemp, flax, and silkworms into America. He was a correspondent of Benjamin Franklin. Their exchange of letters, however, was about other natural phenomena than botany, since Franklin was not much of a botanist. Peter Collinson sent Franklin his first information about electrical experiments being made in Europe, and thus had an indirect hand in Franklin's kite-and-key experiment and other electrical inquiries which, one way and another, eventually led to the lines which now bring electricity to my farm to run my furnace, my refrigerator, even the typewriter on which these words are being written. Peter Collinson, whose name is an obscure entry in the reference books, but who is there in the botany books for all time—*Collinsonia*, rich weed, horse balm, one of the lesser members of the mint family and which grows in my back pasture.

One final word about these lists. Although they include

virtually all the species I have mentioned in this book, they are mere samplings in each category. A list of all the known plants, birds, animals, and insects would literally fill several volumes. As an example, there are about 3,500 identified species of mammals in the world, 389 in North America. There are some 8,600 species of birds, 686 in the United States. There are about 250,000 identified plant species. And when it comes to insects, the number of species is astonishing and an approximation at best; there are 22,000 listed species of *beetles* alone in the United States! Or were when I last looked; the number seems to rise every few months.

Among the taxonomists—the namers and listers—there are two schools, sometimes called "The Lumpers" and "The Splitters." The Lumpers would limit and simplify the listings of species and subspecies, and the Splitters would expand and complicate them. No doubt both factions have sound reasons for their stand, but it does seem to me that the Splitters have strained at quite a few gnats in their passion for diversifying the species. And my layman's complaint is joined by a good many scientists, especially in the fields of ornithology and entomology.

In any case, my combined list of Animals, Fish and Amphibians, Insects, Plants, and Reptiles comes to only about 500. That is what I mean by a sampling.

# Animals

| COMMON NAME | SCIENTIFIC NAME |
| --- | --- |
| Bat, Little Brown | *Myotis lucifugus* |
| Bear | |
|     Black, or Brown | *Euarctos americanus* |
|     Grizzly | *Ursus horribilis* |
| Bobcat—see Lynx | |
| Cat, domestic | *Felis catus* |
| Chipmunk, Eastern | *Tamias striatus* |
| Deer | |
|     Mule | *Odocoileus hemionus* |
|     White-tail; Virginia | *Odocoileus virginianus* |
| Elk; Wapiti | *Cervus canadensis* |
| Fox | |
|     Gray | *Urocyon cinereoargentus* |
|     Red | *Vulpes fulva* |
| Lemming, Northern Bog | *Synaptomys borealis* |
| Lynx | *Lynx canadensis* |
| Mole, Eastern | *Scalopus aquaticus* |
| Moose | *Alces americana* |
| Mouse | |
|     Deer | *Peromyscus maniculatus* |
|     House | *Mus musculus* |
|     White-footed | *Peromyscus leocopus* |
| Muskrat | *Ondatra zibethicus* |
| Opossum | *Didelphia marsupialis* |
| Otter, river | *Lutra canadensis* |
| Panther; Cougar; Mountain Lion | *Felis concolor* |
| Porcupine | *Erethizon dorsatum* |

| | |
|---|---|
| Prairie Dog | *Cyonomys ludovicianus* |
| Pronghorn (Antelope) | *Antilocapra americana* |
| Rabbit | |
|     Cottontail, Eastern | *Sylvilagus floridanus* |
|     Cottontail, New England | *Sylvilagus transitionalis* |
|     Snowshoe (a hare, really) | *Lepus americanus* |
| Raccoon | *Procyon lotor* |
| Rat | |
|     Black | *Rattus rattus* |
|     Domestic; Norwegian | *Rattus norvegicus* |
| Shrew | |
|     Common; Masked | *Sorex cinereus* |
|     Short-tailed | *Blarina brevicauda* |
|     Water | *Sorex palustris* |
| Skunk | *Mephitis mephitis* |
| Squirrel | |
|     Flying | *Glaucumys sabrinus* |
|     Fox | *Sciurus niger* |
|     Gray | *Sciurus carolinensus* |
|     Red | *Tamiasciurus hudsonicus* |
| Vole | |
|     Meadow | *Microtus pennsylvanicus* |
|     Pine | *Microtus pinetorum* |
| Wolf | *Canis lupus* |
| Woodchuck; Ground Hog | *Mormota monax* |

# Birds

| COMMON NAME | SCIENTIFIC NAME |
|---|---|
| Bittern, American | *Botaurus lentiginosus* |
| Blackbird | |
|     Brown-headed Cowbird | *Molothrus ater* |
|     Red-wing | *Agelaius phoeniceus* |
|     Rusty | *Eophagus carolinus* |
|     Yellow-headed | *Xanthocephalus* |

| | |
|---|---|
| Bluebird | *Sialia sialis* |
| Blue Jay | *Cyanocitta cristata* |
| Bobolink | *Dolichonyx oryzivorus* |
| Bob-white; Quail | *Colinus virginianus* |
| Brown Thrasher | *Toxostoma rufum* |
| Bunting, Indigo | *Passerina cyanea* |
| Buzzard; Turkey Vulture | *Cathartes aura* |
| Cardinal | *Richmondena cardinalis* |
| Catbird | *Dumetella carolinensis* |
| Chat, Yellow-breasted | *Icteria virens* |
| Chickadee, Black-capped | *Parus atricapillus* |
| Coot, American | *Fulica americana* |
| Cowbird—see Blackbird | |
| Crow | *Corvus brachyrhynchos* |
| Dove, Mourning | *Zenaidura macroura* |
| Duck | |
|     Black | *Anas rubripes* |
|     Mallard | *Anas platyrhynchos* |
|     Wood | *Aix sponsa* |
| Flicker—see Woodpecker | |
| Flycatcher, Traill's or Alder | *Empidonax traillii* |
| Goldfinch | *Spinus tristus* |
| Goose | |
|     Canada | *Branta canadensis* |
|     Snow | *Chen hyperborea* |
| Grackle | |
|     Boat-tailed | *Cassidix mexicanus* |
|     Common | *Quiscalus quiscula* |
| Grosbeak | |
|     Evening | *Hesperiphona vespertina* |
|     Rose-breasted | *Pheucticus ludovicianus* |
| Hawk | |
|     Red-shouldered | *Buteo lineatus* |
|     Red-tailed | *Buteo jamaicensis* |
|     Sparrow | *Falco sparverius* |
| Heron | |
|     Great Blue | *Ardea herodias* |
|     Little Green | *Butorides virescens* |
| Hummingbird, Ruby-throat | *Archilochus colubris* |

| | |
|---|---|
| Junco; Snowbird | *Junco hyemalis* |
| Kingbird | *Tyrannus tyrannus* |
| Kingfisher | *Megaceryle alcyon* |
| Kinglet, Golden-crowned | *Regulus satrapa* |
| Martin, Purple | *Progne subis* |
| Meadowlark | *Sturnella magna* |
| Merganser | |
|     American | *Mergus merganser* |
|     Hooded | *Lophodytes cucullatus* |
| Nighthawk | *Chordeiles minor* |
| Nuthatch | |
|     Red-breasted | *Sitta canadensis* |
|     White-breasted | *Sitta carolinensis* |
| Oriole, Baltimore | *Icterus galbula* |
| Owl | |
|     Barred | *Strix varia* |
|     Great Horned | *Bubo virginianus* |
|     Screech | *Otus asio* |
|     Snowy | *Nyctea scandiaca* |
| Partridge—see Ruffed Grouse | |
| Pheasant, Ring-necked | *Phasianus colchicus* |
| Redpoll | *Acanthis flammea* |
| Redstart | *Setophaga ruticilla* |
| Robin | *Turdus migratorius* |
| Ruffed Grouse | *Bonasa umbellus* |
| Siskin, Pine | *Spinus pinus* |
| Sparrow | |
|     Fox | *Passerella iliaca* |
|     House, or English | *Passer domesticus* |
|     Song | *Melospiza melodia* |
|     Swamp | *Melospiza georgiana* |
|     Tree | *Spizella arborea* |
|     White-throat | *Zonotrichia albicollis* |
| Starling | *Sturnus vulgaris* |
| Swallow, Barn | *Hirundo erythrogaster* |
| Swift, Chimney | *Chaetura pelagica* |
| Tanager, Scarlet | *Piranga olivacea* |
| Tern, Arctic | *Sterna paradisaea* |

Thrush
    Hermit                 *Hylocichla guttata*
    Wood                  *Hylocichla mustelina*
Thrush, Mimics
    Brown Thrasher     *Toxostoma rufum*
    Catbird            *Dumetella carolinensis*
    Mockingbird       *Mimus polyglottos*
Towhee, or Chewink     *Pipilio erythrophthalmus*
Veery               *Hylocichla fuscescens*
Vireo
    Red-eyed          *Vireo olivaceus*
    Warbling          *Vireo gilvus*
    Yellow-throated    *Vireo flavifrons*
Warbler
    Audubon's         *Dendroica auduboni*
    Bay-breasted      *Dendroica castanea*
    Blackburnian      *Dendroica fusca*
    Blackpoll         *Dendroica striata*
    Black-throated Green  *Dendroica virens*
    Cape May         *Dendroica tigrina*
    Pine              *Dendroica pinus*
    Prothonotary      *Protonotaria citrea*
Whippoorwill         *Caprimulgus vociferus*
Woodcock             *Philohela minor*
Woodpecker
    Downy            *Dendrocopus pubescens*
    Flicker; Yellow-shafted  *Colaptes auratus*
    Hairy            *Dendrocopus villosus*
  Pileated           *Dryocopus pileatus*
Wren, House          *Troglodytes aedon*

## Fish and Amphibians

| COMMON NAME | SCIENTIFIC NAME |
|---|---|
| **Bass** | |
| Large-mouth, Black | *Huro salmoides* |
| Rock | *Ambloplites rupestris* |
| Small-mouth, Black | *Micropterus dolomieu* |
| **Catfish; Horned Pout, etc.** | |
| Bullhead | *Ameiurur nebulosus* |
| Channel | *Ictalurur lacustris* |
| **Frog** | |
| Leopard | *Rana pipiens* |
| Pickerel | *Rana palustris* |
| **Mud Puppy** | *Necturus maculosus* |
| **Perch, Yellow** | *Perca flavescens* |
| **Pickerel** | |
| Barred | *Esox americanus* |
| Eastern, or Chain | *Esox niger* |
| **"Silver Carp"** | |
| Fallfish; Silver Chub | *Semotilus corporalis* |
| Golden Shiner; Chub | *Notemigonus crysoleucas* |
| **Spring Peeper** | *Hyla crucifer* |
| **Sucker, White** | *Catostomus commersonii* |
| **Sunfish** | |
| Bluegill | *Lepomis macrochirus* |
| Pumpkinseed | *Eupomotis gibbosus* |
| Yellowbreast | *Lepomis auritus* |
| **Toad, Common American** | *Bufo terrestris* |
| **Trout** | |
| Brook | *Salvelinus fontinalis* |
| Brown | *Salmo trutta* |
| Rainbow | *Salmo gairdnerii* |

# Insects

| COMMON NAME | SCIENTIFIC NAME |
|---|---|
| **Ants** | |
| Black Carpenter | *Componotus pennsylvanicus* |
| Common Northeast | *Polyergus lucidus* |
| Tiny Black | *Lasius niger* |
| **Back Swimmer** | *Notonecta undulata* |
| **Bees** | |
| Bumblebee | *Bombus americanus* |
| Honeybee | *Apis mellifera* |
| **Birch Moth—see Moths** | |
| **Black Fly** | *Simulidae* |
| **Caddis Fly** | *Ptilostomis semifasciata* |
| **Centipede** | *Scutigera forceps* |
| **Cockroach, Common** | *Blatta orientalis* |
| **Cricket, Common Black** | *Gryllus assimilis* |
| **Damsel Fly** | |
| Black-winged | *Agrion maculatum* |
| Swamp | *Lestes rectangularis* |
| **Deer Fly** | *Chrysops* |
| **Dogbane Beetle** | *Chrysochus auratus* |
| **Dragonfly, Ten-spot** | *Libellula pulchella* |
| **Elm-leaf Beetle** | *Gallerucella xanthomalaena* |
| **Firefly, two common ones** | *Photinus pyralis* / *Photurus pennsylvanica* |
| **Grasshoppers, typical** | |
| Large | *Schistocera americana* |
| Small; Bird Locust | *Schistocera damnifica* |
| Sand-colored | *Spharagemon bolli* / *Trimerotropis maritima* |
| **Housefly** | *Musca domestica* |
| **Japanese Beatle** | *Popillia japonica* |
| **Katydid** | |
| Angular-winged | *Microcentrum retinerve* |
| Common | *Pterophylla camellifolia* |

| | |
|---|---|
| Ladybird Beetle (Cocinella) | *Adalia bipunctata* |
| May Fly | *Ephemeridae* |
| Midges; No-see-ums | *Culicoides* |
| Millipede | *Spirobolus marginatus* |
| Monarch Butterfly | *Danaus plexippus* |
| Mosquito | |
|     Malaria Carrier | *Anopheles quadrimaculatus* |
|     Marsh | *Aëdes sollicitans* |
| Moths | |
|     Birch | *Catocala relicta* |
|     Clothes | *Tineola bisseliella* |
|     Luna | *Actias luna* |
|     Sphinx; Hawk Moth | *Phlegathontius quinquema-culatus* |
|     Woolly Bear; Isabella | *Isia isabella* |
| Potato Beetle; Colorado | |
|     Beetle | *Lema trilineata* |
| Silverfish | *Lepisma domestica* |
| Wasps | |
|     Golden Digger | *Amobia ichneumones* |
|     "Mud Dauber" | *Trypoxylinae* |
|     Paper-maker Wasps which make small, open paper nests (no common name) | *Polistes* |
|     Yellow Jackets and Hornets which make closed paper nests | *Vespa* |
| Water Boatman | *Arctocorixa interrupta* |
| Water Bug; Electric Light Bug | *Benacus grisecus* |
| Water Scorpion | *Nepta apiculata* |
| Water Strider, typical | *Gerris remigis* |
| Woolly Bear—see Moths | |

# Spiders

**(There are about 40,000 species, of which I list only three)**

| COMMON NAME | SCIENTIFIC NAME |
|---|---|
| Black Widow | *Latrodectus mactans* |
| House Web, the common one | *Tegenaria* |
| Wolf | *Lycosidae* |

# Plants

**(Including Flowers, Bushes, Shrubs, Vines, and Trees)**

| COMMON NAME | SCIENTIFIC NAME |
|---|---|
| Alder, Black; Winterberry | *Ilex verticillata* |
| Anemone | |
|     Rue | *Anemonella thalictroides* |
|     Wood | *Anemone quinquifolia* |
| Arbutus | *Epigaea repens* |
| Arrowwood | *Viburnum dentatum* |
| Artichoke, Jerusalem | *Helianthus tuberosa* |
| Ash | |
|     Black | *Fraxinus nigra* |
|     Mountain (not a true Ash) | *Pyrus americana* |
|     White | *Fraxinus americana* |
| Aspen | |
|     Bigtooth | *Populus grandidentata* |
|     Quacking | *Populus tremuloides* |
|     White; Poplar | *Populus alba* |

Aster
    Calico                             *Aster lateriflorus*
    Michaelmas Daisy;
        Heath                    *Aster ericoides*
    New England; Big
        Purple                  *Aster novae-angliae*

| Common name | Scientific name |
|---|---|
| Aster | |
|   Calico | *Aster lateriflorus* |
|   Michaelmas Daisy; Heath | *Aster ericoides* |
|   New England; Big Purple | *Aster novae-angliae* |
| Azalea; Pinkster | *Rhododendron nudiflorum* |
| Baneberry | |
|   Red | *Actaea rubra* |
|   White | *Actaea alba* |
| Barberry | |
|   American, Native | *Berberis canadensis* |
|   European | *Berberis vulgaris* |
|   Japanese | *Berberis Thurnbergii* |
| Basswood; Linden, American | *Tilia americana* |
| Bayberry, Northern | *Myrica pennsylvanica* |
| Bearberry | *Arctostaphylos uva-ursi* |
| Bedstraw, Rough | *Galium asprellum* |
| Beech, Tree | *Fagus grandifolia* |
| Beechdrops, False | *Monotropa Hypopitys* |
| Beggar-ticks | *Bidens frondosa* |
| Bergamot | |
|   Bee Balm; Oswego Tea | *Monarda didyma* |
|   Common Lavender | *Monarda fistulosa* |
| Bindweed, Hedge; Morning Glory | *Convolvulus sepium* |
| Birch | |
|   Black; Cherry; Sweet | *Betula lenta* |
|   Gray | *Betula populifolia* |
|   Red; River | *Betula nigra* |
|   White; Canoe; Paper | *Betula papyrifera* |
|   Yellow | *Betula lutea* |
| Bittersweet, American | *Celastrus scandens* |
| Blackberry, Wild | |
|   Low Running; Dewberry | *Rubus flagellaris* |
|   Tall or Common | *Rubus allegheninesis* |
| Black-eyed Susan | *Rudbeckia hirta* |
| Bladder Campion | *Silene cucubalus* |

| | |
|---|---|
| Bloodroot | *Sanguineria canadensis* |
| Blueberry | |
|     Canada | *Vaccinium canadense* |
|     High-bush | *Vaccinium corymbosum* |
|     Low Sweet | *Vaccinium pennsylvanicum* |
| Blue-eyed Grass | *Sisyrinchium angustifolium* |
| Bluet | *Houstonia caerula* |
| Boneset; Thoroughwort | *Eupatorium perfoliatum* |
| Bouncing Bet | *Saponaria officinalis* |
| Bracken—see Ferns | |
| Buckeye, Sweet | *Aesculus octandra* |
| Buckwheat Family | *Polygonaceae* |
| Burdock | |
|     Common | *Arctium minus* |
|     Great | *Arctium lappa* |
| Bur Marigold | *Bidens laevis* |
| Bur Reeds | *Sparganium* |
| Butter and Eggs—see Toad-flax | |
| Buttercup | |
|     Creeping | *Ranunculus repens* |
|     Early | *Ranunculus fascicularis* |
|     Swamp | *Ranunculus septentrionalis* |
| Butternut, tree | *Juglens cinerea* |
| Canada Mayflower; Wild Lily of the Valley | *Maianthemum canadense* |
| Cardinal Flower | *Lobelia cardinalis* |
| Cat Brier; Bull Brier | *Smilax rotundifolia* |
| Cattail | |
|     Broad-leaf | *Typha latifolia* |
|     Narrow-leaf | *Typha angustifolia* |
| Cedar, Tree | |
|     Dwarf Juniper | *Juniperus communis* |
|     Red | *Juniperus virginiana* |
|     White | *Chamaecyparis thyoides* |
| Celandine | *Chelidonium majus* |
| Cherry, Bird | *Prunus pennsylvanica* |
| Chestnut | *Castanea dentata* |

| | |
|---|---|
| Chickweed (many varieties; two cited) | |
| Common | *Stellaria media* |
| Mouse-ear | *Cerastium vulgatum* |
| Chicory | *Chicorium intybus* |
| Chokecherry | |
| Black | *Pyrus melanocarpus* |
| Red | *Pyrus arbutifolia* |
| Cinquefoil | |
| Common | *Potentilla simplex* |
| Shrubby | *Potentilla fruticosa* |
| Clover | |
| Rabbit's-foot | *Trifolium arvense* |
| Red | *Trifolium pretense* |
| White Sweet | *Melilotus albus* |
| Wild Lupine | *Lupinus perennis* |
| Yellow Sweet | *Melilotus officinalis* |
| Clematis, Wild; Virgin's Bower; Old Man's Beard | *Clematis virginiana* |
| Coltsfoot | *Tussilago farfara* |
| Columbine | *Aquilegia canadensis* |
| Cranberry | |
| High-bush; Pimbina | *Viburnum opulus, var. americanum* |
| Small, Wild | *Vaccinium oxycoccos* |
| Cranesbill—see Geranium | |
| Cress, Wild | |
| Spring | *Cardamine bulbosa* |
| Water | *Nasturtium officinale* |
| Winter; Yellow Rocket | *Barbarea vulgaris* |
| Cucumber, Climbing Wild; Balsam | *Echinocystis lobata* |
| Daisy, Common or Oxeye | *Chrysanthemum leucanthemum* |
| Dame's Rocket | *Hesperis matronalis* |
| Dandelion | |
| Common | *Taraxicum officinale* |
| Dwarf | *Krigia virginica* |

| | |
|---|---|
| Day Lily | *Hemerocallis fulva* |
| Deptford Pink | *Dianthus armeria* |
| Dock, Sour | *Rumex acteosa* |
| Dockmackie | *Viburnum acerifolium* |
| Dogbane | |
|     Indian Hemp | *Apocynum cannabinum* |
|     Spreading | *Apocynum androsaemifolium* |
| Dogtooth Violet; Trout Lily | *Erythronium americanum* |
| Dogwood | |
|     Dwarf Cornel, or | |
|         Bunchberry | *Cornum canadensis* |
|     Flowering (the tree) | *Cornus florida* |
|     Red-osier | *Cornus stolonifera* |
|     Silky; Kinnikinnik | *Cornum amomum* |
| Dutchman's-breeches | *Dicentra cucullaria* |
| Elderberry | *Sambucus canadensis* |
| Elm | |
|     American; New England | *Ulmus americana* |
|     Rock | *Ulmus thomassi* |
|     Slippery | *Ulmus rubra* |
| False Spikenard | *Smilacina racemosa* |
| Ferns | |
|     Bracken; Brake Fern | *Pteridium aquilinum* |
|     Christmas | *Polystichum acrostichoides* |
|     Cinnamon | *Osmunda cinnamomea* |
|     Ostrich | *Matteuccia Struthiopteris* |
| Fireweed; Great Willow-herb | *Epilobium angustafolium* |
| Flag—see Iris | |
| Foamflower; False Miterwort | *Tiarella cordifolia* |
| Forget-me-not | |
|     Small, Wild | *Myosotis laxa* |
|     Large, Escaped Tame | *Myosotis scorpioides* |
| Gensing, Dwarf | *Panax trifolium* |
| Geranium, Wild | |
|     Cranesbill | *Geranium maculatum* |
|     Herb Robert | *Geranium robertianum* |
| Ginger, Wild | *Asarum canadense* |
| Goatsbeard | *Tragopogon pratensis* |

| | |
|---|---|
| Goldenrod | |
| Canada | *Solidago canadensis* |
| Large-leaf | *Solidago macrophylla* |
| Late | *Solidago serotina* |
| Rough-stemmed | *Solidago rugosa* |
| Sweet | *Solidago odora* |
| White | *Solidago bicolor* |
| Goldthread | *Coptis trifolia* |
| Grape | |
| Fox | *Vitis labrusca* |
| River | *Vitis vulpina* |
| Ground Cedar | *Lycopodium tristachyum* |
| Groundnut; Wild Bean | *Apios americana* |
| Hardhack; Steeplebush | *Spiraea tomentosa* |
| Hawkweed | |
| Canada; King Devil | *Hieracium florentinum* |
| Tawny; Devil's-paint-brush | *Hieracium auranyiacum* |
| Hawthorns, the Family | *Crataegus* |
| Hazelnut | |
| American | *Corylus americana* |
| Beaked | *Corylus curnuta* |
| Hemlock, Tree | *Tsuga canadensis* |
| Hepatica; Liverwort | *Hepatica americana* |
| Herb Robert—see Geranium | |
| Hickory | |
| Butternut | *Juglans cinerea* |
| Mockernut | *Carya tomentosa* |
| Pignut | *Carya glabra* |
| Shagbark | *Carya ovata* |
| Swamp | *Carya cordiformis* |
| Sweet Pignut | *Carya ovalis* |
| Holly, American | *Ilex opaca* |
| Hornbeam | |
| American; Blue Beech | *Carpinus caroliniana* |
| Hop Hornbeam; Iron-wood | *Ostrya virginiana* |
| Horsetail | *Equisetum arvense* |
| Huckleberry | *Gaylussacia baccata* |

| | |
|---|---|
| Indian Pipe | *Monotropa uniflora* |
| Indian Tobacco | *Lobelia inflata* |
| Iris | |
|     Common Blue Flag | *Iris versicolor* |
|     Slender Flag (of marshes) | *Iris prismatica* |
| Ironweed | *Vernonia noveboracensis* |
| Ironwood—see Hornbeam | |
| Ivy, Poison | *Rhus radicans* |
| Jack-in-the-pulpit | *Artisaema triphyllum* |
| Jerusalem Artichoke | *Helianthus tuberosus* |
| Joe Pye Weed | *Eupatorium purpureum* |
| Jewelweed; Touch-me-not | |
|     Pale | *Impatiens pallida* |
|     Spotted | *Impatiens biflora* |
| Juniper—see Cedar | |
| Lady-slipper | |
|     Common | *Cypripedium acaule* |
|     Showy | *Cypripedium hirsutum* |
|     Yellow | *Cypripedium calceolus* |
| Lamb's-quarters | *Chenopodium album* |
| Laurel, Mountain | *Kalmia latifolia* |
| Lily | |
|     Day | *Hemerocallis fulva* |
|     Meadow | *Lilium canadense* |
|     Wood | *Lilium philadelphicum* |
| Lobelia | |
|     Great | *Lobelia siphilitica* |
|     Water | *Lobelia dortmanna* |
| Locust, Tree | |
|     Black | *Robinia pseuda-acacia* |
|     Honey | *Gleditsia triacanthos* |
| Manzanita | *Arctostaphylos pungens* |
| Maple, Tree | |
|     Elm-Leaf; Box Elder | *Acer negundo* |
|     Mountain; Elkwood | *Acer spicatum* |
|     Striped; Moosewood | *Acer pennsylvanicum* |
|     Sugar | *Acer saccharum* |
|     Swamp; Red | *Acer rubrum* |

| | |
|---|---|
| Marsh Marigold; Cowslip | *Caltha palustris* |
| May Apple; Mandrake | *Podophyllum peltatum* |
| Meadowsweet | *Spiraea latifolia* |
| Milkweed | |
|     Common | *Asclepias syriaca* |
|     Orange; Butterfly | |
|       Weed | *Asclepias tuberosa* |
| Mint | |
|     Bee Balm; Oswego Tea | *Monarda didyma* |
|     Catnip | *Nepeta cataria* |
|     Gill-over-the-ground; | |
|       Ground Ivy | *Glecoma hederacea* |
|     Selfheal | *Prunella vulgaris* |
|     Wild Mint | *Mentha arvensis* |
| Mistletoe | *Phoradendron flavescens* |
| Moccasin Flower | *Fissipes acaulis* |
| Moneywort | *Lysimachia nummularia* |
| Mountain Ash—see Ash | |
| Mullein | |
|     Great | *Verbascum thapsus* |
|     Moth | *Verbascum blattaria* |
| Mustard, Black | *Brassica nigra* |
| Nannyberry | *Viburnum lentigo* |
| Nettle | |
|     Hedge | *Stachys palustris* |
|     Hemp | *Galeopsis tatrahit* |
| Nightshade, Deadly | *Solanum dulcamara* |
| Oak, Tree | |
|     Black | *Quercus velutina* |
|     Chinquapin | *Quercus muehlenbergii* |
|     Pin | *Quercus palustris* |
|     Red | *Quercus rubra* |
|     White | *Quercus alba* |
| Old Man's Beard—see | |
|   Clematis | |
| Orchis, Showy | *Orchis spectabilis* |
| Oxalis—see Sorrel | |
| Parsnip | |
|     Caraway | *Carum carvi* |

**Parsnip** (*continued*)
    Common Meadow          *Pastinica sativa*
    Cowbane                  *Oxypolis rigidior*
    Poison Hemlock           *Cicuta maculata*
    Sweet Cicely              *Osmorhiza Claytoni*
**Partridgeberry**             *Mitchella repens*
**Partridge Pea**              *Cassia chamaecrista*
**Peppergrass**                *Lepidium virginicum*
**Phlox, Wild Blue**            *Phlox subulata*
**Pigweed**                    *Amarantus retroflexus*
**Pimbina**—see Cranberry
**Pine, Tree**
    Pitch; Jack; Hard        *Pinus rigida*
    Red                    *Pinus resinosa*
    Scrub                  *Pinus virginiana*
    White                  *Pinus strobus*
    Yellow                 *Pinus echinata*
**Pink, Deptford**            *Dianthus armeria*
**Plantain**
    Common               *Plantago major*
    Narrow-leaf            *Plantago rugelii*
**Plum**
    Plain Wild              *Prunus americana*
    Red, or Canada         *Prunus nigra*
**Poison Ivy**—see Ivy
**Poison Oak**—see Sumac
**Pokeweed; Inkberry**       *Phytolacca americana*
**Poplar**—see Aspen
**Primrose, Evening**        *Oenothera biennis*
**Purslane**                    *Portulaca oleracera*
**Queen Anne's Lace; Wild**
  Carrot                    *Caucus carota*
**Ragweed**
    Common               *Ambrosia artemisifolia*
    Great                 *Ambrosia trifidia*
**Raspberry**
    Black-cap              *Rubus occidentalis*
    Purple-flowering      *Rubus odoratus*
**Redwood**                   *Sequoia sempervirens*

| | |
|---|---|
| Robin's Plantain | *Erigeron pulchellis* |
| Rose, Wild; Pasture Rose | *Rosa virginiana* |
| Running Pine | *Lycopodium complanatum* |
| Sagittaria; Broad-leafed Arrowhead | *Sagittaria latifolia* |
| St. John's-wort | *Hypericum perforatum* |
| Sarsaparilla | *Aralia nudicaulis* |
| Sassafras, Tree | |
| Saxifrage | *Sassafras albidum* |
| Early | *Saxifraga virginiensis* |
| Swamp | *Saxifraga pennsylvanica* |
| Scouring Rush | *Equisetum laevigatum* |
| Shadbush; Shadblow; Serviceberry | *Amalanchier canadensis* |
| Skunk Cabbage | *Symplocarpus foetidus* |
| Smartweed Family | *Polygonaceae* |
| Snakeroot, White | *Eupatorium urticaefolium* |
| Snowberry | *Symphoricarpos racemosus* |
| Solomon's-seal | *Polygonatum biflorum* |
| Sorrel | |
| Red; Sour Grass | *Oxalis acetosella* |
| Violet Wood | *Oxalis violacea* |
| Yellow, or Lady's | *Oxalis corniculata* |
| Sour Dock; Curly Dock | *Rumex crispus* |
| Sour Grass—see Sorrel | |
| Spicebush | *Lindera benzoin* |
| Spikenard, False | *Smilacina racemosa* |
| Spruce, Tree | |
| Black | *Picea mariana* |
| Norway | *Picea abies* |
| Red | *Picea rubra* |
| Squirrel Corn | *Dicentra canadensis* |
| Starflower | *Trientalis americana* |
| Steeplebush—see Hardhack | |
| Strawberry, Wild | *Fragaria virginiana* |
| Sumac, Tree | |
| Dwarf; Winged | *Rhus copallina* |
| Poison Oak | *Rhus quercifolia* |

Sumac, Tree (*continued*)
    Poison Sumac               *Rhus vernix*
    Smooth                      *Rhus glabra*
    Stag-horn                 *Rhus tiphina*
Sundrop; Day Primrose     *Oenothera fruticosa*
Sunflower                    *Helianthus annuus*
Sweet Flag                 *Acorus calamus*
Sycamore (native)         *Platanus occidentalis*
Tamarack; Larch          *Larix laricina*
Toadflax; Butter and Eggs  *Linaria vulgaris*
Toothwort                  *Dentaria diphylla*
Tree Clubmoss           *Lycopodium obscurum*
Trefoil, Tick, the Family   *Desmodium*
Trillium
    Nodding               *Trillium cernuum*
    Painted                *Trillium undulatum*
    Wake Robin; Birthroot  *Trillium erectum*
Vervain, Blue            *Verbena hastata*
Viburnum—see Arrowwood;
  Cranberry;  Dockmackie;
  Nannyberry
Violet
    Big White              *Viola blanda*
    Common Meadow     *Viola papilionacea*
    Little Yellow          *Viola pubsecens*
    Marsh                  *Viola palustris*
Virginia Creeper; Woodbine  *Psedera quinquefolia*
Walnut, Black            *Juglans nigra*
Water Plantain          *Alisma subcordatum*
Willow
    Black                  *Salix nigra*
    Pussy                  *Salix discolor*
    Swamp or Bog          *Salix pedicellaris*
    Weeping               *Salix babylonica*
Winterberry—see Alder
Wintergreen               *Gaultheria procumbens*
Witch Hazel              *Hamamelis virginiana*
Yellow Rocket—see Cress

# Reptiles

| COMMON NAME | SCIENTIFIC NAME |
|---|---|
| Copperhead | *Agkistrodon contortrix* |
| Coral Snake | *Micrurus fulvius* |
| Cottonmouth; Water Moccasin | *Agkistrodon piscivorus* |
| Rattlesnake | |
|     Eastern Timber | *Crotalus horridus* |
|     Massasauga | *Sistrurus catenatus* |
|     Western Diamondback | *Crotalus atrox* |
| Turtles | |
|     Snapping | *Chelydra serpentina* |
|     Spotted | *Clemys guttata* |
| Watersnakes | |
|     Brown | *Natrix taxispilota* |
|     Common | *Natrix sipedon* |
|     Green | *Natrix cyclopion* |

# An Armful of Books

IF I were to attempt to compile a bibliography for this book I would have to list at least half the reading I have done since I was a small boy. Even if that were possible, it would be a fantastic list. It would range from the novels of James Fenimore Cooper to Webster's Unabridged Dictionary, from the poetry of William Cullen Bryant to that of Robert Frost, from the romances of Gene Stratton Porter to the Journals of Lewis and Clark, from Aesop's Fables to Zinsser's *Rats, Lice and History*. It would include Thoreau and Audubon, Muir and Burroughs, and dozens of lesser names. I shall omit such a preposterous bibliography. Instead, I shall mention a few of the series of guidebooks and field manuals and suggest individual books in my own library that may be of help or interest in connection with individual chapters of this volume.

First the field guides, the primary purpose of which is identification. There are several series. I can recommend the "Field Book" series published by Putnam and the "Field Guide" series published by Houghton Mifflin with few reservations. I have my preferences among both series, as most readers undoubtedly will also come to have. Doubleday also publishes selected "Guides," of which I use two. The most inexpensive series is the "Golden Nature Guide" group of paperbacks published by the Golden Press. These were brought to my attention by a seven-year-old boy, who was fascinated by them. Though limited in scope, the volumes are well organized, excellently illustrated, and useful especially for youngsters and beginners, interesting for anyone. I have a full set of them. The best broad-scale guide I know of is the fat volume, *The Complete Guide to American Wildlife*, by Henry Hill Collins, Jr. (Harper), which is packed with factual information about birds, animals, fish, reptiles, amphibians, even seashells. Other books in the guide category will be mentioned in the following chapter-by-chapter list:

CHAPTER 1: I have yet to find a wholly satisfactory guide to the insects. Those I know lose me in a maze of anatomical detail. The excellently illustrated *Familiar Insects of North America*, by Will Barker (Harper), is good but limited in scope. *The Living House*, by George Ordish (Lippincott), deals at length with the non-human inhabitants of a country house in England, but much of its material is applicable almost anywhere.

CHAPTER 2: Good roadside books are hard to find. I depend on the guides to birds, wildflowers, trees, and shrubs. John Kieran's *Natural History of New York City* (Houghton Mifflin), while not a guide and although specifically about one city, is packed with information about wild life just outside the door and along urban and suburban streets. Much of its information is true of almost any built-up area in the Northeast.

CHAPTER 3: *Grassroot Jungles* and *Near Horizons*, by Edwin Way Teale (Dodd Mead), although primarily about insects are also good companions for journeys of discovery in any open field. *Weeds*, by Walter Conrad Muenscher (Macmillan), treats wild plants from the agricultural viewpoint but is packed with information. Both *Seeds* and *Grass*, annual publications of the U.S. Department of Agriculture, approach those topics from the farmer's viewpoint but also are well worth attention.

CHAPTER 4: *The Changing Face of New England*, by Betty Flanders Thomson (Macmillan), deals especially well with woodlands as well as with geological history, botany, zoology, and ecology. Though specifically about New England, much of its material is applicable elsewhere. I use the *Field Book of American Trees and Shrubs*, by

F. Schuyler Mathews (Putnam). For ferns I have found *A Field Guide to the Ferns*, by Boughton Cobb (Houghton Mifflin), the best compact volume of its kind. Its illustrations by Laura Louise Foster are superb.

CHAPTER 5: I have found no first-class book dealing with wild life in the bogs and swamps. I use the various guides. Two women who wrote fiction, both now dead, contributed greatly to swamp lore and background. Marjorie Kinnan Rawlings's *The Yearling* (Scribner's), is rich with such material, though it is about Florida. And the all-but-forgotten romantic novels of Gene Stratton Porter, such as *The Harvester* and *A Girl of the Limberlost*, were full of accurate background on the swamps of the Midwest. Mrs. Porter was an ornithologist and good all-round naturalist.

CHAPTER 6: There are many books about human life on rivers and in river valleys, but few about the rivers themselves. Even the "Rivers of America" series (Rinehart) deals primarily with human history and folklore. Thoreau's *A Week on the Concord and Merrimack Rivers* is splendidly alive with nature observation, though insistently interrupted by Thoreau's characteristic social phiolosophic comments. The best recent river book I know is John Graves's *Goodbye to a River* (Knopf), but it is about the Brazos in Texas. *Fishing Lake and Stream*, edited by Ray Schrenkeisen (Doubleday), is a better than average book on the subject. The best compact book on fish identification I have found is Francesca La Monte's *North American Game Fish* (Doubleday).

CHAPTER 7: I have no books dealing extensively or even satisfactorily with the world I see through a hand-glass. There may be one, but I have yet to find it.

CHAPTER 8: There are dozens of animal books, good, bad, and awful. Ernest Thompson Seton's *Wild Animals I Have Known* (Doubleday) has its merits, especially for youngsters. *Familiar Animals of North America*, by Will Barker (Harper), is excellent though limited in scope. I frequently turn to two of the textbooks on my shelves,

*General Zoology,* by Tracy I. Storer (McGraw-Hill) and *Animal Biology,* by Michael F. Guyer (Harper), both of which are more readable than most texts. For night-watchers I recommend *The World of Night,* by Lorus and Margery Milne (Harper). For animal tracks I find Olaus J. Murie's *A Field Guide to Animal Tracks* (Houghton Mifflin) invaluable.

CHAPTER 9: There are hundreds of bird books, good, bad, and impossible. I rely on two guides, *A Field Guide to the Birds,* by Roger Tory Peterson (Houghton Mifflin), and *The Audubon Bird Guide: Eastern Land Birds,* by Richard H. Pough (Doubleday). On my shelves is also the comprehensive *Birds of North America,* edited by T. Gilbert Pearson (Doubleday). For bird songs I have found *A Guide to Bird Songs,* by Aretas A. Saunders (Doubleday), outstandingly good. John K. Terres's *Songbirds in Your Garden* (Crowell) is sound and sensible.

CHAPTER 10: *Why the Weather?* by Charles F. Brooks, Eleanor S. Brooks, and John Nelson (Harcourt Brace), is one of my stand-bys. The "Golden Guide" volumes on *Weather* and *Stars* (Golden Press) are full of clear, concise information. Two volumes in the *Scientific American* series of paperbacks, *The New Astronomy* and *The Planet Earth* (Simon & Schuster), are excellent.

CHAPTER 11: Two books by Lee R. Dice: *Natural Communities* and *The Biotic Provinces of North America* (University of Michigan Press) are unusually worth while. Durward L. Allen's *Our Wildlife Legacy* (Funk & Wagnalls) is both provocative and informative. Almost any book by the late Aldo Leopold throws fresh light on this topic; I often pick up his *A Sand County Almanac* (Oxford) for sheer enjoyment, since Leopold had a poet's tongue and a crusader's vigor. The Betty F. Thomson book previously mentioned, *The Changing Face of New England,* also has much to say in this field.

CHAPTER 12: *Weeds,* the Muenscher book previously mentioned, has a brief section on useful wild plants. *Gar-*

*den Spice and Wild Pot-Herbs*, by Walter C. Muenscher and Myron A. Rice (Cornell University Press), is a big, beautiful, and useful book. Another book packed with material, much of it about the Far West, is *Useful Wild Plants of the United States and Canada*, by Charles Francis Saunders (McBride). Gray's *Manual of Botany*, of course, is a must on any nature reference shelf. I also find *The World of Plant Life*, a textbook by Clarence J. Hylander (Macmillan), invaluable. As for cookbooks presuming to tell how to cook wild food, there are few that deal with wild plants at all, and most of those that deal with wild game are hopeless. The one exception I will make is Raymond Camp's *Game Cookery* (Coward-McCann), which for the most part is sensible and practical. It is the only one I would give shelf space.

CHAPTER 13: The Hylander book I mentioned just above, *The World of Plant Life*, is valuable here. So is the Muenscher book on *Weeds*. The Collins *Field Guide to American Wild Life*, also previously mentioned, has a good, concise section on snakes, both poisonous and harmless.

CHAPTER 14: *An Almanac for Moderns*, by Donald Culross Peattie (Putnam) deals with the natural year, day by day. John K. Terres's *The Wonders I See* (Lippincott) is a naturalist's chronicle of the year. *Rural Free*, by Rachel Peden (Knopf) deals with the events of a typical year in the rural Midwest. My own *This Hill, This Valley* (Simon & Schuster) is about the country year outside the door here in Connecticut.

CHAPTER 15: Most good botany books discuss, or at least explain, taxonomy, the science of naming and classification. Any good biography of Linnaeus is well worth reading; I hesitate to suggest one because most of them are rather dull.

I have intentionally not mentioned many "standard" books by such authors as Thoreau, Audubon, Muir, Burroughs, and many other naturalists and nature writers.

Armchair exploration in that field, like actual exploration in the open, should follow the explorer's bent and provide its own excitement of discovery. I will suggest that recordings of bird songs can be both interesting and useful. My preferences among the recordings I have heard are those of A. A. Allen and P. P. Kellogg: *Songbirds of America* and *American Songbirds*, distributed by Cornell University, and those of N. and J. Stillwell: *Birdsongs of Dooryard, Field and Forest*, distributed by Ficker Records, Old Greenwich, Connecticut.

And I will mention a few periodicals, of which quite a number deal with nature one way or another. Being squeamish, I avoid those that print communications about "birdies," "beasties," and pet skunks named Pansy. But *Natural History* magazine, published by the American Museum of Natural History in New York City, and *Audubon Magazine*, published by the National Audubon Society, are both excellent. Both these organizations, by the way, also publish an assortment of first-rate nature material, most of it for school use but much of it valuable for any nature student, young or old. The Audubon Society's charts and pamphlets on mosses and lichens, for instance, are the best I have seen anywhere, for any age. Generally speaking, the publications of most museums are worth while.

There are also a number of state and regional publications. I mention two that I consider outstanding. For persons living in the Northeast, *The New York State Conservationist*, published six times a year by the New York State Conservation Department, is specially valuable. For Midwesterners particularly, but of general interest too, is the modest but excellent *The Living Museum*, published each month by the Illinois State Museum and edited and largely written by Virginia S. Eifert, an able naturialist and a talented writer.

But even the best books and magazines are essentially no more than a table of contents for the vast volume of material that awaits anyone in the dooryard or just beyond. The big, definitive book about nature is nature itself.

# A Note about the Author

HAL BORLAND, a native of Nebraska who grew up in Colorado, covered the country as newspaperman and magazine writer before settling in New England in 1945 to write books. He and his wife, author Barbara Dodge Borland, live at the edge of the Berkshires in northwestern Connecticut, with half a mile of the Housatonic river and half a mountainside for an outdoor laboratory. A naturalist and ecologist, Borland writes often about that area. Since 1942 he has written the "nature editorial" for *The New York Times* Sunday editorial page. For ten years, 1958–68, he wrote an outdoor column for the *Berkshire Eagle* (Pittsfield, Mass.). He is a contributing editor of *Audubon* Magazine. He has received a number of honors and awards for his writing, among them an honorary Litt.D. from the University of Colorado in 1944, the Westerners' Buffalo Award in 1956, the Secondary Education Board Award in 1957, the Columbia School of Journalism Alumni Award in 1962 and the Journalism Medal in 1965; the Edward J. Meeman Conservation Award in 1967, and the John Burroughs Medal in 1968. His works include essays, fiction, poetry, and autobiography. His *High, Wide and Lonesome* won three nonfiction awards. His best selling novel, *When the Legends Die*, was an A.L.A. notable book selection in 1963 and was chosen for the President Kennedy White House Library and for the one hundred-book libraries sent as U.S. gifts to heads of state overseas. His recent outdoor books include *Sundial of the Seasons, Hill Country Harvest*, and *Countryman: A Summary of Belief*, essays in natural philosophy.